D0039446

ROOT CAUSES OF SUICIDE TERRORISM

Suicide terrorism in its modern form appeared in the 1980s when the Shiite Hezbollah was the first organization to use this strategy in Lebanon. Its subsequent adoption by many organizations in the Middle East and Asia, the majority either Arab or Muslim, led many scholars to emphasize the role of Islam in suicide terrorism's emergence and spread.

Bringing together leading scholars in the field of terrorism studies, amongst them Marc Sageman, Leonard Weinberg, and Mia Bloom, this volume sets out to reassess the root causes of suicide terrorism at elite and rank-and-file levels. Challenging the widespread argument that suicide bombing is tightly connected to Islam, the contributors have approached the topic from a socio-cultural perspective and have juxtaposed the role of religion, and specifically Islam, in generating suicide terrorism with power struggles between elites for state control.

This volume will be essential reading for students of terrorism, security studies, political science, and Middle Eastern politics.

Ami Pedahzur is an Associate Professor at the Department of Government, University of Texas, Austin.

CASS SERIES: POLITICAL VIOLENCE
Series editors: Paul Wilkinson
and David Rapoport

TERRORISM VERSUS
DEMOCRACY: THE LIBERAL
STATE RESPONSE
Paul Wilkinson

AVIATION TERRORISM AND
SECURITY
*Paul Wilkinson and
Brian M. Jenkins (eds)*

COUNTER-TERRORIST
LAW AND EMERGENCY
POWERS IN THE
UNITED KINGDOM,
1922–2000
Laura K. Donohue

THE DEMOCRATIC
EXPERIENCE AND
POLITICAL VIOLENCE
*David C. Rapoport and Leonard
Weinberg (eds)*

INSIDE TERRORIST
ORGANIZATION
David C. Rapoport (ed.)

THE FUTURE OF
TERRORISM
*Max Taylor and
John Horgan (eds)*

THE IRA, 1968–2000: AN
ANALYSIS OF A SECRET
ARMY
J. Bowyer Bell

MILLENNIAL VIOLENCE:
PAST, PRESENT AND FUTURE
Jeffrey Kaplan (ed.)

COUNTER-TERRORIST LAW
AND EMERGENCY POWERS IN
THE UNITED KINGDOM,
1922–2000
Laura K. Donohue

RIGHT-WING EXTREMISM IN
THE TWENTY-FIRST CENTURY
*Peter H. Merkl and Leonard
Weinberg (eds)*

TERRORISM TODAY
Christopher C. Harmon

THE PSYCHOLOGY OF
TERRORISM
John Horgan

RESEARCH ON TERRORISM:
TRENDS, ACHIEVEMENTS
AND FAILURES
Andrew Silke (ed.)

A WAR OF WORDS:
POLITICAL VIOLENCE
AND PUBLIC DEBATE IN
ISRAEL
Gerald Cromer

ROOT CAUSES OF SUICIDE
TERRORISM: THE
GLOBALIZATION OF
MARTYRDOM
Ami Pedahzur (ed.)

ROOT CAUSES OF SUICIDE TERRORISM

The globalization of martyrdom

Edited by Ami Pedahzur

LONDON AND NEW YORK

First published 2006
by Routledge
2 Park Square, Milton Park, Abingdon, Oxon OX14 4RN

Simultaneously published in the USA and Canada
by Routledge
270 Madison Ave, New York, NY 10016

*Routledge is an imprint of the Taylor & Francis Group,
an informa business*

© 2006 Ami Pedahzur

Typeset in Times New Roman by
Newgen Imaging Systems (P) Ltd, Chennai, India
Printed and bound in Great Britain by
MPG Books Ltd, Bodmin

British Library Cataloguing in Publication Data
A catalogue record for this book is available
from the British Library

Library of Congress Cataloging in Publication Data
Root causes of suicide terrorism: globalization of martyrdom /
edited by Ami Pedahzur.
p. cm.—(Political violence)
Includes bibliographical references and index.
1. Suicide bombings. 2. Terrorism. I. Pedahzur, Ami.
II. Title. III. Series.

HV6432.R66 2006
363.325—dc22   2005034792

ISBN10: 0–415–77029–7 (hbk)
ISBN10: 0–415–77030–0 (pbk)

ISBN13: 978–0–415–77029–3 (hbk)
ISBN13: 978–0–415–77030–9 (pbk)

CONTENTS

FIGURES

TABLES

CONTRIBUTORS

Rogelio Alonso is a Lecturer in Politics and Terrorism at Universidad Rey Juan Carlos, Madrid, and coordinator of the Unit for Documentation and Analysis on Terrorism at this University.

Mia Bloom is an Assistant Professor of Political Science at the University of Cincinnati and consults for the NJ Office of Counter Terrorism. She is the author of *Dying to Kill: The Allure of Suicide Terror* (2005).

David J. Brulé is a PhD candidate and member of the Program in Foreign Policy Decision Making at Texas A&M University. He is currently a Visiting Instructor at the University of North Texas. His research interests include the domestic origins of foreign policy decisions, especially the presidential use of force.

J. Tyson Chatagnier is a PhD student at Texas A&M University and a member of the Program in Foreign Policy Decision Making. His research interests include terrorism, decision theory, and political methodology.

Mohammed M. Hafez in a Visiting Professor in the Department of Political Science at the University of Missouri—Kansas City. He is the author of *Why Muslims Rebel: Repression and Resistance in the Islamic World* (2003) and *Manufacturing Human Bombs: The Making of Palestinian Suicide Bombers* (2006).

Alex Mintz is Cullen-McFadden Professor of Political Science and Director of the Program in Foreign Policy Decision making at Texas A&M University. He is also Visiting Fellow at UN studies at Yale University and Distinguished Fellow at IDC Herzliya. He is co-editor of the new ISA journal, *Foreign Policy Analysis* and Associate Editor for Experiments and Simulations for the *Journal of Conflict Resolution*.

Assaf Moghadam is a Research Fellow at the Belfer Center for Science and International Affairs (BCSIA) at Harvard University's John F. Kennedy School of Government and a doctoral candidate in International Relations at The Fletcher School at Tufts University.

Ami Pedahzur is an Associate Professor at the Departments of Government and Middle Eastern Studies at the University of Texas at Austin. He is also a Senior Fellow at the National Security Studies center at the University of Haifa, Israel. His latest book, Suicide Terrorism, was published by polity press in 2005. Currently he is co-authoring a book manuscript entitled The Weapon of the Weak? The Paradox of Jewish Terrorism in Israel. He also serves as Associate Editor of the journals Studies in Conflict and Terrorism as well as Democracy and Security. He is also the Book Review Editor of the Civil Wars journal.

Arie Perliger is Project Coordinator of the Terrorism Project at the National Security Sudies Center. He is a PhD candidate in the School of Political Science at the University of Haifa. His current research interest focuses on terrorism and counterterrorism.

David Rapoport is Founding and Continuing Editor of the *Journal of Terrorism and Political Violence*. He is Professor Emeritus of Political Science at UCLA. He is also the founder of the Center for Religious Studies at this same university.

Fernando Reinares is Professor and Chair in Political Science, as well as Director of the Unit for Documentation and Analysis on Terrorism, at Universdad Rey Juan Carlos (King Juan Carlos University) in Madrid. In May 2004 he was appointed Senior Advisor on Antiterrorist Policy to the Minister of Interior, Government of Spain.

Marc Sageman is a Clinical Assistant Professor of Psychiatry at the University of Pennsylvania and a Senior Fellow at the Foreign Policy Research Institute. He has testified before the 9/11 Commission and has become a consultant on terrorism to various government agencies. He is the author of *Understanding Terror Networks* (2004).

Yoram Schweitzer is Research Associate at the Jaffee Center for Strategic Studies at Tel Aviv University. He is the author (with Shaul Shy) of *An Expected Surprise: The September 11th Attack and its Ramifications* (Hebrew, 2002; English edition, *The Globalization of Terror*, 2003).

Leonard Weinberg is Foundation Professor of Political Science at the University of Nevada and a senior fellow at the National Security Studies Center at the University of Haifa (Israel). Over the course of his career he has been a Fulbright senior research fellow for Italy, a visiting scholar at UCLA, a guest professor at the University of Florence, and the recipient of an H. F. Guggenheim Foundation grant for the study of political violence. He has also served as a consultant to the United Nations Office for the Prevention of Terrorism (Agency for Crime Control and Drug Prevention). For his work in promoting Christian-Jewish reconciliation, Weinberg was a recipient of the 1999 Thornton Peace Prize. In 2005 he participated in the planning for the Madrid Summit Conference on Democracy, Terrorism and Security. His books include *Global Terrorism* (2005), *Political Parties and Terrorist Groups* (2003, with Ami Pedahzur), *Right-Wing Extremism in the Twenty-First Century* (2003, eds. with Peter Merkl), *Religious Fundamentalism and Political Extremism* (2003, eds. with Ami Pedahzur), *The Democratic Experience and Political Violence* (2001, eds. with David Rapoport), *The Emergence of a Euro-American Radical Right* (1998, with Jeffrey Kaplan). His articles have appeared in such journals as *The British Journal of Political Science*, *Comparative Politics*, and *Party Politics*. He is the senior editor of the journal *Democracy and Security*.

PREFACE

The editors of the *Cass Series on Political Violence* are delighted to welcome Ami Pedazhur's fascinating volume, *Root Causes of Suicide Terrorism*. The series, now in its third decade, has published fifteen volumes; all are in print and have significant places in the field.

This work is our first to treat "suicide" or "self-martyrdom" bombing. It grew out of conference of distinguished authorities held at the University of Texas, Austin (May 2005). I attended the meetings, and the intense interactions generated convinced me that a fine volume was in the making, one that would contribute to a much better understanding of contemporary terrorism and how to deal with it. The final product certainly meets these high expectations, and clearly has much more unity than most collections. One important reason is that Professor Pedazhur urged contributors to read all the conference papers they came to Austin, arranged for them to read transcripts of all discussions afterwards, told them to keep in contact, and finally, to utilize each other's comments in their final drafts.

Suicide bombing is the signature tactic of the fourth or "religious wave" of modern terrorism, a wave that began with the Iranian Revolution in 1979. The Viet Cong, the volume points out, did use the tactic in some Vietnam War operations earlier, but although the terrorist groups in the sixties and seventies admired the Viet Cong greatly they ignored the tactic preferring to Kill from a distance. *Hezbollah*, the Party of God, was the first in the fourth wave to use suicide bombing, and it quickly achieved unexpected success by forcing the American and French peacekeeping military forces out of Lebanon (1983). Other groups adopted it soon as their *principal* tactic. Many did so because the tactics they used earlier failed, that is, Sri Lanka, Palestine, and Turkey. No contemporary terrorist method is more important to understand.

The volume provides interesting and very useful accounts of the tactic—definitions, history, sociology, achievements, failures, the relationship to Islam, and various encouraging and discouraging political contexts. Virtually every group that has used the tactic is discussed, but *Al Qaeda* and its affiliated groups, various Palestinian organizations, and the Tamil Tigers (LTTE) of Sri Lanka receive the most attention because they are so important and we do have considerable information about them. How and why individuals are attracted to become suicide martyrs are very important thoroughly discussed questions, ones that probably interest the general public most. One account uses the police records of those who carried out Madrid bombings (March 11, 2004) and then committed suicide *after* their initial success.

Suicide bombing has been used in various ways. Individuals can strap bombs to their bodies and walk to their destinations. Or they can employ different kinds of vehicles or transportation. The choices made depend on the nature of the targets and the assailants' purposes. There are many reasons for employing suicide bombing, and the striking fact is that no weapon in the history of terrorism has produced so many casualties for so little cost.

"Conventional wisdom" too often assumes that terrorists want "our" tools and "technology," particularly those embodied in weapons of mass destruction or WMD. But the fact is that terrorists have always preferred simple, cheap, portable, and easy to use weapons, weapons that provide the "biggest bang for the buck spent."

There are many reasons to explain why terrorist groups find suicide bombing so useful. Bombers can direct their attacks more clearly on the target; even armies with most advanced technology find it difficult to compete in this respect. The assailant rarely survives, and thus a principal or critical source of information will not be available afterwards. The fact that assailants know that success requires them to die generates awe among onlookers. The bombers' potential constituencies are apt to regard the assailant as martyrs and then the problem becomes even more difficult to manage because the blood of the martyrs is the seed of the church. The opposition, moreover, is often driven to "overreact," producing poorly conceived preemption policies with numerous associated abuses.

The martyrdom pattern in the current wave of terrorism is unique and its form is a peculiar perversion of the Islamic tradition; but martyrdom has always been a feature of modern terrorism, which began in 1879. Before that date in the eighteenth- and nineteenth-century Europe and America, organized mobs were the principal creators of rebel terror but they produced no martyrs as the history of the most successful ones, the Sons of Liberty and the KKK, illustrates.

Dynamite changed the character of terror initiating the modern form in which small groups, even individuals, could terrify large numbers. Participants deemed it crucial that the assailants should "claim credit" or accept responsibility for their deeds. Note the table of Vera Zazulich. She committed the first act of modern terror by wounding a Russian official who abused prisoners. "I am not a criminal, I am a terrorist" she told the court, when asked why she threw her pistol to the ground after one shot! An astounded jury declared her innocent and then carried her out of the courtroom on its collective shoulders to a crowd waiting outside. Foreign newspapers predicted that a revolution was in the offing, and Russia abolished the jury system for terrorists.

If the court had behaved differently, Zazulich could have become a martyr, apparently her real goal. Her model, one developed by the Russian anarchists, was a perversion of that developed in the Christian tradition and different than the one described in this volume. Typically, Christian martyrs were prisoners, who accepted death rather than deny their faith. It is worth remembering that nearly 40 percent of the Russian terrorists were children of Russian priests.

In the first wave, when a terrorist threw a bomb, there was a good chance he would be blown up in the process. That would make him a hero but martyrdom was achieved only in court when after gruesome police interrogations, he had the strength to declare his act appropriate knowing that he would die for his statement. Even though women were crucial and prominent members of the first Russian groups, they were forbidden to throw the bomb. Because they could not throw as well as men and were more likely to blow themselves up, and the opportunity for martyrdom which served the cause best was lost. But they could become martyrs if they engaged in hunger strikes, which led to their deaths or if they accepted death for killing with pistols, weapons they were allowed to use.

Terrorist martyrs always generate recruits, revitalize morale, and usually create favorable sentiments among potential supporters. Hunger strikes, a traditional theme in Irish culture, became and IRA feature. Some 8,000 in 1923 went on a hunger strike to oppose the Anglo-Irish treaty. The 1980s hunger strike that Booby Sands led failed to change British prison policy of mixing criminals and terrorists, but it had an enormous impact on Irish constituencies in America, crucial constituencies that had lost interest in the struggle.

Despite events like IRA hunger strikes, the desire for martyrdom kept diminishing among modern terrorists. I remember how disappointed students in my terrorism classes in the 1970s were when Weather Underground members plea-bargained. Europe's most effective group, the Italian Red Brigades, was finally broken after prisoners voiced public repentance to gain pardons.

One would think that the American Christian religious racist terrorist groups, part of the fourth wave and on the scene since the 1980s, would have produced a martyr. But they have not. The irony is heightened by the fact that radical right's canonical text is *The Turner Diaries*, a novel treasured by Timothy McVeigh, the Oklahoma City bomber. Turner's last mission is a form of suicide bombing comparable to the Islamic one; he detonates a nuclear warhead as he flies over the Pentagon telling his supporters, "I offer you my life," and the date of Turner's mission in the text is celebrated as the "Day of the Martyrs."

So disturbed were the Christian racists about their failure to produce a martyr, a Christian Identity meeting in Colorado (1992) decide to "appropriate" persons that they called martyrs, individuals who died at Waco a few months before. Oddly, the beliefs of David Koresh's "Branch Davidians" who perished at Waco were utterly inimical to virtually all that the right-wing Christian religious groups hold dear. Both groups shared apocalyptic visions and similar views on firearms, but hey understood the race question in radically different ways. The Davidians were multi-ethnic and multi-racial. But Davidians "became" Christian Identity martyrs, because Christian identity claimed the US government massacred them!

xvii

This embarrassing appropriation has not produced the effect sought, as the most recent example of a "Christian" terrorist unwilling or unable to become a martyr demonstrates. Eric Rudolph, the bomber in the 2000 Olympics (Atlanta), surrendered recently without resistance, and dismayed his sympathizers by plea-bargaining to save his life (2005).

The world this volume describes is fashioned in a remarkably different spirit. Currently, that world seems to have no shortage of people eager to accept death.

This volume is a special contribution to the literature because no book on the subject has gathered as many knowledgeable and distinguished authorities to explain the complicated and contradictory forces driving suicide bombing. A clear vigorous language also sustains this "Culture of Death" analysis. The authors deserve the gratitude of scholars, officials, students, and the general public.

ACKNOWLEDGMENTS

This volume was completed thanks to the generous support of the Donald D. Harrington Fellows Program as well as the Departments of Government and Middle Eastern Studies at the University of Texas at Austin. Special thanks to Professor John Higley, Professor Ian Manners, and Professor John Dollard for their continuous support and encouragement. Christine Marcine, Julie Ewald, and Lauren Baker devoted a lot of time and effort in putting the conference together and I am grateful to them for that. Hillary Hutchinson made an outstanding contribution to the volume by summarizing the conference presentations, adding her own comments and distributing the summaries among the participants. Nikolay Tabah, a brilliant graduate student at the University of Haifa, worked for days and nights on the manuscript and did a tremendous job.

I would like to express my gratitude to Professor David Rapoport and Professor Paul Wilkinson, the editors of the series, as well to Andrew Humphrys, a wonderful editor, for their invaluable support and assistance. Finally, I would like to thank the conference participants for the outstanding papers and above all for their friendship and for being such good colleagues.

I would like to thank, Assaf Moghadam a dear friend and a wonderful scholar, for allowing us to use his concept "The Globalization of Martyrdom" as a subtitle for this volume.[1]

Note

1 Assaf Moghadam, "The New Martyrs Go Global," *Boston Globe*, 18 November 2005; and Assaf Moghadam, "Suicde Terrorism, Occupation, and the Globalization of Martyrdom: A Critique of 'Dying to Win'," *Studies in Conflict and Terrorism* 29.4 (July–August 2006).

INTRODUCTION

Characteristics of suicide attacks

Ami Pedahzur and Arie Perliger

Suicide attacks appeared in their present form only at the beginning of the 1980s, but in the past twenty-five years, they have proven to be one of the most efficient and least expensive tactics ever to be employed by terror and guerrilla groups. It is no wonder, therefore, that in a relatively short time, this method of operation has been adopted by 32 groups in 28 countries.

Nevertheless, in contrast to other tactics used by terrorists and guerrillas, suicide attacks have a unique quality. The fact that the perpetrator consciously and knowingly faces certain death has attracted attention to the subject by researchers from various disciplines. Thus, as the rate of suicide attacks increased from the mid-1990s, there has been a similar unprecedented development of theoretical approaches and methodologies investigating terrorism and guerilla warfare.

This collection of articles has been written by distinguished experts in the field who, in May 2005, gathered for a two-day workshop under the auspices of the Donald D. Harrington Fellows Program at the University of Texas in Austin. The fascinating discussions provided the seeds which led to the fruition of this project. We hope that the articles will aid readers in dealing with vexing questions and in particular, will scatter the mists and dispel the myths which have evolved around suicide attacks.

However, before relinquishing the stage to the researchers, who focus on defining the phenomenon of suicide attacks and suggesting a variety of approaches, in some cases complementary to each other, to explain it, it seems fitting to present some data concerning the characteristics of the phenomenon. These statistics are based on the dataset of the National Security Studies Center of the University of Haifa in Israel and include descriptions of all suicide attacks which have occurred worldwide between 1982 and June, 2005.[1]

Characteristics of suicide terrorist attacks

Why do terror and guerilla groups make use of suicide attacks when this entails sacrificing their activist members? A preliminary answer is that this is the most efficient way to achieve the highest number of victims. While the average number of victims in a shooting attack is 3.32, and those in a remote-control explosive attack is 6.92, the average number of victims harmed by a suicide bomber wearing an explosive belt is 81.48. When the suicide bomber is driving an explosive-laden car, the number of victims rises to an average of 97.81.[2] Thus, it is only natural that guerilla groups or terror organizations which are interested in increasing the effectiveness of their acts of violence will turn to suicide attacks.

However, in spite of its efficiency, the execution of a suicide attack is not a simple process, and includes the need to prepare and train the potential suicide bomber, as well as assembling intelligence and professional knowledge on preparing reliable explosives. This is, perhaps, the reason that suicide attacks do not usually occur as a result of a personal decision or as a spontaneous act by an individual, but rather as a part of an organized campaign. According to the data presented by Robert Pape, one of the most prominent researchers in the field, in the past few years, 95% of suicide attacks was carried out under the sponsorship of an organization and as part of a well-organized, continuous planned campaign (Pape, 2003).

A close look at the empiric data indicates that this faithfully reflected reality until the beginning of the present decade. However, in the past few years, established organizations which, for the most part, operated to achieve goals of national liberation have yielded the stage to international networks on one hand or sub-national on the other hand.

Analyzing Figure I.1, which presents the distribution of suicide attacks by organizational structure of the groups which activated them, it becomes clear that, beginning in 2000, there has been a moderate decrease in the number of suicide attacks carried out by organizations with a hierarchical structure that includes a clear and established leadership, such as the LTTE or the PKK. At the same time, groups which have adopted a network structure in which the leadership has limited influence on the operative activities of the organizations, including the Palestinian organizations after the start of the al-Aqsa Intifada, or the global network of al-Qaeda, have become the principal groups using suicide attacks throughout the world.

This is due to number of factors. In the case of Palestinian and Iraqi groups, the great military pressure used against these organizations led them to adopt a network structure which improves their survivability, as a blow to one of the cells of the network does not harm the other cells. In addition the fact that, in both places, armies have carried on continuous pursuit, which is sometimes accompanied by targeted assassinations, after the group leaders created a situation where management of the struggle has remained in the hands of local leaders. This led de facto to creation of a network structure, and neutralizes the hierarchical framework of the organization. In the case of al-Qaeda, the desire to operate on an international scale has led it to adopt a network structure. Operative management of an organization which operates in so many different

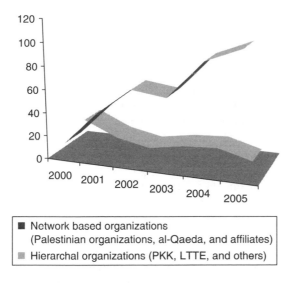

Network based organizations
(Palestinian organizations, al-Qaeda, and affiliates)

Hierarchal organizations (PKK, LTTE, and others)

Figure I.1 Distribution of groups initiating suicide attacks by years and organizational structure.

countries using local cells makes it difficult, if not impossible, to maintain a hierarchical structure.

The change which occurred in the structural characteristics of groups which employ suicide attacks has been accompanied by a change in the groups' strategic aims. It is true that Pape has presented convincing evidence in his research to support the conclusion that the great majority of disputes in which suicide attacks were used have been ethnic conflicts aiming to achieve national liberation, or struggles to expel an occupying army (Pape, 2003). However, in the past few years, there has been a tendency for a variety of Islamic groups to use suicide attacks against pro-western moderate Islamic regimes in order to replace them by extreme Islamic ones.

This was the case, for example, during 1995–8, when the GIA[3] initiated three suicide attacks in Algiers which claimed the lives of more than seventy people. These attacks were carried out in an attempt by the organization to destabilize the secular government in Algeria and to lead to the establishment of an extremist Islamic state. An additional example was the suicide attacks in Morocco during May 2003 at four sites in Casablanca, carried out by various cells of suicide bombers. The common factor among the four sites was that they were either owned by Jews or by foreign nationals. In this case, as well, the bombings were attempting to challenge a moderate Islamic regime which was cooperating with the Western democratic world. The attacks in Turkey in 2003 were carried out by a cooperative effort between al-Qaeda and a local

Islamic organization called the Turkish Hezbollah. They, too, were directed against a moderate Islamic government which not only had a Western orientation, but also allowed the coalition forces to use its military bases to attack targets in Iraq. However, perhaps the Islamic government which has suffered most from suicide attacks has been that of Saudi Arabia. In the past decade, there have been eight suicide attacks, most of which were the result of local cooperation with al-Qaeda operatives. Nearly all of the attacks were carried out in protest against the economic and military cooperation between the Saudi government and Western powers. The fact that the Saudi Arabian government enabled Western military forces to operate from its territory during the allied struggle against Iraq during the two Gulf Wars turned the government, which controls the holiest sites of Islam, into the prime target of extreme Islamic groups employing suicide attacks.

These examples enable us to maintain that, beyond the two central goals presented by Pape—the struggle for national liberation and the expulsion of military occupying forces—in recent years, suicide attacks have been used by various groups to challenge or even to overthrow moderate Islamic regimes. But what leads terrorist groups to believe that suicide attacks more than any other form of violence or struggle, have the potential for destabilizing these governments? It is apparent that they assume that a suicide attack has the potential to create fear and anxiety which will lead to demoralization of the public. The perception by citizens that the government cannot supply them with security will create a legitimacy crisis between governments and military organs, and the citizenry, and will strengthen the readiness of the country's citizens to seek radical solutions, which could include the overthrow of the current regime.

At this stage we would like to ascertain to what extent the change which we have cited in the character of organizational aims is significant and widespread. Hence, we have surveyed the strategic targets of groups which have carried out suicide attacks starting from the 1980s.

As can be seen from Figure I.2, which presents the distribution of suicide attacks according to years and strategic aims, most attacks during the 1980s were carried out against Western military forces which operated in Lebanon. Hezbollah activists, who were trying to achieve the retreat of the international military forces sent by the Security Council in response to the chaos which prevailed in Lebanon after the Israeli invasion to the state, initiated suicide attacks against foreign military installations. After the UN forces had retreated, Hezbollah continued to perpetrate suicide attacks, this time against the Israeli forces and the South Lebanon army. As can also be understood from Figure I.2, the use of suicide attacks in the struggle against occupying forces decreased during the 1990s, when suicide attacks became a dominant tactic in ethnic and territorial disputes in a variety of locations throughout the world, including Sri Lanka, Turkey, and Israel. In these cases, as well, some

4

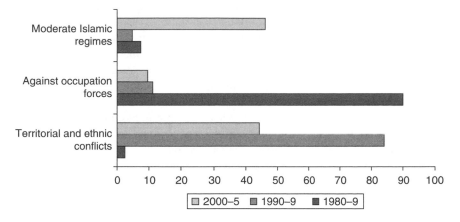

Figure I.2 Distribution of suicide attacks according to years and strategic aims (percentages).

attacks were directed against military forces, but these were attempts to achieve political sovereignty and national liberation, and not only to expel an occupying army. In conclusion, Figure I.2 shows that, in the past five years, while some suicide attacks were still being used as tools in ethnic-territorial struggles, a large proportion has served as a tactic in struggles to topple moderate Islamic governments. Is this only a temporary trend, or does it hint at a real change in the nature of the aims of groups carrying out suicide attacks? For the answer to this question, we will have to wait for a number of years to gain a wider perspective.

Despite the changes which have occurred in the last twenty-five years in the strategic aims of those who initiate suicide attacks, through the years it has been assumed that the type of regimes that were attacked is constant—that is, democratic governments. To a great extent, this was a product of the view which considered terrorism in general as a product of the democratic world. This is because the precise unique components of the democratic environment—including freedom of movement, freedom of assembly, and especially, access to the mass media—grant the terrorists a more convenient arena than in regimes with stronger supervision over the activities of their citizens and where the terrorists' ability to gain publicity for their actions is more limited. Moreover, in democratic regimes the citizens have the ability to force the political system to change its policy, especially by the ballot. Hence, the initiators of suicide attacks believed that their actions have the ability to drive the public to pressure the political leaders to change their policy.

However, is it correct to assume that liberal democracies are the main targets of suicide attacks? Indeed, most of the famous attacks (such as those of September 11 in the United States and the attack in London in July 2005) were

5

directed against democratic governments. But testing the validity of this assumption requires a more meticulous examination. Thus, to examine this assumption, we carried out an analysis consisting of two stages. In the first stage, we checked the distribution of suicide attacks by the type of regime they were directed against, using the triangular typology of Freedom House, which distinguishes between democratic regimes, partially democratic regimes, and non-democratic regimes.[4]

As can be seen in Figure I.3, in contrast to common assumption, more than a third of suicide attacks are directed against regimes which are not at all democratic, and more than a fifth were carried out against regimes with weak democratic infrastructures. In order to strengthen this conclusion, we carried out the second stage of analysis, and we tested the level of democracy in the

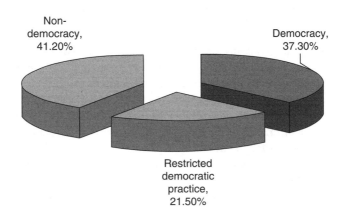

Figure I.3 Distribution of suicide attacks by level of democracy of countries which were attacked.

Table I.1 Level of democracy in the main countries which were targets of suicide attacks

Country	Freedom house (scale between 1–7, 1 = highest level of democracy)	POLITY IV (scale between 10–(−10), 10 = highest level of democracy)	Polyarchy dataset (scale between 0–47, 47 = highest level of democracy)
Lebanon	5	5	13.81
Sri Lanka	3	5	19.27
Israel	3	Military occupation	33.4
Turkey	3	7	31.84
Russia	5	4	29.2
Iraq	5	Military occupation	Military occupation

five main countries which were targets of suicide attacks in the past twenty-five years (and by that, in fact, suffered more than 80% of all suicide attacks which occurred worldwide).

Table I.1, which presents the principal findings, reveals that, in fact, most campaigns are directed systematically at low quality democracies which have not implemented the liberal bases of democratic ideals, but rather focus on the technical-formal practices of democratic regimes. This is true in the case of Israel whose democracy has been widely defined; however most of these definitions view Israel as a formal rather than a liberal democracy. This is also true of Lebanon, where suicide attacks appeared at the same time that the democratic arrangement which had functioned for many years was shattered. Other states which have suffered from systematic suicide attacks, such as Sri Lanka, Russia, and Turkey, are formal rather than fundamental democracies, while Iraq is presently governed by a de facto military government. In addition, in none of these states there is real freedom of information, and there are basic limitations on the media and on the rights of individuals and groups. In all of these states, there is a built-in preference for certain ethnic groups at the expense of others, while there is strong governmental opposition to grant any kind of political autonomy to minority groups.

After surveying the targets of groups which employ suicide attacks and the nature of their organization, the last part of this paper focuses on operative aspects of the phenomenon. Many view the classic model of a suicide attack as an individual who carries explosives on his/her body or drives an explosive-laden car and who sets off the explosives while s/he is still in the car. In fact, wearing an explosive belt (46.2% of all worldwide suicide attacks) or driving a car or truck laden with explosives to a target (37.7% of all suicide attacks) are the most common methods of carrying out an attack. However, there are other less common methods, such as carrying explosives in a handbag (3.6%), using explosive-laden boats (2.9%), exploding hand grenades (2.3%), and the use of booby-trapped bicycles (1.3%). The question arises as to whether different groups in different geographical areas employ different tactics. To answer this question, we analyzed operational methods of six suicide attack campaigns, including attacks of Palestinian organizations against Israel, the LTTE in Sri Lanka and India, the Chechens in Chechnya and Russia, the PKK in Turkey, the Hezbollah in Lebanon, and al-Qaeda and its offshoots in Iraq. Despite the fact that there are other groups which have initiated suicide attacks, these campaigns account for 84.2% of worldwide suicide attacks.

As can be seen in Figure I.4, which presents tactics used in the various campaigns, the basic answer to our question is positive. The various groups which have operated in different geographical areas have preferred different tactics. For example, the Hezbollah, which was active for the most part during the 1980s, focused on employing explosive-laden cars and trucks. Especially remembered is the double suicide attack on the US Marine Base and French forces in Beirut on

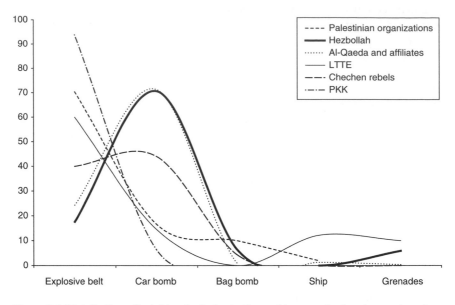

Figure I.4 Distribution of suicide attacks by tactics and by organization (percentages).

October 23, 1982 using two booby-trapped trucks driven by suicide bombers representing Hezbollah; 241 American soldiers were killed in the attack, and 59 French. In the 1990s, the LTTE organization, operating in Sri Lanka, developed two new tactics for carrying out suicide attacks. The first was an exploding boat, steered by a suicide bomber and mainly used against the ships of the Sri Lankan Navy. For instance, in July, 1990, an explosive-laden boat steered by a Tamil suicide bomber collided with a Sri Lankan Navy ship in the port of Trincomalee, killing six sailors. The second tactic was sending out a suicide bomber wearing an explosive belt. This enabled the perpetrator to approach their targets with relative ease. However, the organizations which developed this tactic to its greatest level of sophistication were the Palestinian organizations during the 1990s and at the beginning of the next decade. Using explosive belts which were usually worn under a long coat (or a modest tunic on a woman suicide bomber), these organizations succeeded in infiltrating civilian population centers, such as restaurants, buses, and central urban thoroughfares. The success of this method by the Palestinians led to its use by the Chechens and the PKK. Today, in Iraq, statistics indicate that the local groups prefer to make use of explosive-laden cars and trucks, probably due to the fact that many of their targets are well-guarded army facilities.

It can be concluded from the data presented that, to a great extent, organizations suit their tactics to the nature of the target being attacked. Hezbollah, as an illustration, used booby-trapped cars and trucks because, in contrast to explosive belts, vehicles could be used against military convoys or fortified military bases, which were their main targets. The leaders of the LTTE used operative wearing explosive belts when they carried out hostile encounters and assassinations, and used other tactics, such as exploding boats or cars when they operated against the forces of the Sri Lankan army.

The fact that there is correlation between the types of targets and the operative tactics raises two important questions. First of all, is there really a difference in the nature of the targets attacked among the various organizations which make use of suicide attacks? Second, with the assumption that the answer to the first question is positive, are suicide attacks against army targets acts of terror, or can they be labeled guerilla activity. While the second question has been dealt with widely in the articles which follow, the first question should be answered by a survey of targets of the central suicide attack campaigns throughout the world. The first stage should examine whether, as perceived by the general public, most suicide attacks are directed against civilians, or whether military targets are more common targets of these attacks. The second stage will evaluate what specific civilian targets are most popular among suicide bombers.

Figure I.5 presents the distribution of suicide attacks by civilian or military targets divided into the various organizational campaigns. As previously stated, at the beginning of the 1980s, when Hezbollah was the main organization carrying out suicide attacks, the great majority of attacks were directed against military or police targets, and especially against the Western powers and Israel, which had forces in Lebanon at the time. In the case of the LTTE, the picture is more balanced, but it completely changes when we examine Palestinian groups which have directed most of their attacks against civilian targets. The success of the Palestinians led the PKK to imitate them and focus mainly on civilian targets. Regarding al-Qaeda and the groups operating in Iraq, there is a quantitative

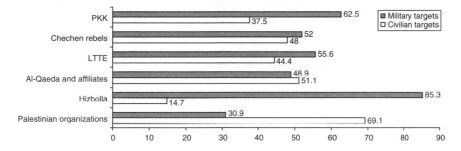

Figure I.5 Division of civilian targets in contrast to military targets by organizational campaigns (percentages).

9

balance among the number of attacks against military targets and those against civilian targets. For example, in February 2004, a Recruiting Center of the Iraqi Army was attacked using an explosive-laden car, resulting in more than forty people being killed. In October of the same year, two suicide bombers blew themselves up at the same time in a market and a coffee shop in Baghdad, killing ten innocent civilians.

In addition to distinguishing between military and civilian targets, it is important to differentiate between various types of civilian targets as, for example, some organizations have focused their attacks against civilian targets with great symbolic significance (such as diplomats and political figures), while others have preferred to focus on anonymous citizens. Figure I.6 presents the distribution of civilian targets that groups initiating suicide attacks decided to attack. Because of the wide variety of civilian targets, we placed them in the figure into four main categories: politicians, foreign diplomats, populated sites (such as restaurants or public transportation), and tourism sites and tourists.

As can be seen, during the early use of suicide attacks by Hezbollah in Lebanon, most civilian targets were diplomats and politicians. To a great extent, the Tamil Tigers adopted this method. Most of their suicide attacks against civilians were directed at assassinating high public officials in Sri Lanka and in India. Striking examples were the assassination of the Prime Minister of India, Rajiv Gandhi, in May 1991, and the suicide attack in October 1994 which led to the death of Sri Lankan presidential candidate Gamini Dissanayake, along with fifty-one other civilians. A real change in the character of civilian targets took place when the Palestinian organizations entered the arena. In contrast to groups which had previously used suicide attacks, they focused their attacks

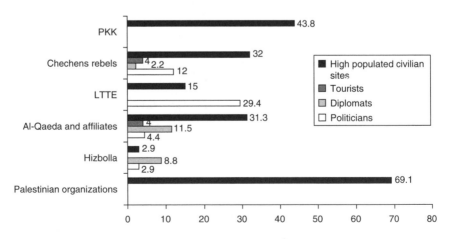

Figure I.6 Distribution of civilian targets by organization (percentages).

10

almost completely against mass civilian targets which enabled them to harm the maximal number of people. The Chechens and the PKK in Turkey imitated them, but with less success. Today, the networks of al-Qaeda are also active against mass civilian targets but, in contrast to the Palestinians, the Turks, and the Chechens, they have renewed the tradition of Hezbollah and the LTTE, and use suicide attacks also against the political leadership in Iraq. For example, in January 2005 a suicide bomber drove an explosive-laden car straight into the home of the Iraqi Justice Minister, Malik Duhan, causing the deaths of twenty-two people.

In summary, the characteristics of suicide attacks which have been discussed point to the fact that, in contrast to common belief, suicide attacks are varied and change from region to region and during different time periods. However, in spite of the differences, there are a significant number of prominent studies which succeed in presenting theoretical frameworks that efficiently explain the general factors involved and their characteristics. The opening chapter of the book presents an attempt to delineate the phenomenon conceptually, and the chapters which follow provide a fascinating journey into the depths of the phenomenon of suicide attacks from a variety of perspectives which we hope will lead the readers to a better understanding, and provide intellectual enjoyment and challenge.

Notes

1 This dataset consists of a list of terror incidents perpetrated by suicide terrorists worldwide. It covers a period beginning in 1982 and concludes on June 2, 2005, in the explosion of a car bomb driven by unknown terrorists in Balad, Iraq. In all, the catalogue includes 624 suicide assaults which took place in 28 different countries and were carried out by 32 different organizations. The database was compiled in several stages and is the property of the National Security Studies Center of the University of Haifa. First, data was collected from various academic sources (articles and books) in order to identify the countries, organizations, and periods which have been characterized by suicide terror. In the second stage, each region and group of organizations was assigned to a researcher, who searched for information on suicide attacks that were relevant to their assigned domain. The sources of information on which the database was established are numerous and diverse: articles and academic texts (Almanac of Modern Terrorism 1991; Encyclopaedia of World Terrorism 1997; Pape 2003), data-banks found on the Internet (CDISS Terrorism Program, MITP Knowledge Base, ICT Database), Internet sites dealing with various terror organizations or terror in the world, as well as a broad use of Israeli and international media sources. In the final stage, the information collected was encoded in an SPSS file according to the specific variables chosen.

2 The number of victims refers to the sum of fatalities and the injured. The data on the average number of victims of different tactics is based on the NSSC Dataset on International Terrorism.

3 Please refer to the description of GIA at Terrorism Knowledge Base—http://www.tkb.org/Group.jsp?groupID=27

4 Please refer to the "Democracy's Century" report—http://www.freedomhouse.org/research/demcent.htm

Bibliography

Chalk, P. (1998) "The Response to Terrorism as a Threat to Liberal Democracy," *Australian Journal of Politics and History*, 44, 3: 373–388.

Doran, M. S. (2004) "The Saudi Paradox," *Foreign Affairs*, 83,1: 35–51.

Karon, T. (2003) "Turkey Bombings Reflect New-Look Al-Qaeda," *Time*, November 20.

Pape, A. R. (2003) "The Strategic Logic of Suicide Terrorism," *The American Political Science Review*, 97, 3: 346–350.

1

DEFINING SUICIDE TERRORISM

Assaf Moghadam

Introduction

On May 16, 2005, the *Associated Press* released a story about a foiled plot by Jewish extremists to fire a missile on the Dome of the Rock, a holy Muslim shrine situated on top of the Temple Mount in the Old City of Jerusalem. Surprising about this plot was not its novelty—in the late 1970s, a terrorist group known as the Jewish Underground (*Makhteret*) had attempted to blow up the same site—but instead the perpetrators' plan, as reported by the Israeli police, to "commit suicide after firing an anti-tank missile at the holy site in Jerusalem and throwing grenades at police who would try to arrest them" (Lavie 2005).

This news story, which appeared a few days after a group of scholars and analysts gathered at a workshop at the University of Texas at Austin to discuss the causes and characteristics of suicide terrorism,[1] heightened a debate among the participants that had begun in the course of the workshop: Exactly what kind of attacks should be considered acts of suicide terrorism?

The present chapter is a direct outcome of discussions held during the workshop, as well as e-mail communications among several participants after the workshop. It is designed to highlight some of the definitional problems related to suicide terrorism. The chapter first describes the problem of terminology, which is particularly acute as scholars oftentimes use the words suicide terrorism, suicide bombings, suicide attacks, suicide missions, martyrdom operations, and other combinations of these terms interchangeably. The second part will describe two categories into which definitions of suicide terrorism generally fall—a narrower and a broader definition. It will also discuss several of the most contentious issues surrounding the definitions of suicide terrorism, and explore the reasons why a universally accepted definition of suicide terrorism has eluded scholars thus far. In the conclusion, I will argue that while scholars are likely to continue to disagree on a definition of suicide terrorism, it is important that they clearly lay out the definition by which they abide if they wish to maximize the scholarly contribution of their work.

Labeling suicide terrorism

One of the terms more commonly used to describe the modus operandi of suicide attacks is "suicide terrorism." Upon closer examination, however, the use of this terminology is not without problems. The most obvious problem is that no agreed upon definition of "suicide terrorism" is possible as long as the word "terrorism" itself is subject to various different interpretations. Terrorism—a pejorative word most organizations refuse to be labeled by—remains a concept that lacks a universally accepted definition, as terrorism scholars have noted (Hoffman 1998; Ganor 2005). The same must therefore also be true for suicide terrorism, a sub-category within terrorism.

Another problem related to the use of the term suicide "terrorism" is that historically, suicide missions as a modus operandi have been used not only during campaigns of terrorism, but also during conventional military campaigns against standing armies. Most definitions of terrorism, however, strictly distinguish acts of terrorism from conventional warfare because the former are generally understood to emanate from non-state actors.[2] Take the case of the Japanese *Kamikaze* suicide pilots. Although clearly a campaign involving suicide missions, *Kamikaze* attacks during the Second World War are not usually considered acts of terrorism because the suicide pilots were acting at the behest of a government in the state of war with the very enemy against whom those suicide attacks were targeted. Similarly, suicide missions—at least as understood in a broader definition as described later—have also been used by the Viet Cong and its North Vietnamese allies in the second half of the 1960s, as Leonard Weinberg describes in Chapter 5. It is less clear whether these attacks, which took place in what was then South Vietnam, are best described as acts of suicide "terrorism," especially in those instances when they were targeted against US troops.

Studies analyzing "suicide terrorism" should therefore be aware of this problem when they include *Kamikaze* attacks and similar missions by conventional armies by either adopting a more suitable title for those attacks or, at the least, explicitly addressing and clarifying their inclusion of attacks that do not generally fall under the category of terrorism.

Even when an attack does emanate from a non-state actor, such an attack should still not be labeled a terrorist attack if targeted against members of an army, since attacks are ordinarily labeled terrorist attacks only when they are targeted at noncombatants.[3] Bombings, shootings, kidnappings, and similar methods are generally labeled guerrilla warfare, insurgency, or low-intensity conflict if they are directed against uniformed men and women on duty.

The need to be precise in one's description of suicide attacks is more than merely a rhetorical exercise, as a recent collection of data related to "suicide terrorism" demonstrates. In his widely quoted book *Dying to Win* (Pape 2005: 39), political scientist Robert Pape has assembled an impressive collection of data, but his terminology is not only confusing, but potentially misleading. Pape labels the 315 suicide attacks he identified between 1980 and 2003 as "suicide terrorist attacks" even though many of these attacks have been targeted against uniformed soldiers that were on duty at the time the attacks took place.[4] As has been noted, however, some of the more frequently cited definitions of terrorism do not regard attacks against uniformed soldiers on duty acts of terrorism. A precise definition of the guidelines one adopts when collecting data on suicide operations, including whether one includes attacks against military targets or not, is extremely important for cross-data comparison among scholars.

It would have been more precise had Pape refrained from using the term suicide "terrorist" attack and instead used the more neutral label "suicide attack." Indeed, the terms "suicide attack," "suicide operation," or "suicide mission" seem to be far better choices of terms than "suicide terrorism." Unlike the value-laden word "terrorism," the terms suicide attack/operation/mission are value-neutral and emphasize the mode of attack—namely one that involves the death of its perpetrator—rather than the type of attack, in this case terrorism, and thus, by association, one's opinion over the legitimacy of the attack.

An additional tricky issue relates to the question of what actually constitutes an attack. It is important to be precise about whether one counts the suicide attack as a single attack even if it consists of multiple attacks performed by several suicide attackers. Strictly speaking, a suicide attack should be counted as multiple suicide attacks if multiple individuals detonated explosive devices. The example of the data collection conducted by Robert Pape again reveals why such accuracy of definition is crucial, because in a large number of cases he lists multiple suicide bombings as a single attack (Pape 2005). The suicide attacks in Istanbul on November 15 and November 20, 2003 were multiple attacks—two car bombs and two truck bombs each exploded on these days, respectively. Pape, however, counts the November 15 and November 20 attacks as one attack each (Pape 2005: 259). Similarly, the May 16, 2003 attacks in Casablanca were aimed at a total of five targets, including a Spanish restaurant, a Jewish-owned Italian restaurant, a Jewish cemetery, a Kuwaiti-owned hotel, and a Jewish community center. Rather than to count the Casablanca bombings as five separate attacks, however, Pape lists them as a single one. He also counts the four separate attacks conducted on September 11, 2001 as a single attack, as he does with the dual bombings of the US embassies in Kenya and Tanzania on August 7, 1998—even though the embassy bombings took place in two separate countries. Pape's method of collecting and utilizing data, meanwhile, can provide a distorted image of the ratio between suicide attacks perpetrated by religious groups versus those perpetrated by what he terms secular organizations. Attacks by Al Qaeda or its affiliates are oftentimes multiple suicide bombings. Yet, counting all of these multiple bombings as a single attack, as Pape does, necessarily reduces the number of attacks that he categorizes as religious, which in turn may support his argument that religion plays a lesser role in suicide bombings than commonly assumed. Clearly, then, as the above example shows, one's methodology can influence one's conclusion.

The label "suicide attack" (as well as the terms "suicide operation" and "suicide mission") is also preferable to the widely used term "suicide bombing" because the former encompasses the widest array of possible ways in which this type of attack may be perpetrated. All suicide bombings are suicide attacks, but not all suicide attacks are suicide bombings. Strictly speaking, the 9/11 attacks were not suicide bombings, since no conventional explosive device was used in the killing of nearly 3,000 people. They were, however, suicide attacks (Lynn-Jones 2005). In this regard, Leonard Weinberg's suggestion to "make a distinction between the act of suicide terrorism itself, and the particular technique used to accomplish it," seems very useful (May 18, 2005).

Another term sometimes used to describe suicide attacks is "homicide bombings" (Ehrenfeld 2002). Writers and news outlets using the term "homicide bombings" argue that unlike the term "suicide bombing," which they say focuses on the individual death and self-sacrifice of the perpetrator, the term "homicide bombing" emphasizes the fact that the bomber kills others. "Homicide bombings" is a politically charged term, however, and thus unlikely to enjoy wide acceptance. More importantly, the term fails to describe the particularity of this type of bombing—namely the death of the perpetrator as an integral part of the attack—thus failing to appreciate that, as Ariel Merari aptly put it, "it is the self-sacrificial rather than the homicidal aspect of suicidal terrorist atttacks that evokes scientific curiosity and public concern" (Merari 1998: 196). In fact, each lethal bombing targeted at people, whether it is conducted by terrorists who die in the process or not, may be considered a "homicide bombing." Thus, this particularly unfortunate term fails to make a basic distinction between, say, the suicide attacks of 9/11, and, on the other hand, an ordinary pipe bomb placed in a trash can that resulted in the death of innocent bystanders. Researchers, however, should make an effort to be as precise as they possibly can in describing the particular modus operandi that was used in an attack. Such accuracy should be abided by not merely for scholarly purposes, but also for practical purposes. Policymakers' job of finding adequate responses to a wide array of terrorist techniques will be significantly streamlined if analysts disaggregate the terrorist tactics to the largest extent possible.

Another terminology for suicide attacks preferred by some scholars, but also by most of the circles who approve of this modus operandi, is "martyrdom operations." This term is used by radical Islamist organizations such as Al Qaeda or Hamas, but also by more secular organizations such as Fatah-Al Aqsa Martyrs Brigades or the Palestinian Front for the Liberation of Palestine (PFLP). "Martyrdom operations" is a term that best describes suicide attacks from the point of view of the attackers, who refrain from calling their death a suicide, which is strictly prohibited in Islam and many other religions (Moghadam 2003). Similar to "homicide bombings," hence, the term "martyrdom (*istishhad*) operations" and related terms such as *shahid* (martyr) are, according to Mohammed Hafez, "highly charged, normative terms that do not aid in the effort to analyze and explain this deadly phenomenon" (May 17, 2005). The term "martyrdom" is therefore unlikely to be universally adopted even though it may well describe the act of dying from the perpetrator's vantage point better than any other term. Unlike the term "homicide bombings," the term "martyrdom operations" does not ignore the element of the attacker's death in its description. It does, however, contain a different problem. From the point of view of the perpetrator—whether radical Islamist or more nationalistic in nature—everybody who dies fighting the Israeli, American, or any other enemy infidel is considered a martyr, whether he is a traditional suicide attacker with a bomb strapped onto his body, a Palestinian trapped in a tunnel while attempting to smuggle weapons into the Gaza strip, an Islamist insurgent dying in a gun battle with US Marines in Falluja, or a Saudi Al Qaeda member shot by the oil kingdom's security forces. Furthermore, even those individuals who volunteer for high-risk missions that do not involve bombs attached to their bodies—and where a tiny chance of survival remains—may think of themselves as no different from traditional suicide bombers. Yoram Schweitzer points out in this regard that a sizable number of Palestinians who carried out shooting spree attacks using rifles have made final preparations similar to those made by traditional suicide bombers, including the shooting of video footage designed for release after the perpetrator's expected death (May 29, 2005).

Suicide attacks: narrow and broad

Suicide terrorism requires the interplay of two conditions: a willingness to kill and a willingness to die (Merari 1998: 196; Moghadam 2003). It is generally assumed that the act of dying and killing occurs simultaneously, although, as will be described later, a broader definition of suicide attacks is more flexible and allows for a certain time lag between the act of killing and the act of dying. There is a consensus, however, that in a suicide attack, the act of killing and the act of dying occur as part of the same mission. Hence, a terrorist responsible for detonating an explosive device in a market, killing innocent bystanders, will not be considered a suicide terrorist even if he later commits suicide in prison. The notorious West German terrorists Andreas Baader and Ulrike Meinhof, both of whom have committed suicide in prison in 1977 and 1976 along with other members of the Red Army Faction, are therefore not considered suicide terrorists. Neither do we consider Bobby Sands and nine other members of the Irish Republican Army (IRA) who starved themselves to death in prison in 1981 suicide terrorists. Instead, they were terrorists who committed suicide.

At times, suicide attackers may have previously conducted conventional, non-suicidal attacks. Joshua Sinai notes that the bombers of the attacks on commuter trains in Madrid on March 11, 2004 aimed to survive those attacks, although they may have planned subsequent suicide operations (June 12, 2005). As Rogelio Alonso and Fernando Reinares describe in detail in Chapter 9, seven members of the Madrid cell, who were involved in the non-suicidal terrorist attacks in Madrid, indeed committed collective suicide on April 3 as the GEO, the Spanish police's counter-terrorism unit, closed in on the apartment in which they were hiding. The police believed that "the terrorists wanted to die while

17

killing as many policemen as possible." The March 11, 2004 Madrid bombings should therefore not be called suicide attacks, and those responsible for placing the bombs on the commuter trains on March 11 bombers were not technically suicide attackers at that moment in time. The April 3, 2004 incident at the working-class area of Leganés at the outskirts of Madrid, on the other hand, can and should be considered a suicide attack, and the attackers, at that point, suicide attackers.

Suicide attacks are traditionally defined as attacks whose success is contingent upon the death of the perpetrator (Creanshaw 2002: 21; Ganor 2002: 140; Schweitzer 2002: 78). According to Schweitzer, for example, a suicide attack is

> a politically motivated violent attack perpetrated by a self-aware individual (or individuals) who actively and purposely causes his own death through blowing himself up along with his chosen target. The perpetrator's ensured death is a precondition for the success of his mission.
>
> (2002: 78)

Boaz Ganor adds that "the terrorist is fully aware that if he does not kill himself, the planned attack will not be implemented" (2002: 140).

According to this definition, suicide operations such as the 9/11 attacks; traditional suicide bombings in Israel and Sri Lanka; and attacks such as the one at a nightclub in Bali in October 2002, the multiple suicide bombings in Casablanca in May 2003, and the November 2003 Istanbul bombings, are clear instances of suicide attacks. Instances such as the shooting spree by Baruch Goldstein, however, who shot twenty-nine Muslim civilians during prayer at a holy site in Hebron in February 1994, are not considered suicide attacks under this "narrow" definition. Although Goldstein probably had no delusion that he would survive the attack, his death was not necessary for the attack to occur—his ability to enter the holy shrine and to fire his weapon before being overrun was the only precondition for success.

Critics of this traditional definition argue that by defining suicide attacks narrowly as attacks that require the death of the perpetrator as a precondition for its success, researchers ignore a wide array of terrorists who were as willing and ready to die as ordinary suicide bombers when they set out for their mission. These critics subscribe to a broader, more flexible definition of suicide attacks that does not make the success of the attack contingent upon the perpetrator's death. Instead, they define suicide attacks as those in which the perpetrator professed a willingness to die in the course of the attack. Alex Mintz, who advocates a broader definition, argues that we should think of suicide attacks comprehensively, by including in such a definition "any attack where the suicide act of the terrorist was an a priori objective of the mission" (August 5, 2005). Likewise, for Merari, "suicidal terrorism," as he calls it, is characterized by one's "readiness to die in the process of committing a terrorist act" (1998: 192). Similarly, Pape writes that a suicide terrorist is an attacker who

> does not expect to survive the mission and often employs a method of attack (such as a car bomb, suicide vest, or ramming an airplane into a building) that requires his or her death in order to succeed. In essence, a suicide terrorist kills others at the same time that he kills himself.
>
> (2005: 10)

Walter Laqueur goes as far as saying that

> prior to World War I, most terrorism was, in effect, suicide terrorism. The weapons used (the dagger, the short-range pistol, the unstable, primitive bomb) compelled the assassin to approach the victim very closely. As such, early terrorists were likely to be apprehended, and since capital punishment was still the rule, the prospect of returning alive from such missions was minimal—a fact well-known to the terrorists.
>
> (2005)

Nevertheless, most suicide terrorism analysts seem to abide by the narrow definition of suicide attacks (Moghadam 2002; Bloom 2005; Gambetta 2005; Hafez 2005). They argue that the ensured sacrifice of the perpetrator must be distinguished from an operation in which there is a high likelihood, but no certainty, of the attacker's death. Even if the perpetrator engages in a high-risk operation that most likely will result in his or her death, we must assume that there is a chance—tiny perhaps, but nevertheless real—that the perpetrator may survive the attack, and indeed may even believe that he will survive the attack. Critics of the broader definition argue that it is impossible to know whether or not a perpetrator had an intent to die in the course of the attack or not. Even if terrorists made it known in advance that they were ready to die, they may have done so for purposes of propaganda, rather than out of genuine volition.

Analysts who abide by the narrow definition of suicide attacks also cite the necessity for a strict conceptual definition in order to be able to collect precise and comparable data across all instances of suicide attacks. They argue that gathering reliable data on suicide bombings is difficult enough already when collected according to a narrow definition, as evidenced by wide discrepancies in the numbers of suicide attacks attributed to particular groups by different scholars.[5] If the notion of what constitutes a suicide attack would be expanded even further, they believe, data would be even more difficult to gather, and different datasets could be expected to manifest even larger discrepancies than those gathered under guidelines of a narrow definition.

It is due to the difficulty in gathering reliable data that most scholars rely on a narrow definition when collecting data even if their overall definition of suicide terrorism may be of the more flexible kind. For the purposes of data-collection,

Robert Pape who, as we have seen, defines suicide terrorism in broader terms, nevertheless counts

> only suicide attacks that meet the classic definition, partly because it is the common understanding of the concept, and partly because suicide missions are hard to identify reliably since we rarely know for certain that an attacker who did not kill himself or herself actually expected to die.
>
> (2005: 11)

Mintz, Chatagnier, and Brule similarly distinguish between a general definition and an operational one. Whereas their general definition of suicide attacks includes "any attack where the suicide act of the terrorist was an a priori objective of the mission," the operational definition codes suicide attacks as (1) instances in which the very act of the attack "is dependent upon the death of the perpetrator" (i.e. the narrow definition), or (2) instances in which the attacker commits suicide in the course of the attack although the very act of the attack is not dependent upon his or her death. While this operational definition minimizes the problem of data-collection associated with a broader definition of suicide attacks, it does not provide a satisfactory answer to yet another problem surrounding both the broader and narrow definitions of suicide attacks. This problem is the inclusion of "false positives," that is, suicide attackers that did not intend to commit suicide voluntarily, or who did not technically kill themselves but were killed by others.[6]

As to the first case of false positives—cases of seemingly unintended suicide— Leonard Weinberg points out that there have been cases reported in Iraq where drivers of suicide vans or cars were not told they were expected to die in the course of their "martyrdom operations," and that the explosives were detonated by remote control (May 26, 2005). Similar cases have been reported, although never fully proven, about Lebanese suicide attackers in the 1980s, where some drivers of bomb-laden cars were apparently unaware they were going to have to die for the attack to be carried out (Merari 1998). In yet other cases, Schweitzer reports, the dispatchers of car bombs had not intended for the driver to detonate himself inside the car, yet the car exploded with the driver anyhow, and the bombing was subsequently coded as a suicide attack (August 3, 2005). With regard to these kinds of attacks that included the seemingly unintended death of the attacker, Weinberg correctly points out that "the death of the driver may very well be a prerequisite for the success of the mission, but it is not an act of suicide in the sense that the perpetrator intentionally killed himself" (May 26, 2005).

Other cases of such false positives—suicide attacks where an individual's awareness of his or her own impending death was lacking, or a death wish was altogether absent—include incidents in which individuals have been physically or psychologically coerced by organizations to detonate themselves along with a chosen target. While outright coercion of suicide bombers has not been proven beyond doubt—in most cases, of course, the attacker does not survive the blast, making his or her interrogation impossible—reports about the use of compellence, threats, or psychological pressure (particularly in the case of female suicide bombers) in driving a person into committing a suicide attack have persisted over the years and across cases of suicide attacks in various locations (*Jerusalem Post* 2002; ABC News 2004; *USA Today* 2005). Several cases, for instance, have been reported of Palestinian and Chechen women who have apparently been subjected to psychological or physical pressure to perpetrate suicide attacks, because they were believed to have brought shame upon their families (Fishman 2004; Murphy 2004). Arguments that such cases of forced self-sacrifice are incompatible with established notions of suicide due to personal distress certainly have validity.

With regard to the broader definition of suicide attacks, "false positives" exist in the sense that some of those individuals defined as suicide attackers by proponents of an expanded definition did not technically kill themselves. Baruch Goldstein, the member of the radical Jewish terrorist organization *Kach* did not commit suicide as it is generally understood—namely by killing himself—but was overrun by a mob. A similar case occurred on August 4, 2005 in the northern Israeli town of Shfaram, when a 19-year-old Israeli soldier who had gone AWOL, Eden Natan-Zada, shot to death four Arab citizens in a bus, wounding 12 others. Zada was beaten to death by enraged residents of Shfaram as soon as he intended to switch magazines. He was called a "suicide bomber" by some journalists (Barnea 2005), although he was technically not taking his own life, and certainly not with a bomb.

A final difficulty apparent in defining suicide attacks is the issue of intercepted suicide attackers—a pool that in some countries is far larger than suicide attackers themselves. In Israel, for example, only around 2 percent of suicide bombers succeed with their intended plans, according to one security expert (Finn 2005). Should we consider these failed suicide bombers to be suicide bombers? Should they be included in data collected on suicide attackers worldwide? It seems sensible to maintain a distinction between successful and intercepted suicide attackers for purposes of data collection, not least because information on intercepted suicide attackers is more difficult to gather than information on successful ones. Alex Mintz makes the useful distinction into two separate codings of suicide attacks, namely that of an ordinary suicide attack (see earlier definition by Mintz) and that of an intercepted suicide attack, the latter labeled as such if (1) the attacker was intercepted on the way to the target and confessed to plan to commit a suicide attack or (2) if the attacker was intercepted on the way to the target and was later on convicted by authorities as attempting to carry out a suicide mission (May 26, 2005).

Conclusion

The purpose of this chapter was to highlight a number of conceptual problems related to how suicide terrorism is commonly defined, not to introduce a new definition of this concept. Given the inability of scholars to agree on a single definition of terrorism after decades of research on this subject, it is unlikely that scholars will agree on a single conception of the sub-category of suicide terrorism. One conclusion reached in this study is that in many cases, it appears preferable to focus on the modus operandi—suicide attacks—rather than the nature of the attack as described by the controversial concept of terrorism. Labeling this tactic "suicide attack" rather than "suicide terrorism" makes particular sense in two cases: First, when scholars include in their research suicide missions targeted not only against civilians, but also against soldiers; and second, when scholars trace the use of this tactic throughout history by including not only suicide missions that were part of campaigns of terrorism (such as in the current attacks by Jihadist groups as occurred in London on July 7, 2005), but also those that were an integral part of conventional warfare, such as the use of *Kamikaze* pilots by Japan during the Second World War. Using a more value-neutral term such as suicide mission or suicide attack helps evade the problem posed by the use of the term "suicide terrorism" in select instances. Such a choice of terms also seems preferable to descriptions of attacks that may be overly political, such as "homicide bombings."

Using the method of data-collection by one contemporary researcher as an example, it has been argued that being precise about how one defines suicide attacks is important for reasons that go beyond scholarly diligence. Counting multiple suicide operations as a single attack because they are seemingly related, rather than regarding them as a series of attacks, is likely to have an impact on how one interprets one's data, and thus one's conclusions about the nature and causes of suicide attacks.

This article has also presented what increasingly crystallizes as two distinct schools of definitions of suicide attacks. According to the established, narrower definition, the attacker's death is a precondition for the success of the mission—in essence, the suicide attacker's death and the death of his victims occur simultaneously. The traditional example for such an attack is a suicide bomber detonating himself among a crowd of people using a suicide belt. A second, broader definition of suicide attacks instead focuses on the perpetrator's principal willingness to die as part of his mission. His own death and that of his victims may not occur simultaneously, and neither does he necessarily take all precautions to ensure his own death, instead relying on others to kill him—be they surviving victims of the attacks, or perhaps security forces arriving at the scene as the attacker continues to carry out his deed.

This chapter has presented arguments both in favor of the narrow as well as the broader definition, and has also introduced legitimate reservations about both of these approaches. Whereas both approaches have their merits, we may conclude that for the purposes of data-collection and statistical comparison across cases, the narrow definition appears more practical. Scholars should be encouraged to continue taking an open-minded approach to the study of suicide terrorism by acknowledging the validity of both approaches. In doing so, it is of utmost importance that the analyst ensures that he explains how he defines suicide terrorism and how he collects his data. An approach of full disclosure is guaranteed to maximize the scholar's intellectual contribution to this growing field of studies.

Notes

1 This was the Donald D. Harrington Workshop, *A Culture of Death: On Root Causes of Suicide Terrorism*, held at the University of Texas at Austin, May 11–13, 2005.

2 This is not to say that terrorism has not been used as a tool by states. State terror has been inherent in the consolidation and maintenance of power of a large number of states, particularly dictatorships, most notoriously visible perhaps during Nazi Germany and the Soviet Union under Stalin. However, the literature generally refers to state-based terrorism as "terror," and reserves the word "terrorism" for the tactic used by non-state actors.

3 There is no universally accepted definition of terrorism, and not all definitions of terrorism define an act of terrorism as an attack on noncombatants or civilians. Some of the more frequently cited definitions, however, do. The US State Department, for example, defines terrorism as "premeditated, politically motivated violence perpetrated against noncombatant targets by subnational groups or clandestine agents, usually intended to influence an audience." Noncombatants include both civilians as well as military personnel who at the time of the incident are unarmed and/or not on duty. See US Department of State, *Patterns of Global Terrorism 2003*, xii. Available online at http://www.state.gov/s/ct/rls/pgtrpt/2003/31880.htm, last accessed December 14, 2004. The full report is available at http://www.state.gov/s/ct/rls/pgtrpt/2003/. For a definition of terrorism that does not include a reference to noncombatants, see Bruce Hoffman, *Inside Terrorism*, New York: Columbia University Press, 1998, 43.

4 Pape, for example, includes the February 27, 2002 suicide attack against an Israel Defense Forces (IDF) checkpoint as a suicide attack; a June 11, 2000 attack by Chechen separatists at a military post in Groznyy; the November 13, 1995 attack by Al Qaeda at a US military base in Riyadh, Saudi Arabia; and a March 19, 1991 suicide truck bomb by the LTTE at a Sri Lankan army camp, to name a few. See the book's appendix, 253–263.

5 Robert Pape, for example, suggests there have been 76 suicide attacks by the Liberation Tigers of Tamil Eelam (LTTE). Although his definition can be categorized as broad, he explicitly states that in collecting his data, he relied on the narrow definition. See Robert Pape, *Dying to Win*, 11. Other sources, on the other hand, report over 150 and up to 220 LTTE suicide attackers. See Rohan Gunaratna, "Suicide Terrorism: A Global Threat," *Jane's Intelligence Review*, October 20, 2000; and Amy Waldman, "Suicide Bombing Masters: Sri Lankan Rebels," *New York Times*, January 14, 2003.

6 I thank Leonard Weinberg for this point.

Bibliography

ABC News (2004) *U.S. Official: Some Iraqi Suicide Bombers may have been Forced*, 23 July.

Barnea, N. (2005) "Not Insane", *Yediot Ahronot*, August 5.

Bloom, M. (2005) *Dying to Kill: The Allure of Suicide Terror*, New York: Columbia University Press, 76.

Chatagnier, D. B. (2005) *Being Bin Laden: An Applied Decision Analysis Procedure for Analyzing and Predicting Terrorists' Decisions*, in the present volume, August 5.

Crenshaw, M. (2002) "Suicide Terrorism in Comparative Perspective," in *ICT, Countering Suicide Terrorism*, 21, Herzliyya, Israel: International Policy Institute for Counter-Terrorism (ICT).

Ehrenfeld, R. (2002) "No Partner: Arafat Cannot be Negotiated with," *National Review Online*, June 11, Available at http://www.nationalreview.com/comment/comment-ehrenfeld061102.asp, accessed July 31, 2005.

Finn, R. (2005) "From Veteran of another War on Terror, a Crash Course," *New York Times*, July 29.

Fishman, A. (2004) "Woman Bomber Sent on Mission as Penance for Adultery," *Yediot Ahronot*, January 18, 6.

Gambetta, D. (2005) (ed.) *Making Sense of Suicide Missions*, Oxford, UK: Oxford University Press, vi.

Ganor, B. (2002) "Suicide Attacks in Israel," in *ICT, Countering Suicide Terrorism*, 140, Herzliyya, Israel: International Policy Institute for Counter-Terrorism (ICT).

—— (2005) *The Counter-Terrorism Puzzle: A Guide for Decision Makers*, New Brunswick: Transaction, 1–24.

Gunaratna, R. (2000) "Suicide Terrorism: A Global Threat," *Jane's Intelligence Review*, October 20.

Hafez, M. (2005) *Manufacturing Human Bombs: The Making of Palestinian Suicide Bombers*, Washington, DC: United States Institute of Peace.

—— (2005) E-mail communication, May 17.

Hoffman, B. (1998) *Inside Terrorism*, New York: Columbia University Press, 13–44.

Jerusalem Post (2002) *Palestinian Man Says Life Threatened by Terrorists if he didn't carry out Suicide Attack*, November 3, "Unwilling Victims?"

Laqueur, W. (2005) "What Makes them Tick?" *Washington Post*, July 24.

Lavie, M. (2005) "Israelis Foil Plot by Jewish Extremists," *Associated Press*, May 16.

Lynn-Jones, S. (2005) Email communication, February 24.

Merari, A. (1998) "The Readiness to Kill and Die: Suicidal Terrorism in the Middle East," in Walter Reich, ed., *Origins of Terrorism: Psychologies, Ideologies, Theologies, States of Mind*, Washington, DC: Woodrow Wilson Center, 192, 194–196.

Mintz, A. (2005) E-mail communication, May 26, 2005, August 5, 2005.

Moghadam, A. (2002) *Suicide Bombings in the Israeli-Palestinian Conflict: A Conceptual Framework*, Project for the Research of Islamist Movements (PRISM), May 11, Available at http://www.e-prism.org, accessed March 2, 2006.

—— (2003) "Palestinian Suicide Terrorism in the Second Intifada: Motivations and Organizational Aspects," *Studies in Conflict and Terrorism*, 26.2, March/April: 69–70.

Murphy, K. (2004) "A Cult of Reluctant Killers," *Los Angeles Times*, February 4.

Pape, R. A. (2005) *Dying to Win: The Strategic Logic of Suicide Terrorism*, New York: Random House, 10, 11, 39, 259.

Schweitzer, Y. (2002) "Suicide Terrorism: Development and Main Characteristics," in *International Policy Institute for Counter-Terrorism (ICT), Countering Suicide Terrorism*, Herzliyya, Israel and New York: Anti-Defamation League and ICT, 78.

—— (2005) E-mail communication, May 29, August 3.

Sinai, J. (2005) E-mail communication, June 12.

United States Department of State (2004) *Patterns of Global Terrorism 2003*, Washington, DC: U.S. State Department, xii.

USA Today (2005) Steven Komarow and Sabah al-Anbaki, *Would-be Bomber Angry at those who Sent him*, January 25.

Waldman, A. (2003) "Suicide Bombing Masters: Sri Lankan Rebels," *New York Times*, January 14.

Weinberg, L. (2005) E-mail communication, May 26, May 18.

2

DYING TO KILL

Motivations for suicide terrorism

Mia Bloom

Why has suicide bombing been effective in some conflicts while in others terrorist organizations have rejected or abandoned it? What motivates organizations to employ this tactic, and how does suicide terrorism inflame or respond to public opinion? By understanding the dynamics of suicide bombing, we are better able to devise strategies to combat it.

The almost daily occurrences of suicide attacks in Iraq, the July 25 attack in Sharm el Sheikh in Egypt—the deadliest in twenty years—coupled with the July 7 and 21 attacks against the London Tube and buses, the first such instance of suicide terror from homegrown cells in the West, raise the question of why a once occasional mode of attack increasingly appears to be the terrorists' weapon of choice. The increase in the number of attacks throughout the world, the proliferation of religious and secular groups using the tactic, and the increasing lethality of the improvised explosive devices themselves require further investigation and understanding.

We can define suicide bombing as a violent, politically motivated attack, carried out in a deliberate state of awareness by a person who blows himself or herself up together with a chosen target. The premeditated certain death of the perpetrator is the precondition for the success of the attack (Schweitzer 2001). Suicide bombing is not, however, a uniform phenomenon (Crenshaw 2003), but rather a subset of terrorism addressing issues relevant to the study of ethnic conflict and asymmetric warfare. Thus, its study provides insight into the larger theoretical issues of ethnic conflict, international security, and contentious politics.

It is important to classify which groups employ suicide terror. These may include states or non-state actors—although the majority of real-world examples of suicide bombing as a tactic tend to be perpetrated by insurgents/terrorists competing with an established state for predominance and/or control. Insurgent groups utilizing suicide bombing tend to alternate between different strategies and vary these tactics with more conventional strategies of warfare.

Suicide bombing is unique in the sense that the organizations which use this tactic reap multiple benefits on various levels without incurring significant costs. On the one hand, the act signals operatives' complete dedication to the group and

25

its cause. This adds a degree of legitimacy to the organization, which can claim the operative as its own, and use his or her dedication to inspire others. While each operation sacrifices one supporter, it enables the organization to recruit many more future bombers. The perpetrator is dead and so can never recant his or her decision. Finally, any potential negative costs associated with an attack (like the deaths of civilians) are mitigated by the logic that argues that the brutal state is so horrendous that its victims (the perpetrators of violence) have no other means of expressing their anger and no other avenues to channel their grievances than this ultimate sacrifice. These people willfully die spectacularly for one another and for what is perceived as the common good of alleviating the community's onerous political and social realities (Atran 2003a: 1534).

Suicide bombing has an additional value: that of making yourself the victim of your own act, and thereby putting your tormentors to moral shame. The idea of the suicide bombing, unlike that of an ordinary attack, is, perversely, a moral idea in which the killers, in acting out the drama of being the ultimate victim, claim for their cause the moral high ground (Margalit 2003). Ultimately, suicide terrorism, like terrorism more generally, is a form of political theatre in which the audience's reaction is as important as the act itself. Suicide terrorism is sometimes used effectively as a form of targeted assassination.

> Suicide bombing as a tactic encompasses attacks of military targets that are immune via ordinary insurgent strategies, the assassination of prominent leaders (who would ordinarily not be accessible by any other means), and the attack of large numbers of civilians—mimicking indiscrimination—in order to create generalized fear...Although a suicide attack aims to physically destroy an initial target, its primary use is typically as a weapon of psychological warfare intended to affect a larger public audience. The primary target is not those actually killed or injured in the attack, but those made to witness it...
>
> (Atran 2003a: 1534)

There are several audiences for suicide terror, targeted at domestic rivals or constituents and an international audience in which suicide terrorism is aimed at potential patrons, funders, and the terrorists' own Diaspora. The obvious audience is the enemy side. The message in many of the ethno-nationalist conflicts is "get off my land." The less obvious audience is their own community for whom the use of violence signals that they are proactive and engaged in the struggle. Using violence may also be a way to prevent defection from within their own ranks for not being sufficiently steadfast and aggressive or for appearing weak. Using violence has a potential financial and public relations pay-off from an international group of funders/patrons that may also provide incentives for terrorists to use suicide terror to grab the headlines and distinguish the group from among a large number of insurgent organizations.

In order to survive, succeed, and achieve political power, insurgent terrorist groups need to mobilize supporters and maintain these support bases (constituencies) over time. If they lose this support, then they are likely to be found, arrested or killed by the opposing government. The terrorist organizations that recruit suicide bombers are identifiable by their constituent population. Their "storefronts" are known locations where supporters can go and volunteer, and their cadres are known members in the community. To the extent that terrorists can continue to move freely among their people, they must sustain their support base and the people's good will. It is also crucial for their survival that the organizations can continue to replenish lost fighters by mobilizing and recruiting new cadres. To use Varshney's theory of ethnic mobilization,

> Mobilization cannot proceed [without] necessary strategies; coalitions must be formed; the response of the adversary—the state, the opposed ethnic group, the in-group dissenters—must be anticipated. And many would join such mobilization, when it has acquired some momentum and chance of success.... The *origins* of...mobilization are thus rational, and its *evolution* may contain a lot of strategic behavior.
>
> (2003: 86)

Constituents' support for terrorist organizations comes in several forms. Supporters are needed to provide food, safe houses, recruits, and ultimately political power (hence the significance of public opinion). Financial support is needed to buy guns and weapons, remunerate the families of martyrs, engage in philanthropic activities to increase the organizations' influence, or pay operatives. In order to raise funds, the insurgents may require the support of external communities, their Diaspora, international sympathizers, or foreign patrons.

Insurgent groups that are not financially independent must search for funds either internally or externally.[1] They have two options: extract money from the broader local population or raise it from a small segment of foreign donors. Extraction, derived largely through taxation or levies, will require the terrorist group to function as a "state in the making," and will circumscribe what can and cannot be done and who can and cannot be killed. If the terrorists engage in activities hostile to the population, their support will dry up. The insurgents provide social services or other benefits to the members of their society to shore up their popularity and increase support. The provision of social services is especially salient when there is little external funding, few weapons from the outside, and the insurgents need to convince the larger population that their cause is just.

This situation is particularly difficult under occupations when the provision of such basic needs by the occupying state is limited or nonexistent. Such conditions create an environment hospitable for the terrorist organizations to recruit and mobilize public support but the poverty of this situation necessitates finding funding to underwrite the costs of the struggle. If the insurgent group is forced to search for money externally from a Diaspora or foreign patron, it will chose tactics that maximize publicity, while garnering greater attention to its cause and to the group employing the tactic. Thus, there are different incentives to resort to suicide bombing, depending from where the bulk of funding comes.

Suicide bombing works when it pays. In the war for public support, when the bombings resonate positively with the population that insurgent groups purport to represent, they help the organization mobilize support. If suicide bombing does not resonate among the larger population, the tactic will fail. If it is applauded, it will flourish. The pattern that emerges from the case studies is that militant groups are more likely to adopt suicide bombing as a strategy, and the tactic is more likely to resonate positively with the population, after other strategies have been tried and failed.[2] If multiple insurgent groups are competing for public support, bombings will intensify in both scope and number as they become both the litmus test of militancy and the way to mobilize greater numbers of people within their community. When competition is especially intense, multiple organizations have occasionally vied with one another to claim responsibility for a particular bombing and identify the bomber as *their* operative. Such spectacular "heroic" attacks garner increased media attention and organizations vie to claim responsibility for martyrs. The more spectacular and daring the attacks, the more the insurgent organization is able to reap a public relations advantage over its rivals and/or enemies. According to Scott Atran,

> Like the best Madison Avenue advertisers, but to ghastlier effect, the charismatic leaders of terrorist groups turn ordinary desires for family and religion into cravings for what they're pitching to the benefit of the manipulating organization rather than the individual being manipulated.
> (2003a: 13)

This process of outbidding between the groups depends on the domestic politics of the minority group and the state counter-terror strategies and responses to the insurgents' violence. The bombings do not occur in a vacuum. In fact, all suicide-bombing campaigns co-exist with regular insurgent tactics (non-suicidal bombings, shooting ambushes, stabbings, assassinations, etc). The organizations that adopt suicide terror do not abandon the other tactics but use it as part of a range of strategies in their arsenal against their (real or perceived) enemies. In fact, even in the most extreme example of a country under virtual siege (Israel), the other traditional insurgent tactics are far more numerous than suicide terror, yet it is the suicide attack that garners the most press and public attention.

Suicide terror plays a greater role in ethnic disputes when the perpetrators and victims belong to different groups. Targeting the other side is easier when its members are of a different race, ethnicity, religion, or nation since the key issues revolve around the control of territory rather than political or party affiliation. Success under such conditions considers the "hearts and minds" of the people on the other (enemy) side to convince the audience that your cause is just (Kaufmann 1996a,b, 1998).

The differences between the insurgents and the state may be an amalgamation of ethnicity, language, and religion. Under conditions of hyper segregation, ideas of *otherness* are easier to promote by the insurgents.[3] It becomes simpler to dehumanize people on the other side and perceive them as legitimate targets and appropriate for suicidal attacks.[4] Suicide terror is less common in political civil wars in which the conflict revolves around party membership or political ideology. Suicide terror, like other forms of atrocity, is successful against civilians when the group employing this tactic is not trying to win over members of the target civilian populace to their ideology or beliefs.

The terrorist organizations do cost-benefit analyses. Their own community provides needed material and support—money, safe houses, recruits—and the terrorist organizations require a hospitable environment in order to survive. There are potential negative *rebound effects* from killing members of your own group. The density of connections between the people and the members of the terrorist groups are more complex within this boundary than across it. This puts constraints on the insurgents as to who should be killed and who should not. The attacks by Al Qaeda in Riyadh and Istanbul in 2003, in which there were significant Muslim casualties, and against children in Beslan in September 2004 and Iraq in July 2005 demonstrate that such "collateral damage" is unacceptable to the larger Muslim community; Al Qaeda's credibility and reputation suffered and the attacks were repudiated by formerly radical Imams. Beslan caused a self-examination and reconsideration of violence throughout the Muslim World. After this attack, even Abu Musab al Zarqawi's own spiritual mentor (Muqdesi) repudiated the use of suicide terrorism and publicly chastised his former student when the attacks in Iraq killed more Iraqis than American and Coalition troops.

However, suicide terror does not occur exclusively as part of ethno-nationalist conflicts. And while it is a mistake to assume that only religious groups use suicide terror, it is equally faulty to view suicide terror as devoid of any religious content. True, many of the groups engaged in equivalently lethal campaigns are decidedly secular and yet in such cases the leadership is canonized to such an extent that they are akin to living gods on earth. The dedication of a Marxist PKK member to Abdullah Ocalan or a LTTE cadre to Villupilai Prabhakaran is no less than a member of Al Qaeda to the Global Salafi Jihad. But it is also not merely a direct response to occupation. Suicide attacks in Iraq have been carried out by Saudi nationals. Attacks in Kashmir are carried out by non-Kashmiris (there is an exception in 2000 when a student from Srinagar drove a truck laden with explosives and crashed into the Badamibagh Cantonment gates). The suicide attacks carried out by Jihadis from Pakistan belong to the Lashkar-i-toiba or the Jaish-e Mohammed. Paradoxically, the leader of Hizbul Mujahideen, Syed Salahudin, considered the "indigenous" opposition compared to these other organizations, has publicly denounced suicide attacks. Kashmir is unique in that suicide missions are executed by non-Kashmiris dying for a perceived Kashmiri cause. Arguably, suicide attacks in Kashmir are religious and not national (Chandran 2003).

In most cases, the organizations fund their activities through a combination of internal and external mechanisms, both legal and illegal. If the local population is paying, they may demand a greater say in who is a legitimate target. In the case

29

of Al Qaeda, suicide attacks are perpetrated by local individuals (immigrants, homegrown sympathizers, or terrorists imported for this specific purpose) but they are funded from abroad; this may limit the degree to which terrorist organizations might consider the impact of public opinion and allow the terrorist to function autonomously. Nevertheless, rather than reap the benefits of suicide terror campaign (in which inappropriate targets are selected) with increased popularity and mobilization, a backlash may result against the organization if the population disapproves of the tactic and publicly repudiates the group's violence. As a general rule, most publics support attacks against occupying forces but this same audience may find this violence unacceptable if directed against civilians—and especially children.

One exception to the *unacceptability* to killing co-ethnics or co-religionists is when suicide attacks are used against the moderate opposition who challenge the dominance of the terrorist/insurgent group or appear more willing to negotiate with the established "enemy" state. Such victims of collateral damage are not necessarily "innocent" in the eyes of the people whose favor the terrorists are trying to win. They may be portrayed as collaborators if they work in government offices, security posts, or for the occupying power. Indeed, one reason for bombing such places may be to coerce people into quitting such jobs. This is most apparent with former regime elements (FREs) in Iraq and now insurgent elements attacking Iraqi policemen, army recruits, and those who work for the coalition provisional authority, or for the Iraqi government. Although, even this "enemy in our midst" justification has its limits. After a year and a half of attacking more Iraqis than Coalition forces, Iraqi public opinion of suicide terror turned against Abu Musab al Zarqawi and even formerly radical Imams made public statements discrediting the tactic in Iraq. A Pew opinion poll released in July 2005 showed the support for suicide bombing in the Middle East was on the decline.[5]

In the cases of Riyadh and Istanbul attacks in November and December 2003, moderate oppositions or "collaborators" had not been the target of the attacks, rather the violence was used indiscriminately against whatever civilians were in the vicinity of the bombings—to create a sense of generalized panic among the population and attack symbolic foreign targets. The Muslim casualties were collateral damage. According to intelligence sources, Al Qaeda loses the war of public opinion in the Islamic world by targeting Muslim women and children in this fashion. This is borne out by the strong condemnation that followed the Chechen attack in Beslan, Ossetia in September 2004 and the emerging split within radical Jihadi circles evident after the London attacks in July 2005 (Pillar 2003; Paz 2005).

The public response to the tactical use of suicide bombing depends on how the tactic is used, against whom, and for what purpose. If suicide terror does not resonate and the domestic environment is antagonistic to it, it will be rejected. Consequently, violence will fail to win over the "hearts and minds" of the public, the insurgent group's goal. It is fairly simple to gage the public's support. In Palestine, every suicide attack is greeted with demonstrations, pamphletting, the naming of streets, schools, and squares after the fallen martyrs and huge funerals attended by hundreds, if not thousands, of supporters. In some instances, human rights organizations and NGOs poll public attitudes about suicide terror and their support or rejection of civilian casualties. If martyrdom is considered a proper response, the larger audience will support suicide terror and it will flourish. If the opposite is true and the environment is antagonistic, acts of suicide terror will only deepen the gap between the insurgents and the masses (Zakaria 2003).

Even the militants themselves differentiate among targets and acknowledge the difference between civilian and military targets. According to one failed suicide bomber, "From our side... innocent women and children are being killed. I don't intend to kill innocents, and I take precautions. I left the vegetable market and didn't detonate because of the presence of women and children" (Argo 2004a,b).

In cases where suicide attacks are considered to be a legitimate military tactic, but the organization targets civilians indiscriminately, the public's response may not be supportive of the organization. In such circumstances, insurgent organizations are highly adaptable and will refocus actions on military (hard) targets, which tend to be more acceptable to a wider audience.

However, when the domestic environment is extremely hospitable to violence, (because of a brutal occupation or state terror) suicide bombing as a tactic may be championed because the hatred for the other side is very high. In such cases, the organization's use of violence will be unrestrained and the insurgents will not make a distinction between civilian and military targets. In fact, the insurgents will choose targets that have the largest impact and are the easiest to reach. This often means civilian targets. Why does the general population accept or reject the violence? The explanation is somewhat endogenous to the cases and results from a variety of personal, economic, structural, and organizational issues. Suicide terrorism fosters a sense of powerlessness within the targeted society. The interplay of domestic politics and external factors like the ongoing conflict, a "hurting stalemate," or the counter-terror strategies employed by the opposing side all affect the extent to which suicide terror resonates positively.

We can contrast short-term and long-term successful strategies. Shimon Peres, in explaining the complexity of the battle against suicide terrorism, listed the two challenges in order to cope with terrorism as follows:

> The first, military-operational—how to fight the suicide terrorists. The second is broader—how to prevent public support for them. The correct way to fight against suicide terrorists is to discover them before they do anything, and this requires receiving intelligence both from our services and from the Palestinians. But the problem cannot be solved only through weaponry. We must produce an economic situation that will divert support for the Hamas to the alternative regime.
>
> (*Yediot Ahronot* 1994)

Harsh Israeli counter-terror measures, including the use of targeted assassination and building a barrier/wall/fence, appear to have stemmed suicide terror in the short term, forced many of the most militant operatives underground, and caused them to spend more time eluding capture than perpetrating acts of terror. However, because terrorists live and work among civilians, attacks against terrorist capabilities can be nearly impossible to execute without significant civilian casualties. In the long term, Israel's heavy-handed tactics, targeted assassinations, "preemptive attacks" to root out the terrorists, and destruction of their infrastructure tend to inflame Palestinian public opinion and supply continual recruits for Hamas and the Islamic Jihad (Stephen 2002; Ma'oz 2004). The outrage caused by anger for personal losses as well as the symbolic humiliation of their "representatives" can be detrimental.

Until the autumn of 2000, Palestinian support for suicide terror never exceeded one-third of the population. Within a few short months, support for suicide terror, including acts against Israeli civilians, increased dramatically. There is empirical evidence that there is a connection between support for violence and domestic politics since the espousal of suicide violence varies over time in different countries. Significantly, the trajectory of support is not fixed as support can decrease (Sri Lanka, Turkey) as well as increase (Chechnya, Palestine) over time.

A growing number of authors are now making an attempt to explain suicide terrorism via theories of insurgency, offensive realism, as an extreme example of social solidarity, or by using econometric approaches of rational choice game modeling (Crenshaw 1990; Gurr 1990; Kydd and Water 2002; Pape 2003).

Martha Crenshaw measures the rationality of terrorist organizations by examining whether they were effective in achieving their goals as compared to other strategies of war. She states that "efficacy is the primary standard by which terrorism is compared with other methods of achieving political goals" (Crenshaw 1990). It appears that suicide terror is rarely, if ever, the strategy of first choice, but tends to follow other strategies deemed less effective through the process of trial and error. Crenshaw continues,

> Organizations arrive at collective judgments about the relative effectiveness of different strategies.... On the basis of observation and experience, as much as on the basis of abstract strategic conceptions derived from ideological assumptions—allowing for social learning.
>
> (1990)

Consistent with Crenshaw's argument, suicide terror often makes its appearance in the second iteration of conflict. Thus, it was not present during the first Chechen War, nor was it present in the first Palestinian Intifada, or in the first Kurdish rebellion, or in the first Gulf War, even though suicide terror as a strategy predates many of these conflicts and its modern manifestation as a tactic of insurgent groups has existed since 1983. Thus, it is not unreasonable to have expected terrorist organizations engaged in conflict after 1983 to use suicide bombing as part of their arsenal of terror after it had been so successful in expelling the Americans and French from Lebanon.

As Crenshaw notes, there is a deliberate imitation of tactics through social learning. Terrorist organizations, often because of the high degree of publicity and media attention engendered by the more spectacular attacks, become familiar with what has worked and what has failed in other circumstances. However, Crenshaw's focus does not take into consideration the role of public opinion and domestic politics in shaping the use of violence or the ensuing competitive atmosphere that can result—something that I emphasize.

Robert Pape has argued that suicide terror is a coercive strategy directed externally (against a more powerful enemy) to coerce democratic governments to change their policies and evacuate a *homeland* territory under their control. Pape argues that liberal democracies can be coerced through the use of sufficient violence and the expectation of future violence when the attacks occur in organized campaigns. Although Pape's explanation is useful for understanding how suicide bombing is directed against an external enemy, it glosses over the domestic political dynamics and organizational motivations for outbidding. Pape's model correctly identifies the motivations of ethno-nationalist-inspired suicide terrorists and the vulnerability of democracies to terrorism; however, it does not fully explain why religious groups (with goals beyond pragmatic territorial demands) might use it (Pape 2005).

Pape's focus on democratic countries should be problematized. He argues that suicide bombings work best against democratic regimes (because of their access to the media, freedom of movement, and the shock value of casualties), although his theory cannot be adequately verified. While there are cases of terrorists in democracies that have not employed this tactic, his argument is hard to assess empirically since most non-democratic regimes do not permit opposition, let alone violent opposition, that would use suicide terror. In instances when illiberal authoritarian regimes have gone head to head against opposition groups (before their strategies have advanced to include suicide terror), the groups are eliminated. For example, when the Muslim Brotherhood in Hama voiced opposition and mobilized against the Ba'ath regime in Syria, the government's response was to eliminate the Islamic opposition and its geographic base of support (Friedman 1990; Peterson 2000).

Seconding this critique is Walter Laqueur who wrote,

> There was no terrorism under Hitler and Stalin, except for state terror from above; there was little if any terrorism under General Franco and the Greek colonels. If Chechens had engaged in terrorism under Stalin or his successors, those surviving the journey would soon have found themselves on the wrong side of the Arctic Circle. Under Ottoman rule, Arab insurgents would have fared no better than did the Armenians.
>
> (2005)

There are definitional issues that emerge with Pape's focus on democracies. The suspension of democratic freedoms and norms in many of the cases, the questionable label of Sri Lanka in the 1980s, Israel in the Occupied Territories,

33

and Russians in Chechnya as "liberal democratic societies" (liberal for whom?) forces us to rethink some of these propositions regarding regime type.

There have been instances where Al Qaeda has attacked targets in non-democracies, which Pape deliberately ignores, such as the cases of Saudi Arabia, Egypt, and Morocco. Pape's interpretation is that the ultimate and real target of these attacks was the United States, although there are questions about the validity of this claim. For Pape, his underlying explanation of motivation for suicide terror is expanded to include foreign occupation, bases, or financial aid. This definitional slip is not at all falsifiable since all of these encompass a range of policies from direct to indirect intervention. If everything causes suicide terrorism, we learn very little. Further, a case like Japan where there has been occupation, bases, aid, and opposition to the US presence, in addition to a historical precedent of suicide bombing, did not resort to suicide terror to expel Americans from Okinawa. Laqueur adds,

> Pape believes that suicide terrorism is essentially a strategy for national liberation from foreign military occupation. This is certainly true in some cases, such as Chechnya, Kashmir and Palestine but in many cases—from Algeria to Central Asia and the Philippines—it is not. It is not even true with regard to Iraq, where in recent months more than 90 percent of the victims of such attacks have been the terrorists' fellow Muslims—not by accident but quite intentionally.
>
> (2005)

Moreover, fewer than 10 percent of the suicide attackers in Iraq have been Iraqi nationals (Bloom 2005).

Pape argues that the conflict is not about an evil ideology, but about troops stationed in Iraq or Saudi Arabia. However, much of this rhetoric from Osama Bin laden and the Al Qaeda network is merely that, slogans allowing for mobilization and recruitment and finding hot button issues that can unite disparate radical Muslims groups (Crenshaw 1990; Sprinzak 2000; Post 2001; Blanchard 2005). To blatantly ignore the ideological aspect of Al Qaeda and especially the Salafi Jihadi rhetoric in favor of territorial pragmatism is foolish. Pape's portrayal of a centralized Al Qaeda completely misses the effects of the war in Afghanistan and the disruption of the Al Qaeda network. He also wrongly portrays Osama as some mastermind kingpin when every expert on Al Qaeda argues that Al Qaeda has been transformed into a decentralized, franchise like operation of loosely affiliated groups that share the precise ideology that Pape repudiates.

Finally, Pape's model cannot explain why moderates who share the same ethnicity as the terrorists are targeted, because this approach reifies the opposition engaged in suicide terror. This approach glosses over how some groups target the enemy and others target moderates willing to negotiate with the enemy or those who pose a challenge to the leadership of the terrorist group. By lumping together all the attacks in "campaigns" Pape cannot explain the competitive environment that emerges in some cases and not in others—all of which requires an analysis of domestic level variables.

Suicide bombing should be disaggregated into three levels of analysis—the individual bombers who blow themselves up, the organizations that send them, and the environment in which they operate, all of which interact with each other in an Eastonian feedback loop (Moghadam, this volume). To varying degrees, the individuals and the organizations are acting rationally (in terms of *value rationality* and *instrumental rationality*) in the strictest sense of the term since they are pursuing goals consistent with picking the option they think is best suited to achieve their goals.

According to Varshney,

> Instrumental rationality entails a strict cost-benefit calculus with respect to goals, necessitating the abandonment or adjustment of goals if the costs of realizing them are too high. Value-rational behavior is produced by a conscious "ethical, aesthetic, religious or other" belief, "independently of its prospects of success." Behavior, when driven by such values, can consciously embrace great personal sacrifices.
>
> (2003)

The organizations strategically adapt to changing circumstances to maximize their popularity and their ability to influence the "electorate" is based on resonance; specific tactics are either applauded or rejected. This underscores a significant rational calculation—those terrorist groups that are not rational, and do not adjust to circumstances, can lose support and may cease to exist.

My focus on the organizations fits the available empirical evidence from the Japanese Kamikazes of the Second World War to most of the Palestinian and other suicide bombers of today. All of the bombers are first and foremost members of organizations that train them, select their targets, buy their explosives, issue orders for when to launch an attack, and try to convince the larger population that their cause is just.

Motivations for suicide terror

Individuals

In the terrorists' society, a necessary precondition for suicide terror is the existence of a population that believes in violence or thinks that other (more peaceful) strategies have failed. Thus, there needs to be some preexisting level of violence, which has become institutionalized and taken on life of its own. The individuals who perpetrate suicide attacks have social, cultural, religious, and material incentives. These include spiritual rewards in the afterlife, the guarantee of a place with G-d for the attackers' families, celebrity, and even cash bonuses. Although some have argued that suicide bombers are coerced, this is not borne out by the evidence. The individuals may be subject to intense group pressure to sacrifice for the greater good.

> You can't let it happen that you feel shame—that you are always talking of the struggle but don't make anything of it.
>
> (Hamas supporter, Gaza, July 2003
> (Argo 2004a))

Although it is impossible to devise a profile for suicide bombers, individuals most easily manipulated by terrorist organizations for such purposes tend to be young and impressionable—such people would be equally susceptible to joining cults or abusing drugs. This is not a recent phenomenon. The Japanese relied on impressionable youths as well.

> The kamikaze ("divine wind") first used in the battle of the Philippines (November 1944) were young, fairly well educated pilots who understood that pursuing conventional warfare would likely end in defeat.... Few believed they were dying for the emperor as a war leader or for military purposes. Rather, the state was apparently able...to convince the pilots that it was their honor to "die like beautiful falling cherry petals."
>
> (Atran 2003a)

At the individual level, people appear to be driven by a sense of humiliation or injustice (Stern 2003). Some argue, for example, that perceptions regarding the plight of the Palestinian people influence the willingness of young Egyptians, Saudis, Iraqis, and others to participate in suicide attacks (Golden 2002). Others argue that it is actually the conflict in Iraq or Kashmir that motivates generally peaceful Muslims to go on Jihad. At the individual level, these people appear to be driven by the desire for personal revenge because they have suffered the loss of a loved one. Interviews of failed suicide bombers in Israeli prisons elucidate the connection between loss and revenge: When asked why they became martyrs or *shahids*, the interviewees responded with personal accounts of moments that sparked them into action:

> Pictures of dead kids had a major affect on me. Many were killed [right] before me, like my friend [whose body] I had to carry in my own arms.... [A]fter the *istishhad* (martyrdom) of a friend of mine, and after the murder of a baby.... These two cases made me think that human life is threatened every moment without good cause...without distinction between those [of us] who are soldiers, civilians, adults, or kids.
>
> (Argo 2004a)

The truth is that beforehand I saw pictures of dead and wounded children on television.... One day my cousin came and told me: "What do you say to us doing an *Istishhad* [martyrdom] operation?"...the next day we went into town, to a restaurant...with another guy, and then I went with him and I put on the explosive belt and he said it would be in the name of Fatah.

(Hass 2003)

It is unclear as to whether suicide attackers suffer from a form of Post Traumatic Stress Disorder (PTSD). Many attackers have often been drawn from widows or bereaved siblings who wish to take vengeance for their loved one's violent death (Speckhard 2004). There is an empirical regularity in Chechnya, Palestine, and Sri Lanka wherein suicide bombers have lost a family member to the "unjust state" and feel that their only meaningful response to express their outrage is to perpetrate an act of suicide terror. The insurgent organization might also suppose that people who have lost relatives are potential recruits because they are unlikely to change their minds at the last minute or defect.

David Laitin has identified defection as the principal strategic problem that the insurgents must guard against:

"Clubs" of a certain type (most easily formed through religious membership) are able to deal with defection...and to use suicide attacks effectively. Radical religious sects should have an advantage in recruiting suicide attackers if they can design signals of commitment that will distinguish members who have the "right" beliefs from those that will pull out or even defect.

(Berman and Laitin 2002)

The surviving family members of people tortured by the security apparatuses have filled the ranks of suicide bomber volunteers, and human rights abuses by the state only serve to shore up the justifications for violence made by the most extreme organizations. There have been allegations that Tamil women raped by the Sinhalese security services and Sinhalese military at check points join the LTTE as the "Birds of Paradise" unit of female suicide bombers.

However for Nichole Argo, the personal connection to the person killed might be a distant one if any connection existed at all. For some would-be Palestinian suicide bombers, watching the deaths of children from other villages or towns was particularly poignant and crucial to their mobilization. The images broadcast from Jenin or Nablus made personal and real every casualty of the Al 'Aqsa Intifada.

There have been other less altruistic reasons to become a suicide bomber. From the perspective of the individual attacker, the act of martyrdom in the pursuit of honor may offer an opportunity to impress a wider audience and be remembered as a hero.

Sacrifice and risk—when employed on behalf of the group—become valuable virtues, rewarded by social status. Thus, the culture...transforms

37

individual risk and loss into group status and benefit, ultimately cycling that status back onto the individual. The higher the risk, the higher the status.

(Argo 2003)

This symbolic act may be a powerful incentive for individuals who perceive that their lives have little significance otherwise (Crenshaw 1990). Jessica Stern has argued that engaging in such activities affords a way out of a life of boredom, poverty, despair, and likens becoming a suicide martyr to a sort of "Outward Bound" for radicalized Muslims (Stern 2003). Bruce Bueno de Mesquita and Alan B. Krueger have examined whether financial incentives might motivate Palestinian bombers (Plotz 2001; Krueger and Malekova 2002), whereas other authors have discussed how Islam and the heavenly reward awaiting the martyrs in the afterlife explain the phenomenon and enthusiasm for martyrdom (Haddad and Khashan n.d.). A longing for religious purity and/or a strong commitment to the welfare of the group may drive individuals to engage in suicide terror. Even this explanation contains an element of altruism if by perpetrating an act of martyrdom seventy of your relatives are guaranteed a place in heaven. This partly explains the relatives' glee when a family member commits a martyrdom operation.

Religious ideology or political culture can be crucial. Suicide attacks in some contexts inspire a self-perpetuating subculture of martyrdom (Brooks 2002). Children who grow up in such settings may be subtly indoctrinated into a culture glorifying ultimate sacrifice in the service of the cause against the enemy people or in the service of a cult-like leader such as Villupilai Prabhakaran or Abdullah Öcalan. According to Victor, Palestinian children as young as six (both male and female) report that they want to grow up and become *Istishhadis*—often not yet understanding the full impact of what that means. By the age of twelve, they are fully committed and appreciate what becoming a martyr entails (Victor 2003b).

There are two kinds of individuals who become suicide bombers: those people produced by an organization under this subculture and educated outsiders who flock to the organization to volunteer because of personal motivation. These two groups are often comprised of very different kinds of individuals, with varying educational backgrounds, abilities, and profiles. Clearly, different would-be suicide bombers have different motivations, some rational and others irrational, and may be provoked by any number of overlapping incentives for their actions and resist mono-causal explanations.

Organizations

Regardless of the motivations and calculus of the individual bomber, the terrorist organizations coordinate the attacks and aim to gain the attention of the target audiences. The organizations adapt to changing political circumstances and are sensitive to the public reactions to suicide operations. In several of the country studies of Israel, Sri Lanka, Turkey, and Lebanon, the organizations that perpetrated the violence increased or decreased operations in response to the reactions of the larger population.

Flexibility to changing circumstances is far from a handicap since a sustained consistency in the organizations' ideology that use suicide terror is not required. Hamas committed itself at the start of the 1990s not to kill Israeli civilians: when the organization reneged on its commitment in 1994, it found ample reasons for justifying the shift (Hroub 2000). In an act of intellectual acrobatics, Rantisi argued that every Israeli was either a current, past, or future soldiers so that there were no civilians in Israel. The PFLP (Popular Front for the Liberation of Palestine) initially eschewed the tactic and George Habash decried suicide terror in many published interviews. However, when the organization began losing support and credibility, the PFLP hopped on the suicide bandwagon in 2001. Should Palestinian public support for suicide terror return to the pre-2000 levels, the PFLP and Hamas would likely modify their tactics again.

According to one senior intelligence analyst, "Despite its rhetoric, Hamas' primary interest is having and keeping political power. It won't relinquish this for 'ideology'. Most Hamas leaders know very well that they will never push Israel into the sea (Pillar 2003)." Thus, even the most religious organization that employs suicide terror is pragmatic and power seeking. Their political survival is ultimately more important than any ideology.

As part of their propaganda, suicide terrorists are trying to portray themselves as fanatical, and irrational, because they want their potential victims to believe that nothing can be done against such an adversary. Terrorist organizations overwhelmingly claim that violence is a tool of last resort and is a sign of desperation, and this might be the case when states utilize suicide terror as a strategy of war. Although the actual number of states that have engaged in the tactic is too small for the claim to be statistically verified, states that use suicide terror appear to do so only when they are losing military conflicts decisively (e.g. the Japanese Kamikaze or the Iranian shock troops during the First Gulf War). Most suicide terrorism, however, is perpetrated by insurgent opposition groups struggling against an established and much more powerful state. It is used after other strategies have been tried and found wanting but it is rarely the last ditch attempt in the face of certain defeat. Thomas Friedman has argued, "Let's be very clear: Palestinians have adopted suicide bombing as a strategic choice, [and] not out of desperation" (*New York Times* 2002).

In several cases, insurgent organizations tend toward the use of atrocities when the military conflict has reached a deadlock or there is a hurting stalemate and something shocking is needed to tip the balance between forces. Crenshaw confirms this when she writes, "extremists seek a radical change in the status quo" (Crenshaw 1990).

At first blush this might appear contradictory since terrorism is the quintessential "weapon of the weak" and the terrorists claim they are using terror as a last resort, not to end a deadlock. This seeming inconsistency can be summed up as follows: non-state actors tend to resort to atrocities in the second iteration (or more) of conflict after the other strategies have failed to yield the desired results, and when faced with a hurting stalemate.

Ehud Sprinzak summarized the organizational logic of using suicide terror in the following manner: "Our enemy possesses the most sophisticated weapons in the world and its army is trained to a very high standard.... We have nothing with which to repel killing and thuggery against us except the weapon of martyrdom. It is easy and costs us only our lives.... [H]uman bombs cannot be defeated, not even by nuclear bombs" (Sprinzak 2000).

However, much of the success of this strategy—whether it will take root or be rejected—will depend on the existing domestic political backdrop against which these actions take place. Sprinzak argues that the institutionalization of suicide terrorism is temporary and conditional: "Leaders who opt for this type of terrorism are usually moved by an intense sense of crisis, a conviction in the effectiveness of this new tactic, endorsement by the religious or ideological establishment, and the enthusiastic support of their community" (Ibid.).

Ultimately, there is a complexity of motivation behind this particular form of violence. But regardless of objectives, it is a form of "contingent violence." That is to say, the next iteration of violence is shaped by both the reactions of the state and the behavior of the target audiences during the previous iteration.

> The highly publicized attacks engaged in by Chechens against Russian civilians have been designed to draw attention to their cause. They have also played a crucial role in shaping the timing and form of the state response. What is less commonly recognized is that the state's response to terrorism is also targeted at an audience. The actions of the Russian government demonstrate that state counterterrorism can be as consciously directed toward shaping perceptions as are the terrorist attacks to which it responds.
>
> (Cronin forthcoming)

This pattern is repeated among Palestinians who admit that violence can be used to force the state's hand and demonstrate that they are the real victims of the conflict. An art history graduate student preparing for a suicide bombing admitted that

> At the moment of executing my mission, it will not be purely to kill Israelis. The killing is not my ultimate goal.... My act will carry a message beyond to those responsible and the world at large that the ugliest thing for a human being is to be forced to live without freedom.
>
> (Jaber 1997)

This same explanation is true of Al Qaeda. According to one of Osama Bin Laden's closest advisors, (name) one of the reasons for the 9/11 attacks was to force the United States to overact and massively retaliate against the Muslim World thus unleashing a Huntingtonian Clash of Civilizations (Blanchard 2005).

This logic can be extended to explain the counterfactual cases in which organizations did not resort to suicide bombing (although they did engage in insurgency) by examining public reactions to civilian casualties that resulted from conventional bombing campaigns. If the public repudiated civilian casualties, the organizations learned that increasing violence against civilians would not be a welcome tactical shift as was the case for the Basque ETA in Spain and the Provisional IRA in Ireland.[6]

Domestic politics and public support

Popular support for suicide bombing depends on who is targeted and the environment in which the terrorists operate. Suicide operations vary along a spectrum that encompasses the targeting of civilians, military personnel and bases, infrastructure, and, recently, international organizations and other NGOs.

The rejection or acceptance of such violence by the larger population (of Palestinians, Kurds, Tamils, Irish Catholics, etc.) depends on what strategies and counter-terror policies are enacted by the opposing side. The larger population will either support the tactic of suicide terror or reject it and make distinctions between the targets: civilian versus military targets, settlers versus civilians located in the area not part of the disputed homeland, men of military age versus women and children.

> I do not intend to kill innocent women and children, but to kill Israeli soldiers and all that support them in their mission to: take our lands, to kill us, to plant settlements. These people carry the responsibility for these crimes exactly like the soldier that executes [them]. Therefore we don't kill innocents. But when a kid is being killed, here [in Palestine] or there [in Israel], this is distressing. He is killed incidentally [sic] with no intent. I do not intend to kill children.
>
> (Preempted bomber, Shikma prison,
> May 2003 (Argo 2003))

Interestingly enough, in several cases, public support shifted in favor of suicide terror (including when used against civilian targets) when the targeted state engaged in specific counter-insurgency tactics. Thus relying on "targeted assassinations" by using helicopter gun-ships increases the chances that civilians will be killed because such tactics are less effective in distinguishing the combatants from noncombatants. If one side's civilians are fair game, the targeted community will believe that civilians on the other side are not sacrosanct.

After a Palestinian mob lynched two Israeli reserve soldiers who had mistakenly entered Ramallah, Israel used helicopter gunships to carry out aerial attacks on targets in Gaza and Ramallah, the first time they had used this tactic in many years.[7] During the same period, the IDF (Israeli defence forces) carried out targeted assassinations against Tanzim activists in Fatah, in addition to Hamas and Palestinian Islamic Jihad operatives. Israel once again began to raze the houses of those suspected of carrying out attacks (Drucker 2002). A thorough study of whether the use of helicopter gunships and other airpower instigates terrorist groups to bring the fighting and death back to the oppressor's doorstep—to make the war real for them again—would be illuminating (and useful with regard to US foreign policy in Iraq). There is a supplementary psychological factor for the terrorists: if the enemy state feels safe attacking from high above, suicide terror against the enemies' civilians increases the intimacy of the violence. In both Chechnya and among the Palestinians, the Russian and Israeli switch to heavy-handed tactics using aerial bombardment and helicopter gun ships in the second Intifada or the second Chechen war correlates with the rise of suicide terror and support for suicide operations among the general civilian population or mass public.

In Chechnya, the Russian shift toward a more offensive approach to counterterrorism mirrors that of Israel.

> The second Chechen war accompanied with total air bombing and barbarous mop-ups is producing thousands of suicide bombers.... After the Nord-Ost ordeal...we should be glad that [suicide attacks] do not happen every day.... Since the Khasavyurt agreements, Moscow has followed only one policy—sowing death and making the people hold a referendum and elections. It is the road to a deadlock making Chechens fight in the Palestinian way.
>
> (Milstein 2003)

From the perspective of the Chechens, they "have a complete moral right to retribution after what Russia and the Russians have done to them. It is very difficult to expect humanism from the victims of Russia's concentration camps who have suffered torture by electric shock" (Kavkaz-Tsentr 2004).

Finally, military targets become increasingly problematical to attack over time as states harden these targets and, as a result, civilians become a more obvious choice for insurgent groups. It is more difficult to breach the security of a military base or attack a soldier who can defend himself. The PKK (Kurdish Workers party) targeted police and state representatives; the LTTE (Tamil Tigers) largely aimed at politicians and military targets, whereas Palestinian groups have overwhelmingly and deliberately targeted civilians by attacking shopping malls, buses, discotheques, pizzerias, and locations frequented by teenagers and children. Israeli responses have exacerbated the violence.

Israel's strategy of hunting down Islamic militants, including several of the organizations' leaders—Fathi Shiqaqi, Sheikh Ahmed Yassin, and Dr Abdel Al Rantisi, infuriate the wider Palestinian audience, increase the group's ability to mobilize popular support, decrease the ability of more moderate secular groups to rein in the terrorists, and provide "defensive" justifications for future attacks. In fact, according to some bombers, previously disliked leaders become popular because of the targeted assassination.

> We ha[d] a *Hudna*, (ceasefire) but two days later they went after Rantisi.
> I don't like Rantisi—in the first Intifada he tried to kill my brother and

I tried to kill him. But after they attempted to shoot him—in the middle of the street as people carried out their day—I can't think these bad things about him anymore.

(Bomber Interview Gaza City,
July 15, 2003 (Argo 2004a))

Rather than undermine the groups using suicide terror, such tactics have several unintended consequences that end up encouraging terrorism rather than demobilizing it. For one theorist, Israel's use of limited coercion is a deliberate baiting strategy to force a Palestinian reaction in response to which it can escalate conflict.

The process of controlled escalation through targeted assassinations was designed to deal with what the IDF considered a key problem in the management of the conflict: the ability of the Palestinians to develop an elaborate infrastructure for the production of materials and explosives for suicide bombings in Israel.

(Ma'oz 2004)

In several instances when Hamas has ostensibly shifted from targeting civilians (albeit temporarily) or has made pronouncements of its intention to do so (e.g. declaring a *Hudna* or ceasefire), Israel's targeted assassination of a Palestinian leader provided them the justification to renew attacks against Israeli civilians and certainly mobilized support for the organization (Ibid.).

Thus, the fashion in which the state responds to suicide terrorism will have a significant impact on whether bombers and the sponsoring organizations *win the hearts and the minds* of the larger population they purport to represent. The fashion in which a state responds to the threat will also impact international public opinion and international support for the terrorist organization and the targeted state.

Part of the suicide bombers' strategy anywhere is to provoke the government into undertaking actions that the terrorists feel they can manipulate for propaganda purposes, which will also portray them as the victims rather than as the perpetrators... for the first time in the history of terrorism, terrorists have gotten people to sympathize much more with the perpetrators of the violence than with the victims. The [Israel's] activities in the West Bank have turned large swatches of foreign public opinion against Israel in a way that nothing else has in the very long and tortured dynamic of the Israeli-Palestinian relationship.

(Hoffman 2003)

IRA Leader Tom Barry expressed this best when he said,

It would be wrong to suggest that at the beginning of the Anglo-Irish War a majority of the people supported armed action against the British.

43

They did not, mainly because they considered such a campaign as hopeless and suicidal... [T]he savagery of the British and the deaths of their neighbours' children for the peoples' freedom roused them, and from the middle of 1920 they loyally supported the IRA.

(Ryan 2003)

In sum, these domestic strategies of counter-terrorism create the backdrop (receptive or hostile) against which suicide attacks take place, especially when the goal of terrorism is the draw afoul and force the government to behave in ways that will alienate the population further and drive them into the hands of the terrorist network. The domestic environment will have an enormous impact on whether it continues to be used, whether it is abandoned, or whether there is an explosion in the number of organizations using suicide terror to mobilize the population and increase their bases of support. "Struggles won by states against terrorism may not so much involve military victories as the winning of psychological contests in which terrorists lose the support of the people in whose name they are acting" (Argo 2004a).

The goals of suicide bombing: group competition, and outbidding

Under conditions of group competition, there are incentives for further groups to jump on the "suicide bandwagon" and ramp up the violence in order to distinguish themselves from the other organizations.

Outbidding is partly the result of the structural conditions of domestic politics. How many insurgent groups are involved, is one group clearly dominant, or is there a multiplicity of groups engaged in competition to win over a future or emerging electorate? When there is a multiplicity of actors and insurgent groups, outbidding becomes more likely. In cases where one group is clearly dominant, there are fewer incentives to outbid. Suicide bombing is less likely to proliferate and will not become the litmus test against which the organizations and individuals measure themselves. However, even when one group is clearly dominant, defection of smaller organizations from the main group pose the danger of outbidding and thus defection may have dangerous unintended consequences.

Historically, we can observe that suicide terror was adopted when multiple organizations ramped up insurgent violence with increasing degrees of lethality. Where there are multiple groups, violence is a technique to gain credibility and win the public relations competition.

In such circumstances, outbidding will result as groups try to distinguish themselves from the crowd of groups and from one another to establish or increase a domestic constituent base. If the domestic popularity of the organization using suicide terror increases, we observe an increase in bombings. If the domestic environment supports the use of suicide terror and an insurgent group does not use the tactic, they tend to lose market share and popularity. A 21-year-old bomber described his experience in this way.

> The first time I attempted *istashhad* I didn't go to [through] organization, but did it on my own initiative. Second time, I went to the Islamic Jihad—where my brother was in charge.... Myself, I belong to Fatah [But] Fatah in that time would not do istashhad.
>
> (Argo 2004a)

Thus, when and if the group alters its tactics and adopts suicide terror, its popularity can sometimes be resuscitated. The case of the PFLP is illustrative. PFLP leader George Habash repudiated suicide terror for years and refused to engage in such tactics (Habash 2002; JMCC May 20, 2002).

Support for the PFLP declined significantly and, in 2001, the PFLP began to use suicide terror and the language of Jihad and martyrdom. By the time next public opinion poll was taken (within three months), support for the PFLP returned to its former percentage. Since the groups are motivated to win the public relations game, and to win over as many adherents as possible, the tactics that garner them the most support win out.

The question revolves around whether there is a dominant political opposition or whether there is a diffusion of support because no one group has captured the imagination of the people. This reflects a degree of legitimacy (Arafat and Fatah were far more popular before the corruption of the Palestinian Authority became obvious) as well as the extent of coercion used against opponents (Prabhakaran and the LTTE simply kill anyone who defects or joins a different Tamil organization). In March 2004, an East Coast commander named Colonel Karuna defected from the organization and tried to establish an independent support base. Karuna was quickly reigned in and threatened (LTTE 2004). Coercive bargaining is directed at the enemy to force them to leave the homeland territory; the outbidding is directed toward the domestic population who sponsor, join, support, or "vote" for these organizations. The objectives of suicide bombing are, thus, multiple and may reinforce or undercut each other depending on specific conditions endogenous to each case. The goals are directed against the international opponent (get out of the "homeland"), against the domestic rivals (to achieve dominance), and/or against a negotiated settlement to which they might not be party (spoil the peace).

There are indicators that popularity which results from violence is not ingrained and the domestic population can distinguish between killing civilians and military personnel. In some cases, military targets are acceptable whereas civilian casualties are not. Organizations recognize this and adapt their strategies accordingly. The LTTE has adapted to such limitations because of similar constraints on its behavior.

Recognizing the impact of public opinion opens up different avenues of response for counter-terrorism. Shabtai Shavit, former head of Israel's intelligence apparatus, the Mossad, states that the range of decision making vis-à-vis counter-terrorism is restricted by public opinion of the targeted community, noting, "The main problem today when combating terror is not to exceed the limit set by public opinion which is willing or unwilling to accept means that you use against terror" (Ganor 1999). Public opinion not only determines the range of activity, but also affects the types of steps taken against terror, as well as their scope and frequency.

Counter-terrorist policies can be directed at thwarting successful outbidding by the terrorist organizations. The target state could favor moderate factions and not induce support for the militant insurgent groups advocating extreme violence. Thus, where there is a condition of support for suicide bombing, reacting to it harshly directly supports the outbidders' strategy (as has been the case in Israel and Russia).

The conditions of support must be analyzed carefully. A possible counter-terror strategy is to "outbid the outbidders" and engage in policies that emphasize elements of domestic politics that the suicide groups cannot deliver. The ultimate Achilles' heel of terrorist organizations is in its overall negative empowerment dynamic (stemming from desperation or hopelessness). The state can undercut the despair by responses designed to empower. The state can reward the community without rewarding the terrorists themselves. Jailing the leaders rather than targeting them for assassination might prove to be a superior strategy, in that it could drain the lake in which the insurgents swim by encouraging the domestic population to turn away from them.

Algeria, for example, managed to outbid the outbidders by separating the terrorists from the larger Algerian public. "It was only then when the people turned against the terrorists that counter terror strategies were effective" (Baali 2003). The targeted state can go over the heads of the terrorists and outbid them to the domestic population. This path would include, for example, Israel pulling out of Palestinian Territories and the Sri Lankan Government negotiating with the LTTE. You outbid the suicide terrorists and return the objective of a negotiated settlement to prominence by giving the public a stake in the process (i.e. giving it something to lose).

The danger of outbidding has important ramifications for whether policies aimed at democratizing previously authoritarian structures and regimes should be enacted. It may well turn out that they will have unintended negative consequences. A case in point has been the attempts to democratize Iraq under the American and British occupation. This theory would predict that Iraq is potentially ripe for outbidding. If a central Iraqi authority does not emerge with control over patronage and legitimizing functions, weaker factions will find incentives to outbid and use violence (killing Americans) to gain credibility and popularity. In fact, there might be an outbidding dynamic already at play in Iraq as groups vie to become the major opposition faction in Iraq. Indeed, there has been a proliferation of suicide bombings since the declared end of the US-led war in Iraq in 2003.

Religious versus nationalist suicide bombers

It is important to distinguish whether the nature of the organizations engaged in suicide terror is religious or nationalistic. Nationalist groups tend to be vying for the control of territory. Their goal is to recapture the *homeland* and rid the area of what it perceives as a foreign occupation. Territory is often divisible although sacred areas are difficult to divide and the extent to which an area is designated as hallowed will complicate a negotiated settlement. Having said that in the secular contest for power, far less territory is viewed as *terra sancta*. In religious conflicts, these areas might be the focus of the dispute for both sides whether it is Najaf, Karbala, Kosovo, Jerusalem, or the Hedjaz.

In the game of "outbidding the outbidders," it is possible to offer the insurgents a negotiated settlement and give the larger community a stake in the process. In Sri Lanka, the government finally concluded that the North and East Coast of Sri Lanka were divisible under a devolution of central powers. The LTTE accepted the model of a negotiated settlement and agreed to autonomy, although they had previously assassinated moderate Tamils willing to accept such schemes. Devolution and autonomy were less than the complete independence they initially fought for and yet the LTTE reduced its violence, stopped perpetrating suicide terror, and sat down to negotiate with the government.[8]

Religiously oriented groups are more complicated and dangerous negotiating partners. Their ultimate goal may include the spread of religious holy war, to end Evil as interpreted by them, or the pursuit of some heavenly millenarian reward. Religious purity as an ideological goal is not divisible and it is thus more difficult to create incentives to deter the terrorists by appealing to the public. Additionally, it appears easier for religious groups to mobilize operatives to commit suicidal violence than it is for secular nationalist groups, and a growing number of groups are adapting their strategies and techniques accordingly. According to a Rand survey, religious groups have been far more successful in killing large numbers of people than nationalistic ones.[9]

Barbara Victor argues that some of the secular groups in Palestine had great difficulty mobilizing suicide bombers. Logically, before the Nationalist and Marxist groups switched to suicide bombing tactics, anyone predisposed toward martyrdom already belonged to a religious militant group like Hamas or the Islamic Jihad or aligned with them to volunteer for martyrdom.[10]

The Islamic groups prohibited women's participation and so this became the pool from which the groups drew their new operatives. Victor alleges that this explains why women were finally permitted to participate in martyrdom operations (rather than simply play a supportive role) and the Al Aqsa Martyrs' Brigades were able to emerge onto the scene as a contender by tapping a previously unexploited constituency. However, the groups in question appear highly adaptable. In 2003, the Palestinian Islamic Jihad claimed responsibility for two women bombers and Hamas' initial ideological rejection of women *shuhada'a* (martyrs) shifted over a period of two years. Sheikh Yassin finally claimed responsibility for a female martyr, Reem Riashi, on January 14, 2004 (Regular 2004).

Finally, the issues of capabilities and resources come into play. Terrorist groups that can fund suicide bombing and reward their operatives accordingly can generate financial incentives to become martyrs. Organizations that are resource poor might be induced by powerful external actors to jump on the suicide bombing bandwagon if there are financial rewards attached to perpetrating acts of suicide bombing (conventional bombing campaigns do not garner the same degree of external support from Hizb'allah or Al Qaeda as suicide terrorism). Scott Atran writes that after Ayat Akras bombed the Supersol in Jerusalem, a Saudi telethon raised more than 100 million dollars for the Al 'Aqsa Intifada (Atran 2003b).

When the non-state actor or insurgent group must raise money for operations from within its own ranks, a different dynamic comes into play. When the group suffering from the perpetuation of conflict is also subsidizing the struggle, there is a greater likelihood that the larger population will grow war weary and may exert pressures on the terrorists to abandon military operations and negotiate a settlement.

In cases where the money to support the organizations comes from outside the conflict zone, almost as a form of rent, the terrorist group is less beholden to the will of the people. This war weariness was a crucial element bringing all sides to the negotiating table in Sri Lanka. This is due in part because the LTTE has resorted to domestic taxation, levies, and tolls of the Tamils who reside in Sri Lanka once expatriate financial contributions were precluded by anti-terror laws promulgated after 9/11. Following from Charles Tilly, the LTTE's reliance upon taxation increasingly transforms the organization into a "state in the making" responsible to its constituency, rather than a terrorist organization operating above the population (Evans 1985; Tilly 1992). The LTTE must be more responsive to the will of the people, their desire for a peace dividend, and their opposition to the targeting of civilians. In response, the LTTE has also become more pragmatic and amenable to negotiation.

From the perspective of the terrorists themselves, taxation plays a role in justifying why civilians are not sacrosanct. According to the Chechens, it is precisely the people of Russia who, by supporting the authorities and their taxes, are sponsoring this war and this genocide. The people of Russia say nothing, they know nothing, and they want to know nothing of the truth about Chechnya, their brains have been reliably washed by the propaganda.... Silent complicity with the genocide, refusal to protest actively, from a civic position, from conscience and truth—this is what the "civilians" of Moscow are dying for. The submissiveness of the slave goes hand in hand with the aggressiveness of the invader (Kavkaz-Tsentr 2004).

This final element sheds greater light on potentially more productive counter-terror strategies than the heavy-handed approaches preferred by the Russians, Israelis, and, previously, the Turks. If terrorist organizations are severely handicapped by the loss of financial support from abroad, and they are forced to rely on internal financial resources which limit their ability to carry on the fight, there is an opportunity for the targeted state to outbid the outbidders by providing the civilian population with the material benefits, infrastructure, and autonomy that would erode the insurgents' support base. If the terrorist leader can be captured, imprisoned, and made to denounce his/her organization, this is a proven effective strategy. The loss of leadership in this fashion takes the steam out of the organization (e.g. Abdullah Öcalan of the PKK in Turkey, Abimael Guzman of Peru's Shining Path, and Michael (Mickey) McKevitt of the Real IRA).

In contrast to this, killing terrorist leaders appears to serve the purposes of the outbidders, creates nationalist myths, martyrs, and cults of personality. Among the Palestinians, Israel has tended to prefer a policy of targeted assassination, since they rightly assume that to capture their targets alive would be very costly in terms of Israeli life. In Turkey, the assassination of Hizb'allah Sheikh Huseyin Velioglu might have been a factor in the rise of suicide terror in Turkey in 2003. The strategy of killing a leader, rather than imprisoning him and making him renounce violence, has yet to be proven productive in the long term since new groups or units emerge among the terrorists named after the slain martyr—who becomes a symbol and source of inspiration and emulation. Targeted killing further reduces moderates' ability to control the extremists (or self-police) (Fearon and Laitin 2003) since they lose credibility among the larger audience and undermine them overall.

There are no easy solutions to the problem of suicide terror. To paraphrase Scott Atran, policies aimed at empowering moderates from within, supporting certain values (like the respect for life), and similar behavior may produce emotional dissatisfaction with the existing terrorist leaders which could lead to lasting change from within. However, some of the more heavy-handed counter-terrorist tactics of certain states, such as the preemptive attack on the supporters of terrorism, is likely to backfire and mobilize greater support for terror. An alternative counter-terrorist strategy is to change the targeted state's behavior by addressing and lessening the minorities' grievance and humiliation, especially in asymmetric ethno-nationalist conflicts. There is little evidence (historical or otherwise), which indicates that support for suicide terrorism evaporates without the realization of some of the fundamental goals that suicide bombers and their supporting communities share (Atran 2003a). Thus, it is imperative to understand the complexity of motivations, processes, and the inner workings of the organizations to suggest alternative policies to combating suicide terror—making it less effective and less popular.

Notes

1 Bell suggests four ideal models of terrorist funding: (1) popular support model (donations), (2) criminal proceeds (drug dealing, bank robbery), (3) state sponsor model, (4) entrepreneurial model (where businesses generate funding), to which my argument would add (5) the domestic taxation model, Bell, R. E. "The Confiscation, Forfeiture and Disruption of Terrorist Finances" in the *Journal of Money Laundering Control* (2003).

2 *Resonance* can result from desperation (after other strategies have failed) or because of intense outrage (hatred of "the other" because of their actions—real or perceived).

3 It should be noted that hyper segregation is caused by a variety of state practices which include discrimination in residence, land tenure, economic opportunities, or access to education. The hyper segregation is a necessary though insufficient precondition of ethno-nationalist violence.

4 I am grateful to Jeff Goodwin for this observation.

5 On July 15, the *Los Angeles Times* reported a new poll done for the Pew Global Attitudes Project that found a sharp drop over the past two years in the number of people in 4 of 6 predominately Muslim countries surveyed who believe that bin Laden will "do the right thing regarding world affairs." The survey also showed less support for violence against civilian targets in 5 of those 6 Muslim countries. Thirteen percent of people surveyed in Morocco this spring thought it was justified "often" or "sometimes" to defend Islam from its enemies, down from 40 percent a year earlier. In Pakistan, the share who approved of violence "often" or "sometimes" fell from 33 percent in 2002 to 25 percent this year, and in Indonesia that figure fell from 27 percent in the summer of 2002 to 15 percent. Only in Jordan where there are close ties with Iraq's Sunni minority, did support rise for the statement that "violence against civilians to defend Islam was justified 'sometimes' or 'often.'" See http://pewglobal.org/.

6 The IRA briefly attempted to use suicide car bombs, employing coerced Protestant Ulster Orangemen as drivers, but this tactic was renounced by the general population and was quickly abandoned.

7 Although beyond the scope of this present study, a project regarding the effects of counter-terror strategies could be undertaken in the future to test which military tactics are most efficient.

8 The adjournment of democracy in Sri Lanka by President Chandrika Kumaratunga in November 2003, suspension of Parliament, and military reoccupation of the capital was a step in the wrong direction for the negotiations between the LTTE and the Sri Lankan Government. In July 2005 the Government accused the LTTE of violating the MOU 2000 times while admitting that it had likewise violated the MOU 200 times. This work posits that the only solution to end suicide bombing is to appeal to the rank and file, offer an alternative solution, and negotiate to avoid an endless spiral of violence.

9 If the instance of 9/11 is excluded then both types of groups have fairly equal degrees of lethality. Hoffman and Rand identify the religious-based groups as dominant and increasing while nationalist groups appear to be receding.

10 Several formerly secular individuals joined religious groups to volunteer for martyrdom operations. Nichole Argo, Interview with the author, November 23, 2003.

Bibliography

Argo, N. (2003) *The Banality of Evil, Understanding Today's Human Bombs*, Policy Paper, Preventive Defense Project, Stanford University.

—— (2004a) *Interview with a 26 year old Palestinian suicide bomber, July 2003*, in *Understanding and Defusing Human Bombs: The Palestinian Case and the Pursuit of a Martyrdom Complex—A Working Paper*, Paper prepared for presentation to the International Studies Association Meeting, Montreal, March 17–20: 6–7, 10, 21.

—— (2004b) "Expressive Purpose and the Palestinian Martyrdom Complex," *Jaffe Center Report*, April 8.

Atran, S. (2003a) "Genesis of Suicide Terrorism," *Science*, vol. 299, March 7: 1534, 1535, 1538.

—— (2003b) "The Strategic Threat from Suicide Terror," *AEI-Brookings, Joint Center for Regulatory Studies*, December 13.

Baali, A. (2003) Representative, Permanent Mission of Algeria to the U.N. Interview with the author, November 13.

Bell, R. E. (2003) "The Confiscation, Forfeiture and Disruption of Terrorist Finances," *Journal of Money Laundering Control*, 7 (Autumn): 2.

Berman, E. and Laitin, D. (2002) *Rational Martyrs: Evidence from Data on Suicide Attacks*, ISERP Paper, Contentious Politics Seminar, Available at http://www.iserp.columbia.edu/news/calendars/contentious_politics.html

Blanchard, C. M. (2005) "Al Qaeda: Statements and Evolving Ideology," *Congressional Research Service*, CRS Report, June 20: 4, 14.

Bloom, M. (2005) "Saudis Grim Exports—Suicide Bombers," *LA Times*, July 17.

Brooks, D. (2002) "The Culture of Martyrdom," *Atlantic Monthly*, 289, 6 (June 20): 18–20.

Chandran, S. (2003) *Suicide Terrorism in South Asia: From Promised Land to Presumed Land*, Article no. 1085, July 26.

Crenshaw, M. (1990) "The Logic of Terrorism: Terrorist Behavior as a Product of Strategic Choice," in Walter Reich, ed., *Origins of Terrorism: Psychologies, Ideologies, Theologies, States of Mind*, New York: Cambridge University Press, 7–24, 8, 10, 26.

—— (2003) *Observations Regarding the Need to Create a Typology of Suicide Terror*, Discussions with the author, November 6.

Cronin, A. (forthcoming) *Studies in Counter Terrorism: Russia and Chechnya*, in Art, Richardson and Stares.

Drucker, R. (2002) "Harakiri (Hebrew)," *Yediot Ahronot*, Tel-Aviv, 310.

Evans, E. (1985) "War-making and State-making as Organized Crime," in Dietrich Rueschemeyer and Theda Skocpol, eds, *Bringing the State Back In*, New York: Cambridge University Press, 169–191.

Fearon, J. and Laitin, D. (2003) "Ethnicity, Insurgency, and Civil War," *American Political Science Review*, Fall.

Friedman, T. (1990) *From Beirut to Jerusalem*, New York: Anchor Books, ch. 4, "Hama Rules," 76–105.

Ganor, B. (1999) Interview with Shabtai Shavit, The former head of the Israeli "Mossad," November 4.

Golden, T. (2002) "Young Egyptians Hearing Calls of 'Martyrdom' For Palestinian Cause," *The New York Times International*, April 26: A1.

Gurr, T. R. (1990) "Terrorism in Democracies: Its Social and Political Bases," in Walter Reich, ed., *Origins of Terrorism: Psychologies, Ideologies, Theologies, States of Mind*, New York: Cambridge University Press, 86–102.

Habash, G. (2002) Interview, June 20, Available on PFLP website http://www.pflp-pal.org/opinion/habash29-6-02.html, Accessed on May 20, 2003.

Haddad, S. and Khashan, H. (n.d.) *Accounting for Palestinian Perspectives on Suicide Bombings: Religious Militancy, Poverty, and Personal Attributions*, Unpublished manuscript.

Hass, A. (2003) *"Confessions of a Dangerous Mind," Ha'aretz Magazine*, March 14.

Hoffman (2003) *The Atlantic Monthly*, April.

Hroub, K. (2000) *Hamas: Political Thought and Practice*, Washington, DC: Institute for Palestine Studies, 245–249.

Jaber, H. (1997) *Hezbollah*, NY: Columbia University Press, quoted in Jaber, H., "Inside the World of a Palestinian Suicide Bomber," *The Jordan Times* cited by Argo (2004a).

JMCC public opinion polls *Palestinian Opinion Pulse*, 2, no. 4 (June 2001); 2, no. 6 (October 2001); 3, no. 7 (January 2002); 3, no. 8 (April 2002); Available at www.jmcc.org/publicpoll.opinion.html, Accessed on May 20, 2002.

Kaufmann, C. (1996a) "Possible and Impossible Solutions to Ethnic Civil Wars," *International Security*, 20, 4 (Spring): 136–175.

—— (1996b) "Intervention in Ethnic and Ideological Civil Wars: Why One Can Be Done and the Other Can't," *Security Studies*, 6, 1 (autumn): 62–100.

—— (1998) "When All Else Fails: Ethnic Population Transfers and Partitions in the Twentieth Century," *International Security*, 23, 2 (Fall): 120–156.

Kavkaz-Tsentr (2004) News Agency Web Site in Russian, February 8.

Krueger, A. B. and Malekova, J. (2002) *Education, Poverty, Political Violence and Terrorism: Is There a Causal Connection?*, Princeton University Working paper, July.

Kydd, A. and Walter, B. F. (2002) "Sabotaging the Peace: the Politics of Extremist Violence," *International Organizations*, 2, 56 (Spring).

Laqueur, W. (2005) "What Makes Them Tick?" *Washington Post*, July 24.

LTTE (2004) Representative Interview with the author, March 6, name withheld.

Ma'oz, Z. (2004) *The Unlimited Use of the Limited Use of Force: Israel and Low Intensity Warfare, 1949–2004*, paper prepared for presentation to the International Studies Association Meeting Montreal, March 17–20, 16.

Margalit, A. (2003) "The Suicide Bombers," *The New York Review of Books*, 50, 1, January 16, Available at: http://www.nybooks.com/articles/15979#fnr1

Milstein, I. (2003) "A Female Suicide Bomber is more Dangerous than a Nuclear Power," *Gazeta*, October.

Moghadam, A., Chapter 4 in this volume, for a full elucidation of levels of analysis approach.

New York Times (2002) March 31.

Pape, R. A. (2003) "Strategic Logic of Suicide Terrorism," *American Political Science Review*, 97, 3 (August): 343–361.

—— (2005) *Dying to Win: the Strategic Logic of Suicide Terror*, New York: Random House.

Paz, R. (2005) *Islamic Legitimacy for the London Bombings*, Global Research in International Affairs (GLORIA), The Project for the Research of Islamist Movements (PRISM) Volume 3 (2005) Number 4 (July 2005).

Peterson, S. (2000) "How Syria's Brutal Past Colors its Future," *Christian Science Monitor*, June 20.

Pillar, P. (2003) Interview, NYC, November.

Plotz, D. (2001) "The Logic of Assassination: Why Israeli Murders and Palestinian Suicide Bombings makes Sense," *Slate Magazine*, Friday, August 21.

Post, J. (2001) *The Mind of the Terrorist: Individual and Group Psychology of Terrorist Behavior*, Testimony Prepared for the Subcommittee on Emerging Threats and Capabilities, Senate Armed Service Committee, November 15.

Regular, A. (2004) *Mother of Two Becomes First Female Suicide Bombers for Hamas*, Available at: http://www.haaretzdaily.com/hasen/pages/ShArt.jhtml?itemNo=383183& contrassID=1&subContrassID=5&sbSubContrassID=0&listSrc=Y, January 15, Accessed on March 29, 2004.

Ryan, M. (2003) *Tom Barry; Column Commander and IRA Freedom Fighter*, Cork: Mercier Press.

Schweitzer, Y. (2001) *Suicide Bombings: The Ultimate Weapon?* Institute for Counter Terrorism (ICT) website (*www.ict.org.il*) published on August 7.

Speckhard, A. (2004) work on Chechen Black Widows, *Understanding Suicide Terrorism: Countering Human Bombs and Their Senders*. Paper presented to the Atlantic Council's, "Topics in Terrorism: Toward a Transatlantic Consensus on the Nature of the Threat," conference held on November 29 and 30, in Brussels, Belgium.

Sprinzak, E. (2000) "Rational Fanatics," *Foreign Policy*, September/October: 66–73.

Stephen, D. (2002) *Fatal Choices*, Policy Paper, The Begin-Sadat Center for Strategic Studies.

Stern, J. (2003) *Terror in the Name of God: Why Religious Militants Kill*, New York: Harper Collins.

Tilly, C. (1992) *Coercion Capital and European States AD 990–1992*, New York: Blackwell, 1992.

Varshney, A. (2003) "Nationalism, Ethnic Conflict and Rationality," *Perspectives on Politics*, 1, 1 (March): 86.

Victor, B. (2003a) *Army of Roses: Inside the World of Palestinian Women Suicide Bombers*, New York: Roedale Press.

—— (2003b) Interview with the author, October 24.

Yediot Ahronot (1994) (Hebrew), March 11, 13.

Zakaria, F. (2003) *Suicide Bombings Can Be Stopped*, Available on MSN op ed, http://www.msnbc.com/news/953555.asp (August 2003) www.fareedzakaria.com

3

DYING TO BE MARTYRS

The symbolic dimension of suicide terrorism

Mohammed M. Hafez

Introduction

The phenomenon of suicide bombings has so far produced many studies that aim to *explain* why ordinary young men and women sacrifice themselves in order to kill others. Some point to rational calculation of insurgent organizations (Pape 2005); others point to the religious fanaticism of militants, organizers, or societies (Israeli 2003; Shay 2004); still others use a multi-level approach that looks at individual and organizational variables that produce suicide bombers (Moghadam 2003 and Chapter 4 in this volume). We have yet to encounter many studies that seek to *understand* the social meaning of martyrdom for the actors involved (Khosrokhavar 2005). How do suicide bombers view their actions? What meaning do they give to their sacrifice? What meanings do sympathetic observers give to acts of suicide terrorism?

The act of seeking to understand is a controversial one because it requires a degree of empathy with the human bombers that kill and maim civilians, including women, children, and the elderly. The terrorist attacks of September 11, 2001 on the United States have complicated attempts to understand suicide bombers because the act of empathy can easily be confused with outright sympathy for murderous attacks. However, one cannot get into the mind of suicide bombers to discover the layered or interwoven meanings of their sacrifice without immersing oneself in their grievances, religious rhetoric, and symbolic universe. Understanding and explaining are not necessarily opposed methodological positions, although their research requirements can differ significantly. I argue that to explain suicide terrorism, at least as they relate to why individuals become human bombs, we need to first understand the social meaning given to these acts of extreme violence by their perpetrators. Thus, we must, first and foremost, seek to understand the symbolism of self-sacrifice.

The prevailing explanations of suicide bombings focus on the strategic aspects of this form of terrorism, including its kill-rate, psychological affect on target audiences, efficacy in relation to alternative tactics, ability to enhance the standing of groups competing for political legitimacy, and signaling potential in a protracted conflict (Sprinzak 2000; Pape 2003; Hoffman and McCormick 2004; Bloom 2005). These theories explain why organizations choose suicide terrorism as a preferred method from a repertoire of terror tactics. However, they do not explain why individuals agree to play the role of "martyrs" in this game of *real politic*. Are individual suicide bombers motivated by the strategic effectiveness of self-immolation? Do they frame their sacrifice in terms of comparing the costs and benefits of different courses of action or choosing the best means to an end, or are they inspired by more emotive, nationalist, and religious inspirations that have little to do with instrumental rationality?

This chapter argues that individuals are driven to suicide terrorism by motives different than those held by their organizers. One should not conflate the goals of organizations with the motives of individuals. Moreover, while organizations deploying human bombs are, generally speaking, strategically-oriented, this is not the case for individual bombers. Individuals often express motivations rooted in religious identities, nationalist appeals, group commitments, vengeance, or emotive factors associated with personal suffering and empowerment in the context of generalized helplessness. In some instances, radical organizations generate high rates of volunteerism for suicidal missions by fostering a culture of martyrdom in their broader social setting. Rather than manipulate or brainwash individuals to become human bombs, they engender the myth of the "heroic martyr" in public discourse and debates. Strategically oriented organizations employ religion, ritual, and ceremony to legitimate and honor martyrdom; frame their tactics as a continuation of accepted and revered historical traditions; and enshroud their worldly goals with a transcendent morality associated with national salvation or religious redemption. The symbolism of martyrdom becomes the vehicle through which individual bombers frame or give meaning to their different motivations for self-sacrifice.

In this chapter I draw upon the case of the Palestinian suicide bombers in the second uprising, known as *Al-Aqsa Intifada*, to demonstrate how insurgent groups seek to generate volunteers for suicide attacks by engendering a culture of martyrdom. Specifically, I will seek to show how they use religious texts, historical narratives, rituals and ceremonies to foster the myth of the "heroic martyr." Furthermore, militant groups rely on the symbolism of national salvation, retributive justice, and community empowerment to induce volunteerism for suicide bombings. Insurgent groups seek to permeate their culture with symbols that appeal to visceral, not rational, aspects of human needs. These appeals by themselves are not sufficient to generate suicide bombings; one must look at the broader political context and polarizing conflicts that create fertile ground for such appeals. My aim here, therefore, is not to offer a comprehensive discussion of suicide terrorism. I have done that elsewhere (Hafez 2006a,b). My aim, rather, is to point out the often ignored symbolic dimension of suicide terrorism and the social meaning of such action to the human bombers.

Moreover, this chapter is partly intended to raise an anomaly for the emerging rationalist paradigm for studying suicide terrorism. Some may object that a focus on a single case involves a selection bias and, therefore, one cannot generalize the conclusions of this study. This is true. My aim in this chapter is not to present a

55

generalizable theory of individual motivations in suicide terrorism. My aim, rather, is to argue that if we are to accept rationalist explanations of *individual* motivations for carrying out suicide attacks, rationalist theories must be able to explain the motivations of Palestinian suicide bombers, which constitute a significant test case given that approximately 116 suicide attacks using 127 bombers took place between September 2000 and February 2005. This chapter, therefore, has two objectives. First, it seeks to present a test case for theories that solely rely on rationalist explanations of suicide terrorism and, second, it seeks to demonstrate how researchers may proceed to understand the social meaning of suicide terrorism in the mind of its perpetrators.

Is dying to kill rational? The limits of rationalist explanations

How could human beings, young men and women, strap explosives around their bodies, walk into crowed public places, and blow themselves up with the intent of killing and maiming others? Can recourse to human rationality and instrumental calculation explain this type of simultaneous sacrifice and murder? Can reference to costs and benefits explain why upright and well-integrated individuals turn themselves into human bombs?[1]

These are puzzling questions indeed. A number of writers claim that despite its seemingly fanatical and irrational aura, suicide bombings are rational, strategic decisions taken by insurgents or terrorists seeking to defeat a powerful enemy. For example, Iraqi insurgents use suicide bombers against Iraqi police recruitment centers to derail the efforts of American and coalition forces to establish security under occupation; Palestinian factions deploy human bombs against "soft targets" in Israel because it is much more difficult to launch hit-and-run operations against well-trained and better-equipped Israeli Defense Forces; and Chechen rebels use suicide attacks to blow up airplanes, metro stations, and concerts inside Moscow to raise the cost of Russia's control over Chechnya. These are situations of asymmetrical conflicts in which the weak innovate tactically to circumvent the superior military capabilities of its adversaries. They are also examples of how suicide terrorism is purposeful and calculated to produce an intended effect, and where the means chosen are logically connected to organizational objectives.

Suicide bombers, it is often said, are "smart bombs," perhaps the smartest ever invented. They can select the time and place of their detonation in order to inflict the greatest damage in the enemy camp. Human bombs can make last minute changes to ensure their operation is successful. Their psychological affect on those observing the act of "martyrdom," whether friend or foe, is powerful. Suicide bombers send a message to one's constituency that the struggle is alive and well because there are heroic figures welling to sacrifice for the cause. It also delivers the message that such heroic sacrifices must not go in vain; others must step forward to carry the torch of liberation through similar sacrifices. As for one's enemies, suicide attacks deliver the unmistakable message that we will fight to the death; we shall not be deterred.

There are other rationalist explanations of why people become human bombs. Some maintain that suicide attacks are relatively inexpensive because they inflict the greatest amount of damage with the least number of cadres. Others point out that suicide attacks do not require an escape plan and leave no one behind to be tortured into informing on one's recruiters. Still others point to how human bombs could generate revenues for the families of bombers by states that support their cause. Suicide terrorism could also be useful in factional competition over public support and legitimacy. Finally, suicide bombings are dramatic events that are guaranteed to capture media attention, thus generating publicity for the attacking group. This type of attack tells international observers that "something must be wrong" for ordinary young men and women to voluntarily kill themselves. No matter how much one abhors the killing of civilians, the neutral observer cannot help but feel sympathy for the cause of the bomber.

All these are logical and plausible explanations. The problem, however, is that these explanations work at the level of organizational motivations; they do not explain why *individuals* accept the role of the "martyr." For instance, why would an individual agree to kill himself in order to improve the competitive stance of his faction? What benefits does he derive from such an act? Suppose his group becomes the most influential on the political scene. Any benefits that could be gained from this new situation are unrealizable for the dead bomber. He incurred the ultimate cost without attaining any benefit to himself. Similarly, why would an individual blow herself up to deliver a message to her enemies? If her enemies heed the message, she gains nothing because she is dead. Her people may enjoy the fruits of her sacrifice, but she cannot take in any of the "public goods" generated by her action.

Classical rational actor models—rooted in methodological individualism—posit that individuals will be inclined to free ride rather than participate in collective action in situations where the collective effort produces public goods that are not excludable to those who participate (Olson 1965; Sandler *et al.* 1983). For example, a person being asked to go out on a demonstration to express his opposition to a violent regime may say to himself, "If I demonstrate, I may get killed; but if I stay home and others go out to demonstrate, I may gain new freedoms without risking my life." Rational individuals are likely to forgo the risks of incurring costs such as wasting their personal time and resources or putting themselves in harms way if they could stand on the sidelines and reap the benefits when collective action by others succeeds. For individuals to move from the sidelines into the center of action, they must be given selective incentives to participate—benefits given only to those who participate in the collective effort. Selective incentives could be in the form of salaries paid to rebels, loot taken during riots, or positions in a revolutionary organization. Absent selective incentives or coercion, people will free ride.

Later theorizing in collective action moved away from a strict notion of selective incentives and spoke of how public goods could compel individuals to participate, as long as the individuals are able to benefit from those public goods (Mason 1984; Muller and Karl-Dieter Opp. 1986). Examples of collective action that produce public goods include workers striking for higher wages, civil rights groups marching to end racism, citizens rioting to overthrow a dictator, or rebels attacking to liberate their country from foreign occupiers. Individuals in those and other instances may be willing to take a chance—not free ride—if they believe that their action, along with others, will produce the public good. Cost-benefit calculations, in this instance, are shaped by the importance of the public good for the individual taking the risk, the probability of group success, and the perceived importance of personal participation in achieving the overall goals of the group (Finkel *et al.* 1989; Muller *et al.* 1991). These considerations make the act of calculating costs, benefits, and probabilities much more complex. Nonetheless, at their core is the idea that net benefits (benefits minus the costs) must exist for individuals to undertake the risks of collective action in the first place. If the contenders' cost of collective action increases due to state repression or lack of participation from others, these costs serve as a selective disincentive to engage in high-risk activism (Oberschall 1973; Tilly 1978; Oliver 1980). Unless the probable outcome promises greater benefits to outweigh the selective disincentives incurred by the act, rational individuals will forgo the trouble of participating. If the costs become too prohibitive, or if the likelihood of group success is too low, individuals will opt to free ride rather than assume the risk of collective action (Muller and Weede 1990).

The point of the aforementioned literature is that both classical and revised models of rational action assume that costs and benefits are important determinants of one's decision to participate in high-risk activism. It is not enough to point to organizational benefits to explain the decision of individuals to participate in collective action. Individuals must be shown to benefit from organizational gains, either in the form of selective incentives or public goods. Therefore, organizational benefits stemming from successful suicide attacks *cannot* outweigh the ultimate sacrifice (cost) of giving up one's life. Both the classical rational actor model and later innovations assume the individual will be around to reap some of the benefits derived from his or her sacrifice. In the case of suicide bombers, there are only costs, no benefits.

Recent innovations in the rational actor model may offer a way out for rationalist explanations of suicide bombings, but unconvincingly. Rational actor theorists have begun to incorporate non-material, "selfless" or normative ends such as perceived heavenly rewards or concern for one's reputation or social standing (Chong1991; Noll and Weingast 1991; Varshney 2003). The key here is that people are presumed rational insofar as they seek to maximize something of value to themselves, even if that value is altruism toward others or achieving an otherworldly good (Green and Shapiro 1994; Yee 1997).

For instance, Berman and Laitin argue that rewards in the afterlife promised by religion serve as the prerequisite selective incentives for rationally calculating costs and benefits of self-sacrifice. Suicide bombers calculate that their "heroic" leap will avail them in the afterlife and bestow upon them heavenly rewards that cannot be achieved on earth. This rationality is problematic for rational actor theorists because both the *ends* (rewards in afterlife) and *means* (martyrdom in the path of God) are contingent on the bomber's deep religious faith. The rationality of self-sacrifice is possible because of a transcendent belief system that links death with heavenly rewards, not just the instrumentality of human reasoning. What is determinative here is not the act of calculating costs and benefits, but the religious underpinnings that shape people's preferences and modes of operation. The wall separating religious fanaticism and instrumental rationality withers away.

Another way rationalists could explain individual motivations to engage in suicide bombings is by arguing that community honor and respect for "martyrs" and their families factor into the cost-benefit calculations of suicide terrorists. In other words, the bombers sacrifice themselves to enhance their reputation and respect for their families. They also do it because their families might reap financial rewards from a supporting public or a sponsoring organization or state. There are three problems with this line of reasoning. First, it does not seem logical for individuals to seek rewards (such as enhancing one's reputation) that they cannot enjoy because the rewards are dependent on their self-immolation; dead bombers cannot relish in greater community respect bestowed upon them following an attack. This explanation is implausible unless the mere thought that "people will think highly of me after I'm dead" is enough to outweigh the cost of self-sacrifice. It is possible that the attention and respect bombers receive the days or weeks before an attack is what they are seeking after; in effect, they are trading off a long, supposedly meaningless life for few weeks or months of peer attention. This is possible, but it does not seem likely, especially given the fact that many of these bombers come from well-integrated social settings and are often college students in the hard sciences, which means their odds of leading relatively successful careers and making a family of their own in the future are decent.

Second, even if reputational rewards for surviving family members can inspire self-sacrifice, then we must explore the cultural norms that constitute martyrdom as an honorable act deserving respect in the first place. In this instance, there is no escaping the role of culture as constitutive of rewards and utilities in human rationality. What is of interest and significance here is not the act of calculating costs and benefits, but the symbolic context and cultural innovations that make people think that destroying oneself to kill others is an honorable act worth emulating.

Third, regarding material and reputational rewards for surviving family members, it is known that many of the suicide bombers in the Muslim world are religious or at least receive religious training prior to their missions. The two leading organizations deploying suicide bombers in the Palestinian-Israeli conflict since 1993 are Hamas and Islamic Jihad. Even Al-Aqsa Martyrs Brigades, which is a secular nationalist group, often justifies its attacks with reference to religion and its bombers are Muslims, some of whom are quite devout Muslims. The Islamic background of the bombers is important because in the Islamic tradition one does not enter paradise if his or her act of martyrdom is intended for vanity, honor, material rewards, or mere expression of courage. Martyrdom in the eyes of God, according to the tradition, can only be achieved if the fighter is sincerely battling and is killed in the path of God.[2] Self-sacrifice for something other than raising God's word on earth is not only rejected, it is considered suicide, which entails eternal damnation.

The requirement that self-sacrifice be in the path of God leaves three possibilities open, none of which is favorable for rationalist explanations. First, the bomber could be unaware of the religious requirement to sacrifice only for the sake of God and his trainers hide this fact from him. One could term this scenario the "duped rational martyr." This scenario is hardly plausible given the extensive religious discourse surrounding these operations in the public arena and the religiosity of many of the militants that perpetrate these acts. Second, the bomber could be aware of this requirement (fighting only in the path of God), but subconsciously he or she is committing the act of sacrifice for family honor and community rewards. We can term this the "subconsciously rational martyr." This is indeed possible, but not rational. Rationality assumes a conscious attempt to calculate costs and benefits, even in the context of imperfect information. Purpose and intent is one of the cornerstones of rationalist analysis. As Fiorina puts it, "the only thing that all [rational choice] people would agree upon is that their explanations presume that individuals behave purposively (Morris 1996)." In this sense, people are acting with intention and consciousness as opposed to behaving habitually or acting on their subconscious. According to March, "Action is presumed to be consequential, to be connected consciously and meaningfully to knowledge about personal goals and future outcomes, to be controlled by personal intention" (March 1986).

The third possibility is that of the "altruistic rational martyr." He is making the ultimate sacrifice in order for his family to enjoy financial rewards after his martyrdom. In the case of Palestinian suicide bombers, this scenario applies to few cases at best. In each instance, the Israeli authorities destroy the homes of the bomber's family, often arrest surviving family members to interrogate them, and impose travel and work restrictions on them, thus causing tremendous hardship for the family. Also, the sums of money rewarded tend to off-set the costs of lost income from employment and to replace the destroyed home. Given that many of the bombers come from middle-class backgrounds and are in college studying engineering or some other field in the hard sciences, financial concerns do not appear to be their overriding concerns. Thus, rather than being a vehicle for enrichment, financial rewards from martyrdom, at best, compensate for the disrupted status quo following a suicide attack.

In sum, the preceding analysis suggests that rationalist approaches can explain organizational decisions to employ suicide terrorism, but they cannot explain why individuals accept the role of "martyrs" in fulfilling organizational objectives. We must look beyond rationality, into the realm of symbolic framings, to understand and explain, at least in part, why individuals become martyrs.

The role of religion, nationalism, and community in constituting a culture of martyrdom

Research on political violence and social movements shows that organizers of violence must draw on religion, culture, or identity to give meaning to extreme violence (Friedman and McAdam 1992; Hoffman 1995; Loveman 1998; Tololyan 2001). Religion, culture, and identity serve as "tool kits" from which organizers of collective action strategically select narratives, traditions, symbols, rituals, or repertoires of action to imbue risky activism with morality. Moreover, militant groups must align their rhetoric and ideological appeals with cultural norms and expectations, lest they fail to resonate with their target recruits (Swidler 1986; Ross 1993; Emirbayer and Goodwin 1994; Jasper 1997; Williams and Kubal 1999, 2002; Wood 1999; Polletta and Jasper 2001). Finally, the act of cultural or religious appeals to motivate collective action always involves a degree of innovation, whereby old ideas are presented in new ways that appear to be simultaneously authentic and relevant for contemporary times. As Sidney Tarrow eloquently put it,

> symbols of revolt are not drawn like musty costumes from a cultural closet and arrayed before the public. Nor are new meanings unrolled out of whole cloth. The costumes of revolt are woven from a blend of inherited and invented fibers into collective action frames in confrontation with opponents and elites.
>
> (1998)

In the Palestinian territories, militant groups deploying suicide bombings foster a culture of martyrdom in order to generate volunteers for suicide missions. Simple notions of brainwashing and manipulated individuals must be abandoned in this case. Militant organizations have succeeded in framing self-immolation as a meaningful act of redemption. Redemption has two meanings in this context. In one sense, redemption is adherence to one's avowed identity in times when loyalty to this identity is brought into question. In this respect, redemption is about keeping a commitment to one's values and fulfilling the promises implied by those values. Rather than shy away from the challenge, individuals choose to redeem their identity through acts of heroism and sacrifice. For example, soldiers in intense combat situations, or firefighters in emergency conditions, often explain their extraordinary courage in terms of doing their job because that is who they are and what they are trained to do. In another sense, redemption is about salvation of the self or valued others from perceived dangers or errors. From a religious point of view, redemption is about saving oneself or loved ones from grave sin that could result in eternal damnation. From the point of view of nationalism, redemption is about taking extraordinary measures to save one's country from existential threats. Militant groups often call on people to engage in violence to fulfill their duty to their own values, family, friends, community, or religion.

Failure to act, consequently, creates dissonance because it is perceived as a betrayal of one's ideals, loved ones, country, God, or sense of manhood.

Palestinian insurgent organizations draw on three cultural and political contexts to equate suicide attacks with opportunities for redemption: religious revivalism, nationalist conflict, and community ties. Religious revivalism allows religious appeals that equate self-sacrifice with the imperative of martyrdom in the path of God to resonate in society. Nationalist conflict allows militant groups to argue that extraordinary acts of heroism are necessary for national salvation. Community ties create bonds of friendship and family loyalty that motivate individuals to seek vengeance when loved ones are killed, traumatized, or humiliated by external enemies. The statements of bombers and their organizers often weave these three elements together, so it is difficult to segregate individual motivations into a clear hierarchy of motives. Moreover, it is difficult to determine whether these elements are sufficient to motivate suicide bombings or are mere subconscious discursive ploys by which to give acts of sacrifice meaning after one has already taken the decision to kill oneself. Insights from psychology and other disciplines are needed to specify the causal weight of these apparent motivations in suicide bombings. Whatever the case, there can be no doubt that religion, nationalism, and community ties have played important roles in engendering a culture of martyrdom that underpins the campaign of suicide bombings against Israel.

Religious redemption

One cannot understand the prevailing acceptance of suicidal violence in Palestinian society—and in the Muslim world in general—without comprehending the cultural shift that has characterized Muslim societies since the 1970s. After decades of Western secularization, the Muslim world has witnessed an Islamic revival characterized by the spread of public displays of piety, growing mosque attendance, and the spread of Islamic networks, social movements, and political parties. Young men and women in the universities gravitated toward Islamic social clubs and unions, and Islamic activists reaped the benefits by expanding their representation in local student elections. Where and when allowed, Islamists organized political parties and played an active role in Islamizing their politics. Networks of charity and nongovernmental mosques were created by Islamic activists who saw an opportunity to present viable public spaces free from the "corrupting" influence of the secular state, as well as to foster legitimacy for the Islamic movement through tangible provisions to the public. The Iranian revolution in 1979 and the liberation of Afghanistan from Soviet forces in the late 1980s reinforced the trend toward Islamic resurgence and activism as Islamists appeared to be effective agents of social change.[3]

Palestinian society did not escape this phenomenon. Significant segments of Palestinians living in the West Bank and Gaza have become more religious as a result of Islamic revivalism (Ziad 1994; Milton-Edwards 1996; Robinson 1997; Mishal and Sela 2000). The rise of Hamas as a viable competitor of the nationalist camp in 1988, the success of the Islamic Bloc in various universities in the West Bank and Gaza since the 1980s, and the proliferation of Islamic charity networks, especially in Gaza, created resources and a palpable legitimacy for the Islamic movement (Roy 2000; Fisher 2003; ICG 2003). Although Fatah remained the dominant organization representing Palestinian aspirations for independence, the stock of Hamas rose quickly during the first uprising.

We cannot draw a straight causal line between religious revivalism and suicide bombings. Islamic fundamentalism created a context whereby religious appeals and symbolism resonate much more readily than in previous decades. Whereas in the 1950s and 1960s religious groups were marginalized by the spirit and policies of secular nationalism, socialism, and Nasserism (after Gamal Abdel Nasser of Egypt), since the 1980s religious interpretations of the multiple crises facing the Muslim world have gained privileged legitimacy among the wider public. Militant Palestinian factions find in Islamic revivalism a cultural opportunity that allows them to frame their suicide attacks as fulfillment of sacred imperatives to fight injustice.

Hamas and Islamic Jihad, the two main organizers of suicide attacks since the early 1990s, employ five means by which they link self-sacrifice to Islamic identities. First, Hamas and Islamic Jihad insist that jihad in Palestine is an individual obligation (*fard ayn*) as opposed to a collective obligation (*fard kifaya*). Islamic scholars construe individual obligation to mean that it is the duty of every Muslim to wage jihad in the path of God in defense of Islam, its lands, religious institutions, people, and property. Individual obligation usually arises when Muslim lands are besieged by powerful foes that cannot be easily repelled with a small force. Under these circumstances, jihad is the religious obligation of every Muslim capable of fighting, just as all Muslims are obligated to pray, fast, and pay alms. In contrast, collective obligation means that the duty of jihad on individual Muslims is fulfilled if a sufficient number of Muslims arise to make additional fighters unnecessary for the task. Collective obligation usually applies in campaigns of conquest (*futuhat*) that Muslims are powerful enough to undertake without the need to burden all of society.

Islamists in Palestine maintain that Islamic lands have been stolen by the Jews in alliance with powerful Western forces. Given the magnitude of the injustice, it is an individual obligation on every Muslim inside and outside Palestine to wage a jihad of liberation. Hamas's position has been influenced by the writings and personal example of Sheikh Abdullah Yussuf Azzam, a Palestinian who dedicated his earlier life to fighting against Israel and, later, against Soviet forces in Afghanistan. Although the current military wing of Hamas calls itself the "Militias of the Martyr Izzedin Al-Qassam," which was the title of its armed groups in Gaza before the official formation of Hamas's military wing in January 1992, Hamas militants in the West Bank carried the title "Militias of Abdulla Azzam." When the Gaza and West Bank military wings joined together, there was a debate whether to keep the West Bank wing's title in honor of Sheikh Azzam (Al-Deif 2004). Azzam wrote a pamphlet entitled "Defense of Muslim Lands: The First Obligation after Faith." In the fifty-two-page pamphlet, he argues that all the Quranic commentators and scholars of all four Islamic legal traditions (Maliki, Hanafi, Shafai, and Hanbali) agree that when Muslim lands are threatened,

> *jihad* under this condition becomes a personal religious obligation [*fard ayn*] upon the Muslims of the land which the infidels have attacked and upon the Muslims close by, where the children will march forth without the permission of their parents, the wife without the permission of her husband, and the debtor without the permission of the creditor. And, if the Muslims of this land cannot expel the infidels because of the lack of forces, because they are dragging, are indolent or simply do not act, then the individual obligation spreads in the shape of a circle from the nearest to the next nearest. If they too are dragging or there is again a shortage of manpower, then it is upon the people behind them, and on the people behind them, to march forward. This process continues until it becomes a personal religious obligation upon the whole world.
>
> (Ahle Sunnah Wal Jama'at n.d.)

This notion of *jihad* as an individual obligation is also proclaimed by Fathi Shiqaqi, one of the founders of the Palestinian Islamic Jihad (Hatina 2001). It also received support from the popular Sheik Yussuf al-Qardaqwi and many other Islamic scholars.[4]

Second, to substantiate their claim for the necessity of sacrifice in Palestine, Hamas and Islamic Jihad draw on the abundant Islamic texts concerning jihad and martyrdom in the Quran and prophetic traditions. These passages urge Muslims to fight persecution and injustice in the path of God and not to fear death, because those killed in battle will be rewarded by God (Al-Qasimi 1982; Mehdi and Legenhausen 1986; Shadid 1989; Lewinstein 2001). A systematic reading of the communiqués from Hamas and Islamic Jihad, in which they claim responsibility for attacks and present the last will and testament of the bombers, reveals that each communiqué invariably begins with one or more Quranic verses that either urge Muslims to embrace God's command to carry out jihad in the path of Allah and strike at the enemy without concern for one's own weaker military status, or expound on the benefits of martyrdom:

> 2:154—And call not those who are slain in the way of Allah "dead." Nay, they are living, only ye perceive not.

> 8:17—So you slew them not but Allah slew them, and thou smotest not when thou didst smite (the enemy), but Allah smote (him), and that He might confer upon the believers a benefit from Himself. Surely Allah is Hearing, Knowing.

> 9:14—Fight them; Allah will chastise them at your hands and bring them to disgrace, and assist you against them and relieve the hearts of a believing people.

9:111—Surely Allah has bought from the believers their persons and their property—theirs (in return) is the Garden. They fight in Allah's way, so they slay and are slain.

In addition to these Quranic verses, many prophetic traditions venerate martyrdom in the path of God. In one prophetic saying (*hadith*), the prophet Muhammad is reported to have said that "no slave [of God] who dies and has goodness with God wants to return to the world, even if he would have the world and all that is in it, except the martyr, for when he sees the greatness of martyrdom, he will want to return to the world and be killed again." In another, the prophet Muhammad is said to have been approached by a man who asked him, "Where am I, Apostle of God, if I am killed [in battle?]" The prophet replied, "Heaven." The man "threw away the dates that were in his hand and fought [in battle] until he was killed."[5] According to the prophetic tradition, the benefits of martyrdom include:

1   Remission of one's sins at the moment the martyr's blood is shed.
2   Immediate admission into heaven, so martyrs do not suffer the punishment of the tomb.
3   The privilege of accompanying prophets, saints, and righteous believers.
4   Marriage to heavenly maidens (*houri al-ayn*).
5   The right to intercede with God on behalf of seventy relatives.
6   Protection against the pain of death.
7   Entry into the highest gardens of heaven (*jannat al-firdaous*).

To be sure, the Quranic verses and prophetic traditions are subject to competing interpretations; they cannot serve as justifications for suicide bombings without the mediation of authoritative interpretation. Nonetheless, Hamas and Islamic Jihad present many of these texts as unproblematic grounds for suicide attacks, even against civilians.

Third, Hamas and Islamic Jihad draw on the narrative of faith and persecution that characterized the prophetic career of Muhammad. In the first twelve years of his mission, beginning in AD 610, the prophet Muhammad preached monotheism to the polytheists of Mecca. He endured ridicule and persecution without calling for a violent jihad against his oppressors. When the danger against the embryonic Islamic community of Mecca grew to an unbearable level, the prophet Muhammad and his followers left for the town of Yathrib (or al-Medina al-Munawara). In the ten years that followed, until the death of Muhammad in AD 632, the Muslims were initially given permission to fight back against the onslaught of Meccan invasions and, later, to take the initiative against the unbelievers (Firestone 1999; Bonney 2004). Despite being initially outnumbered, the Muslim community in the Medina was able to stave off the superior Meccan forces and ultimately triumph over them. Had the first Islamic community succumbed to persecution, Islam as a world civilization would have died in its infancy. The dominant symbolism of this narrative is the defeat of unjust authority by dispossessed, righteous victims who did not recoil in the face of martyrdom and who relied on their faith to help them triumph over a superior enemy.

In interviews with members of the Islamic Bloc (generally Hamas supporters) at al-Najah University in Nablus and Bir Zeit University in Ramallah, I made it a point to ask about the wisdom of militarizing the uprising and deploying suicide bombers against the powerful Israeli state, which has not shown any willingness to give an inch in the face of Palestinian violence. Invariably, someone fires back that the early Islamic community of Medina faced a similarly powerful enemy, yet they prevailed despite the odds, because they had something stronger than guns, tanks, and fighter planes; they had faith and a love for the afterlife. It is interesting to note that one of the Quranic passages most cited by suicide bombers is verse 8:17 (So you slew them not but Allah slew them...). This verse comes from the battle of Badr, which was the first major battle between the Muslims of Medina and the invading Meccan army of about 1,000 men. Although the Muslims could only muster 314 fighters, the verse speaks of direct divine intervention to aid the Muslims, which was God's way to show his blessings upon the faithful. Indeed, God sent angels from heaven to fight alongside the Muslims. Militants frame their contemporary struggle against Israel as part and parcel of the Islamic tradition of jihad and martyrdom by the weak against the strong, the righteous over the unjust.

Fourth, Hamas and Islamic Jihad circumvent the suicidal aspect of human bombings by euphemistic labeling. Instead of calling their operations "suicide bombings" (*tafjirat intihariya*), they term them "martyrdom operations" (*amaliyat istishhadiyya*) because in Islam, as in other Abrahamic traditions, there are strict prohibitions against suicide. Sheikh Ahmed Yassin, the founder and assassinated leader of Hamas, when asked about the permissibility of committing suicide in an operation, replies, "If there are individuals that claim these operations are suicide, there are hundreds that say they are martyrdom" (2002). He and others insist that suicide is about escapism, the deviation of weak minds. Martyrdom, on the other hand, is about noble sacrifice by strong-willed individuals. Suicide is the pathetic end to depression and despair; martyrdom is a new beginning for hope and deliverance. Suicide is shameful and something to be discouraged; martyrdom is honorable and worth emulating. Indeed, organizers of suicide bombings honor the mothers and fathers of "martyrs" by giving them the title of "*umm al-shahid*" (mother of the martyr) or "*abu al-shahid*" (father of the martyr), instead of "*umm Ahmad*" or "*abu Omar*." Such honor is not conferred on those who commit nonpolitical suicide. By putting the emphasis on martyrdom as opposed to suicide, it becomes very difficult to criticize the bombers directly. One may question the goals and tactics of their organizations, just as one may question the policies of states at war, but one rarely questions the heroism of individual martyrs, just as societies rarely question the gallantry of their fallen soldiers. Iyad Sarraj, a Palestinian psychiatrist, perhaps put it best: "You can say, 'I condemn terror, I condemn killing civilians', but you can't say, 'I condemn martyrs', because martyrs are prophets" (Bennet 2002).

Fifth, organizers of suicidal violence utilize ritual and ceremony to amplify the value of martyrdom in society. Ritual is symbolic behavior and prescribed procedure that is dramatic, socially standardized, and repetitive. It aims at arousing emotions, deepening commitments, and inculcating the values of collective ethos. It links individuals with broader goals and identities and may even link worldly time with sacred history. Ceremony is a formal, public ritual to commemorate a special event, celebrate human accomplishments, and honor solemn occasions with reverence. By setting apart an occasion or persons for special recognition, it implies social acceptance and veneration of one's action, position, or identity. Ceremony is intended as much for those observing the honor as for those honored. It is society's stamp of approval, one way of setting standards for action (Kertzer 1988; Santino 2001).

Proponents of suicide bombings create posters, Web sites, and public exhibits to honor their "martyrs" and publicize their "heroic" sacrifice. At al-Najah University in Nablus, a place that has produced many suicide bombers, I saw many posters and murals for "martyrs" exhibited on nearly every wall and entrance. This is also the case through the numerous towns, villages, and refugee camps of the West Bank and Gaza. One can hardly walk or drive without coming across the posters of the "martyrs" or their names written in graffiti-style on the walls. Sermons are dedicated to commemorate the lives of the bombers and speak of their virtues.

Ritual and ceremony permeate all aspects of preparing "living martyrs" (suicide bombers in waiting) and burying dead ones. The videotape to record the last will and testament of the bombers and solidify their commitment to martyrdom; the white shrouds that covers the bombers from head to toe to simultaneously symbolize their purity and preparedness for the grave; the headband and banners emblazoned with Quranic verses to decorate the living martyrs' quarters before they declare their intention to go on a mission; the guns and bombs that serve as props for their last photos, to symbolize empowered individuals making a free choice to self-sacrifice for the cause; the mass procession to commemorate the death of the martyr, often featuring other militants dressed as martyrs in waiting and strapped with fake explosive belts; the chants of marchers and loud speakers during burial processions: "With our soul, with our blood, we sacrifice for you o'martyr" (*bil rouh, bil damm, nafdika ya shahid*); the melodramatic music to celebrate the heroism and sacrifice of the martyrs; the mourning ceremony where the women ululate and distribute candy or sweet coffee to celebrate the martyr's entry into heaven, and where men receive congratulatory handshakes because their sons or daughters have achieved eternal salvation; the posters on a wall, and electronic links on a web site to immortalize the bombers— all these actions are undertaken repeatedly, routinely, and with procedural rigor. These practices idealize the act of martyrdom and elevate its underlying values in the eyes of potential recruits, to inspire future missions. Ritual and ceremony imbue acts of extreme violence with meaning, purpose, and morality. Violence becomes a vehicle to uphold one's religious values and prove one's self-worth. It transforms cruel terror into sacred missions in the minds of potential militants and their sympathetic observers.

Rituals have many powerful effects on recruitment—not in a direct way, but by fostering an image of a heroic martyr that inspires others to emulate the dead bombers:

1 Rituals and ceremonies engender identification between individuals and organizations. Rituals communicate collective ethos in an emotional way as to appeal to our visceral senses, not our intellect.
2 They can simplify complex political realities by creating narratives of good and evil, right and wrong, honorable and disgraceful.
3 Rituals and ceremonies elevate the status of some individuals over others; they say that a person or category of persons is to be exalted.
4 Rituals build solidarity without necessarily building consensus. Rituals are inherently ambiguous, allowing people to fix different meanings to them.
5 Rituals connect seemingly mundane worldly struggles with sacred time and history.
6 Public rites can be festive, breaking the monotony of everyday routine, creating social incentives to participate in them. They draw people into a network of activists.

These five strategies have fostered a culture of martyrdom that legitimizes self-immolation. Consequently, the religious framing of suicide bombings permeates many of the last wills and testaments of the suicide bombers. Groups like Hamas and Islamic Jihad choose bombers who exhibit deep religious commitments, partly because the discourse of heavenly rewards associated with martyrdom depends on a sincere belief in God and the afterlife (Weinberg *et al.* 2003). The statements of the bombers reveal at least three themes. The first is their insistence that "martyrdom operations" are necessary to fulfill one's commitment to God and the prophet Muhammad, who urged Muslims to fight persecution and not fear death. Suicide bombers emphasize the need to embrace martyrdom in order to achieve liberation, end injustice, seek vengeance, or fulfill one's duty to country and God.

Ismail al-Masoubi, a suicide bomber who killed two Israelis and injured one in Gaza on June 22, 2001, wrote in his last will and testament,

> Love for jihad and martyrdom has come to possess my life, my being, my feelings, my heart, and my senses. My heart ached when I heard the Quranic verses, and my soul was torn when I realized my shortcomings and the shortcomings of Muslims in fulfilling our duty toward fighting in the path of God almighty.

Mahmoud Sleyman Abu Hasanein, who was bent on achieving martyrdom and sought after his wish in March 2002, wrote to his father, "Dear Father: If I do not defend my religion, my land and holy sites, and another person does not, and another, then who will liberate the land and the holy places."

It is important to note that this discourse is not limited to Hamas and Islamic Jihad bombers. Al-Aqsa Martyrs Brigades (AMB) uses the same Islamist discourse in its last wills and testaments. Abdel Salam Hasouna, a member of AMB, begins his last will and testament with the following words:

> After placing my trust in God almighty, and with faithful intentions toward the Lord of the world, I yearn for meeting God...I give myself in the path of God and for the sake of the two domes, and the third noble sanctuary, which is the gateway of our great Prophet. [I give myself] to continue the march of our venerable martyrs that have superseded us in their faith so that the word of God reigns supreme and the word of the infidels is low.

Dareen Abu Ayshe, another AMB bomber, writes in her last will and testament,

> The time has come for the Muslim Palestinian women, whose role is no less important than the role of our fighting brothers. I have decided to be the second (female) martyr to continue in the path that was forged by the martyr Wafa Idris. I give my modest self in the path of God...in revenge for the limbs of our martyred brothers, and in revenge for the sanctity of our religion and mosques, and in revenge for the sanctity of the *Aqsa* mosque and all of God's places of worship that have been turned into [alcohol] bars in which all that has been forbidden by God is pursued in order to spite our religion and to insult the message of our prophet.

Mahmoud Saalem Muhammad Siyam, a 20-year-old militant from AMB, writes,

> I write to you my last will and testament while I am alive, before my martyrdom (God willing). I write it with my tears, not with the ink of my pen. I write it with my tears not out of fear for myself, but in sadness for my mother, who I urge not to cry when she hears the news of my meeting my Lord. I ask her to rejoice and raise her head high in the sky. O mother, I know that being nestled in your lap is gentler and kinder on me than my burial grave, but this is God's calling and the calling of my country. For know with certainty that I did not die; I am no longer in a insignificant world that is not worth the wing of an insect, but in a soaring paradise whose fruits hang low, in the company of the God-fearing and the pure, the righteous, the Prophets, and the martyrs, God willing.

The second theme that emerges from the discourse of suicide bombers and their supporters is the redemptive act of martyrdom. Suicide bombing is not only an opportunity to punish an enemy and fulfill God's command to fight injustice; it is also a privilege and a reward to those most committed to their faith and their values. To be selected for "martyrdom operations" is akin to receiving a stamp of approval or a certificate of accomplishment from one's peers. It is a form of endorsement of one's moral character and dedication. Hiba Daraghmeh, a female suicide bomber dispatched by Islamic Jihad, killed three Israelis and wounded forty-eight on May 19, 2003. When her family inquired about her upbeat mood the day before the attack, she told them, "I feel that I am a new person. You will be very proud of me" (Bennet 2003; Ghazali 2003). I encountered many stories or statements of bombers that refer to their missions euphemistically as "a test" or a challenge to prove their courage and manhood. Fouad Ismail Muhammad al-Houwarni, who blew himself up on March 9, 2002, killing 11 Israelis and injuring 54, wrote in his last will and testament, "Can there be men of truth if we are not (willing to be) men? A believer without courage is like a tree without fruit." The mother of Abdel Muti Shabana, who carried out the bombing on June 10, 2003, killing 17 Israelis and injuring over a 100, tells of how, on the day of the operation, her son asked her repeatedly to pray that God make him successful in his upcoming test. (She thought he was referring to a school examination.)

Moreover, the act of martyrdom is seen as an attempt to redeem society of its failure to act righteously. Words expressed by revered martyrs carry a great deal of weight. Thus, some suicide bombers use their statements to express their view of how individuals and communities should act to overcome the malaise that characterizes their condition. Some urge their mothers, fathers, brothers, and sisters to pray regularly (especially the dawn prayers), to wear the *hijab*, and to be among the best Muslims on earth. Shadi Sleyman al-Nabaheen, who carried out a failed suicide mission on May 19, 2003, wrote in his last will and testament,

> My dear brothers and sisters: Forgive me for any mistake or lapse in judgment toward you...I urge you to be supportive of my mother and father and do not fall short (of your duty) toward them.... Be from among the patient and steadfast and hold tightly to the religion of God. Guide your children to the mosque and instruct them to read the *Quran* and attend the recitation lessons, and teach them to love *jihad* and martyrdom.

Mahmoud Siyam, a member of AMB, writes in his last will and testament,

> Mother and father, I urge you to pray, fast, and rise for the dawn prayers...I urge you to recite and chant [God's name], and entreat [God] to have mercy on me and forgiveness. I urge you to be pleased with me and mention me in your prayers. I know I will leave a void in your lives, but this is the calling of my God and my country.

Others use their martyrdom to urge fellow Muslims to follow in their example in order to redeem Muslims in their moment of weakness. Shadi Sleyman al-Nabaheen, who carried out a suicide operation on May 19, 2003, injuring three Israelis, declared in his last will and testament, "The tree of Islam is continuously nourished with the blood of martyrs so that it can provide shade to those who come after us..." He rhetorically asks fellow Muslims around the world,

> how long will the Muslim nation continue in its stupor and paralysis?...I say to you [Muslims] we are coming from the midst of the pile [of fallen martyrs], we will arise from our wounds and limbs, for a pure and virtuous Muslim youth took upon themselves the burden of their nation to get rid of its oppression in order to raise high in the sky its banner "There is no God but Allah, and Muhammad is His Prophet."

Jihad Walid Hamada, who carried out an operation on August 4, 2002, killing 10 and injuring 40 Israelis, is equally eloquent in his last will and testament:

> I write this testament in the depth of *jihad*, waiting for the ultimate battle against those who violated our homeland. I ask God to bless his soldiers and give me the strength to sever the heads of Jews from their bodies...Heaven is calling upon its people...so do as I did and make a promise to God to pursue *jihad* and liberate our Palestine and blessed Noble Sanctuary....Let us make the Zionists regret the day they contemplated the assassination of our leader and preacher Salah Shahada....O'brothers, embark on the path of the holy fighters that preceded you....May our blood become a lantern that lights up for those around us the path towards liberation, to raise the banner of truth, the banner of Islam. O'sons of Palestine, O'sons of Qassam: the path is ahead of us.

This testament, as we shall see further later, contains three elements that are common in other testaments: (1) religious devotion and belief in the duty and honor of jihad and martyrdom, (2) explicit call to avenge previous killings, and (3) appeal to others to carry out similar operations as well as lead moral lives that will ultimately vindicate the Islamic community and make them victorious in the eyes of God as well as in this world.

The third theme that emerges is that of reward in the afterlife. Kamal Abdelnasser Rajab, an Islamic Jihad suicide bomber, cites the following Prophetic tradition in his last will and testament: "In heaven, God has prepared 100 ranks for those holy fighters that fight in His path. The difference between one level and another is akin to the difference between heaven and earth." He goes on to declare: "O'father and mother, dearest to my heart; o'brothers, sisters, and friends, life near God is the best of lives and better than life itself, especially one dominated by arrogant tyrants." Bombers also speak of heavenly rewards for their families. In many communiqués the bombers ask their mothers and fathers to forgive them and remind them that God has promised martyrs the privilege of interceding on behalf of seventy family members on judgment day. Hamed Abu Hejleh, a suicide bomber who blew himself up at a bus stop in

71

Netanya in January 2001, injuring sixty Israelis, tells his family in his last will and testament,

> If I have fallen short in my duty toward you in this world, I will not fall short during judgment day, God willing. For know that the Prophet Muhammad, peace be upon him, has said that the martyr intercedes (with God) on behalf of seventy of his family members.

Shadi Sleyman al-Nabaheen, who was mentioned earlier, wrote to his mother and father in his last will and testament, "I wanted to beat you to heaven so I can intercede with my God on your behalf...."

Suicide bombers and their organizers urge their families to celebrate, rather than mourn, their "martyrdom" after a suicidal mission to rejoice their entry into heaven. The previously mentioned bomber Hamed Abu Hejleh, whose oversized picture was mounted in one of the main staircases at al-Najah University, where he studied civil engineering, wrote in his last will and testament, "My last wish to you my family is that none of you should weep in my procession to heaven. Indeed, distribute dates and ululate in the wedding of martyrdom." The mother of Muhammad Fathi Farhat, who was videotaped with her son before his operation, wishing him success, was also videotaped after he completed his mission, distributing sweets to neighbors who came to "celebrate." She reproached those who sobbed, asking them to leave because she would not accept tears on this joyous occasion.

Nationalist conflict and community ties

The discourse of Hamas and Islamic Jihad is not purely religious; they, along with secular groups like AMB and the PFLP, draw on deep nationalist feelings to inspire people to die for the nation. To be sure, the secular groups rely on the culture of martyrdom fostered by the Islamists. Similarly, many of the suicide bombers of Hamas and Islamic Jihad reference nationalist goals and desire for defiance and revenge in the face of repressive Israeli measures. It would be a mistake, therefore, to claim that the bombers of Hamas and Islamic Jihad rely on religious motivations while the bombers of AMB and PFLP rely on nationalism; the motives of the bombers are much more complex and interwoven.

One theme that emerges from a systematic reading of statements made by bombers is their desire to shake their people as well as fellow Muslims and Arabs into action by a drastic act of heroism. Muhammad Hazza al-Ghoul, a Hamas member who blew himself up on a bus on June 18, 2002, killing 19 Israelis and injuring 74, wrote in his last will and testament,

> How beautiful for the splinters of my bones to be the response that blows up the enemy, not for the love of killing, but so we can live as other people live.... We do not sing the songs of death, but recite the hymns of life.... We die so that future generations may live.

This theme of sacrifice for the sake of others is echoed in the eulogy given to two suicide bombers from Nablus by Qais Adwan, a Hamas organizer of suicide attacks killed by Israelis in April 2002: "It's amazing that man sacrifices himself so as to enable his nation to live" (Rubin 2002).

The symbolism of martyrdom is seen as perhaps sufficient to awaken the consciousness of Arab nations to compel their governments to act in unison against Israel and its allies. Muhammad al-Habashi, who blew himself up on September 9, 2001, killing 3 Israelis and injuring 90, wrote in his last will and testament, "I ask God almighty that my martyrdom is a message to all the Arab and Muslim nations to get rid of the injustice of their rulers that weigh heavily on their shoulders, and to rise to bring victory to Muslims in Jerusalem and Palestine, and in all conquered Muslim lands...." Mahmoud Sleyman Abu Hasanein, mentioned earlier, concludes his last will and testament with words directed toward all Arab and Muslim nations of the world: "Why are you committed to this transient world? Why the fear? We only die once, so let it be for the sake of God." Ayat Akhras, a female suicide bomber who blew herself up in a Jerusalem supermarket in March 2002, killing a body guard and a young women nearly her age, declared in her videotaped message, "I am going to fight instead of the sleeping Arab armies who are watching Palestinian girls fight alone."

Nationalism is as much about an imagined community as it is about shared borders, language, and culture. Imagined community, following Benedict Anderson, refers to how members of disparate communities come to identify themselves as a unified nation despite the fact that they have never met and are not likely ever to know one another on a personal level (Anderson 1991). Others refer to this phenomenon as *fictive kin*, whereby individuals who do not know each other personally develop emotional ties based on social identification, especially in times of crisis or trauma (Speckhard 2005). The events of September 11 undoubtedly generated such feelings among Americans, who grieved together regardless of whether they lost loved ones in the tragic attacks of that day.

Israel's response to Palestinian violence generated additional grievances, humiliations, and traumas that resulted in a desire among ordinary people to avenge loved ones as well as those they identified with on a personal level. Closures, curfews, checkpoints, home demolitions, targeted assassinations, military incursions, and the security barrier/wall of separation had a dual effect of building bonds of solidarity among communities and increasing the desire for defiance and vengeance (HRW 2000, 2001; Hass 2002, 2003; Moore 2002, 2003; Pedatzur 2002; Anderson 2003; Eldar 2003a,b; Levy 2003; Rubinstein 2003a,b). Daily killings that were televised by local and satellite media resulted in a multiplier effect, whereby the pain of one community reverberated in other communities. Many Palestinian bombers insist that their violence is a response to the overwhelming injustices perpetrated by Israeli forces. If the Israelis did not kill old men, women, and children, the Palestinians would not be compelled to attack Israeli civilians in retaliation, they argue.

Jamal Abdel-Ghani Nasser, a suicide bomber that carried out an operation on April 29, 2001, killing no one but himself, wrote this message prior to his mission:

> Who amongst us was not enraged and did not seek vengeance when witnessing the mothers, wives, and sons and daughters of the martyrs on television; who from among us did not feel as one of the homeowners that had their homes destroyed lately in Khan Yunis and Rafah; who amongst us did not feel rage when children were killed, trees uprooted, and towns bombarded.

Muhammad al-Habashi, who was mentioned earlier, cites in his last will and testament the names of children that have been killed during the uprising and received a great deal of media attention, including Muhammad al-Dura, Iman Hujou, and Diya al-Tamizi. He also cites historic episodes in which massacres against Palestinians took place, including Kafr Qasim, Dir Yassin, Qina, and Sabra and Shatila.

Mahmoud Ahmed Marmush, who carried out a suicide attack on May 18, 2001, killing 7 and injuring over 120 in Netanya, begins his last will and testaments with these words:

> The Palestinian people are encountering the cruelest times, enduring daily killings, bombardment, displacement, and the most extreme forms of violence. Everyday its suffering increases. A group must arise to sacrifice itself and strive in the path of God to defend its honor and its people....

Fuad Qawasmeh, 21 years old, carried out an operation for Hamas on May 17, 2003, killing two Israelis in a Hebron city center. According to his cousin, Fahid Qawasmeh, Fuad spent seven months in an Israeli prison and lost two close friends in the uprising. This experience transformed him from an apolitical and irreligious person to a nationalist and pious young man. He began spending hours each day reading the *Quran* and listening to music extolling *jihad* and martyrs fighting Israel (Myre 2003).

In an investigative report by the *Guardian* newspaper, the friends and families of twenty-one suicide bombers were interviewed. It is reported that all the families described that the bombers were influenced emotionally by daily images of killings, sometimes "breaking down in tears or shouting before their television sets" (Goldenberg 2002).

Perhaps one of the better-known stories is that of the 27-year-old apprentice lawyer Hanadi Jaradat, one of the female suicide bombers of Islamic Jihad. On October 4, 2003, she blew herself up in the Maxim restaurant in the Israeli sea-side town of Haifa, killing 19 Israelis and injuring 60. Like Hiba Daraghmeh before her, she, too, appeared to her family to be happy the day before the attack. There can be little doubt about what motivated her action. Four months before, her

23-year-old brother Fadi and her 31-year-old cousin, both members of Islamic Jihad, were killed in Israeli military actions. After those deaths, she became radicalized. She was always intensely religious, but the killings of her brother and cousin, along with the refusal of Israeli military authorities in Jenin to grant her father a permit for medical treatment in Haifa for his liver ailment, resulted in deep trauma. Her mother reports that she "was full of pain.... She saw them taking the body [of her brother] from the hospital to the morgue, and she was different after that. Some nights, she woke up screaming, saying she had nightmares about Fadi." The reaction of her family reflects how community ties could lay the basis for societal support for suicide attacks. Her mother tells reporters that "She has done what she has done, thank God, and I am sure that what she has done is not a shameful thing, she has done it for the sake of her people." Her father had a similar reply:

> I don't want to talk about my feelings, my pain, my suffering. But I can tell you that our people believe that what Hanadi has done is justified. Imagine yourself watching the Israelis kill your son, your nephew, destroying your house... they are pushing our people into a corner, they are provoking actions like these by our people.
>
> (Burns 2003)

All these statements reflect the underlying sense of moral righteousness derived from the act of self-sacrifice. They also show that one cannot simply disaggregate nationalism and religious revivalism; the bombers are dying for God and country. Religious revivalism, nationalist conflict, and community ties underpin the culture of martyrdom that emerged during the second Palestinian uprising. Organizations drew on these three sources of identity to engender the myth of the heroic martyr. These identities were interwoven by militant groups to frame martyrdom as an act of redemption, empowerment, and defiance against unjust authorities. Volunteers for suicide attacks were not brainwashed victims of opportunistic organizations or manipulated individuals that were fooled by calculating terrorists; nor were they rational actors calculating costs and benefits of different options and choosing the path that maximizes their preferences. Instead, it is more appropriate to say that they were *inspired* by the symbolism of martyrdom and opportunity to fulfill their obligation to God, sacrifice for the nation, and avenge a grieving people.

Conclusion

This chapter addressed Palestinian suicide bombings against Israelis, so its conclusions may not extend beyond this case. However, the analysis presented by the case study raises serious doubts about rationalist explanations of individual motivations for carrying out suicide attacks. Strategic calculus helps explain why organizations choose to dispatch human bombers, but it cannot explain why ordinary men and women accept the role of the "martyr." To explain why individuals do it, we must go beyond instrumental rationality and we must first seek to understand the social meaning bombers give to their actions. To do so, we must immerse ourselves in the symbolic universe of perpetrators of extreme violence. This chapter illustrates one way to approach the study of individual motivators in suicide terrorism.

The case of Palestinian suicide bombers during al-Aqsa uprising supports the view that, at the level of the individual, religious and nationalist appeals that equate self-sacrifice with martyrdom and national salvation are instrumental in producing volunteers for suicide attacks. Individuals are not inspired to carry out suicide bombings because they are the optimal tactic given the constraints of the political environment or calculations of costs and benefits; rather they are inspired by the redemptive nature of self-sacrifice. The religious and nationalist framings of Hamas, Islamic Jihad, and Al-Aqsa Martyrs Brigades go beyond mere manipulation of individual minds; they combine religious texts and historical narratives with ritual and ceremony to foster a culture that venerates martyrdom. The cultural context of Islamic revivalism and the context of violent nationalist conflict allow those appeals to resonate with the broader public and potential bombers. Militant groups also draw upon the desire for national empowerment in the context of powerlessness to motivate individuals to undertake "heroic" acts to shake the passive public into action. Finally, militant groups draw upon the desire for vengeance that arises when individuals perceive members of their actual or imagined community humiliated or traumatized by hated enemies.

A neat hierarchy of motivations will not serve us well in this case. The statements of the bombers and those that know them well show how motivations often weave together religion, nationalism, and a desire for vengeance. Moreover, this case shows that one cannot simply allocate religious motivations to religious groups and nationalist motivations to nationalist groups. Both Islamist and nationalist factions fostered and benefited from the myth of the heroic martyr that simultaneously fulfills his obligation toward God, country, and people.

Notes

1 Many studies have shown that suicide bombers are, generally speaking, normal human beings with no diagnosable psycho-pathological inclinations. Moreover, many tend to be educated, socially-accepted at their universities and among their peers, and are not suffering severe economic distress. See, for instance, Douglas Davis, "Aksa Bombers Educated, Middle-Class," *Jerusalem Post*, March 25, 2002; Scott Atran, "Genesis of Suicide Terrorism," *Science*, March 7 (2003): 1534–1539; Nasra Hassan, "An Arsenal of Believers: Talking to 'Human Bombs'," *The New Yorker*, November 19, 2001.

2 See Nawaf Hayel al-Takrouri, *al-Amaliyat al-Istishhadiyya fi Mizan al-Fiqhi* [Martyrdom Operations in Islamic Jurisprudence] (Damascus, Dar al-Fikr 2003). This is one of the most important books to be published on this subject by an author supportive of "martyrdom operations." He cites historical and contemporary Islamic scholars that affirm that martyrdom is dependent on religious faith and striving in the path of God only.

3 A full discussion of the causes and dynamics of Islamic revivalism witnessed since the 1970s is outside the scope of this book. For a good introduction to theories explaining Islamic activism, see Hafez (2003, ch. 1) and Wiktorowicz (2004).

4 Yussuf al-Qaradawi's declared jihad in Palestine as the individual obligation of every Muslim on many occasions during his weekly program on al-Jazeera entitled *al-Sharia wal-Haya* (Islamic Law and Life). His religious rulings regarding "martyrdom operations" aired on December 23, 2001 in a show entitled *al-Amaliyat al-Istishhadiyya fi Falastin* (Martyrdom Operations in Palestine) and on May 31, 2004 in a show entitled *al-Muslimun wal-Unf al-Siyasi* (Muslims and Political Violence). Yussuf al-Qaradawi's blessing for suicide bombings can be found in interviews with the Kuwaiti-based weekly, *Majallat al-Mujtama'a*, no. 1201, 1996 and the London-based monthly, *Falastin al-Muslima*, March 2002. In the latter, he rules that it is permissible for women to engage in suicide bombings. His religious rulings and publications can be found on his web site www.qaradawi.net. Al-Takrouri, in his book *al-Amaliyat*, cites at least thirty-two religious rulings (*fatwas*) by Islamic scholars around the Muslim world supporting "martyrdom operations" in Palestine.

5 These prophetic traditions and others concerning the desire to die as a martyr are quoted by al-Takrouri, *al-Amaliyat*. This book provides justification for suicide attacks and insists that they are legitimate martyrdom operations that can be equated with martyrdom during the time of the prophet Muhammad. It is advertised on Hamas's Web site, www.palestine-info.net/arabic/hamas/.

Bibliography

Abu-Amr, Z. (1994) *Islamic Fundamentalism in the West Bank and Gaza: Muslim Brotherhood and Islamic Jihad*, Bloomington, IN:Indiana University Press.

Ahle Sunnah Wal Jama'at (n.d.).

Al-Deif, Muhammad (2004) General Commander of Hamas's Military Wing, available on www.alqassam.info/ or www.palestine-info.net/arabic/hamas/, accessed March 8, 2004.

Al-Takrouri, Nawaf Hayel (2003) *Martyrdom Operations in Islamic Jurisprudence*, Arabic, Damascus: Dar al-Fikr.

Anderson, B. (1991) *Imagined Communities: Reflections on the Origin and Spread of Nationalism*, London and New York. Verso.

Anderson, J. W. (2003) "Israel's Fence Mixes Security and Politics: As Scope Grows, So Does Hostility," *Washington Post*, September 23.

Atran, S. (2003) "Genesis of Suicide Terrorism," *Science*, March 7: 1534–1539.

Bennet, J. A. (2003) "Scholar of English Who Clung to the Veil," *New York Times*, May 30.

—— (2002) interview, "The Bombers," *New York Times*, June 21.

Bloom, M. (2005) *Dying to Kill: The Allure of Suicide Terror*, New York: Columbia University Press.

Bonney, R. (2004) *Jihad: From Qur'an to bin Laden*, London and New York: Palgrave Macmillan.

Burns, J. B. (2003) "For Bomber's Parents, a Smile for a Goodbye", *New York Times*, October 7.

Chong, D. (1991) *Collective Action and the Civil Rights Movement*, Chicago, IL: University of Chicago Press.

Davis, D. (2002) "Aksa Bombers Educated, Middle-Class," *Jerusalem Post*, March 25.

Dhafer al-Qasimi (1982) *al-Jihad wal-huquq al-dawliya al aama fi al-Islam* [Jihad and Universal International Rights in Islam], Beirut: dar al-ilm lil-malayeen.

Donald P. and Shapiro, P. (1994) *Pathologies of Rational Choice Theory: A Critique of Applications in Political Science*, New Haven, CT: Yale University Press.

Eldar, A. (2003a) "*If Only the Bullets Could Talk*," *Ha'aretz*, March 4.

—— (2003b) "What Suffering? The Fabric of Life is Not Torn," *Ha'aretz*, October 29.

Emirbayer, M. and Goodwin, J. (1994) "Network Analysis, Culture, and the Problem of Agency," *American Journal of Sociology*, 99: 1411–1454.

Finkel, S. E., Muller, E. N., and Karl-Dieter Opp. (1989) Personal Influence, Collective Rationality, and Mass Political Action: Evaluating Alternative Models with Panel Data," American Political Science Review 83, March: 885–903.

Firestone, R. (1999) *Jihad: The Origin of Holy War in Islam*, New York: Oxford University Press.

Fisher, I. (2003) "Defining Hamas: Roots in Charity and Branches of Violence," *New York Times*, June 16.

Friedman, D. and McAdam, D. (1992) "Collective Identity and Activism: Networks, Choices, and the Life of a Social Movement," in Aldon D. Morris and Carol McClurg Mueller, eds, *Frontiers in Social Movement Theory*, New Haven, CT: Yale University Press, 156–173.

Ghazali, S. (2003) "The Palestinian Extreme," *The Independent*, May 27.

Goldenberg, S. (2002) "A Mission to Murder: Inside the Minds of the Suicide Bombers," *The Guardian* (London), June 11.

Green, D. P. and Shapiro, I. (1994) *Pathologies of Rational Choice Theory: A Critique of Applications in Political Science*, New Haven: Yale University Press.

Hafez, Mohammed M. (2003) *Why Muslims Rebel: Repression and Resistance in the Islamic World*, Boulder, CO: Lynne Rienner.

Hafez, M. (2006a) *Manufacturing Human Bombs: The Making of Palestinian Suicide Bombers*, Washington, DC: United States Institute of Peace Press.

—— (2006b) "Rationality, Culture, and Structure in the Making of Suicide Bombers: A Preliminary Theoretical Synthesis and Illustrative Case Study," *Studies in Conflict and Terrorism*, 29: 137–157.

Hardin, R. (1982) *Collective Action*, Baltimore, MD: Johns Hopkins University Press.

Hass, A. (2002) "Deterrents That Haven't Deterred," *Ha'aretz*, August 28.

—— (2003) "We don't raze homes for no reason," *Ha'aretz*, June 5.

Hassan, Nasra (2001) "An Arsenal of Believers: Talking to Human Bombs," *The New Yorker*, November 19.

Hatina, M. (2001) *Islam and Salvation in Palestine: The Islamic Jihad Movement*, Moshe Dayan Center for Strategic Studies in Tel Aviv University, ch. 2.

Hoffman, B. (1995) " 'Holy Terror': The Implications of Terrorism Motivated by a Religious Imperative," *Studies in Conflict and Terrorism*, 18: 271–284.

—— (2004) "Terrorism, Signaling, and Suicide Attacks," *Studies in Conflict and Terrorism*, 27, July–August: 243–281.

Human Rights Watch (HRW) (2000) "Investigation into the Unlawful Use of Force in the West Bank, Gaza Strip and Northern Israel—October 4 Through October 11," *A Human Rights Watch Report*, 12, October.

—— (2001) *Center of the Storm: A Case Study of Human Rights Abuses in Hebron District*, New York: Human Rights Watch.

International Crisis Group (ICG) (2003) Islamic Social Welfare Activism in the Occupied Palestinian Territories: A Legitimate Target? *Middle East Report*, 13, April 2: 1–31, available on www.icg.org

Israeli, R. (2003) *Islamikaze: Manifestations of Islamic Martyrology*, London: Frank Cass Publishers.

Jasper, J. M. (1997) *The Art of Moral Protest: Culture, Biography and Creativity in Social Movements*, Chicago, IL: University of Chicago Press.

Kertzer, D. (1988) *Ritual, Politics and Power*, New Haven, CT: Yale University Press.

Khosrokhavar, F. (2005) *Suicide Bombers: Allah's New Martyrs*, London: Pluto Press.

Levy, G. (2003) "The Ill Wind Blowing from the Border Police," *Ha'aretz*, May 11.

Lewinstein, K. (2001) "*The Revaluation of Martyrdom in Early Islam,*" in Margaret Cormack, ed., *Sacrificing the Self: Perspectives on Martyrdom and Religion*, New York: Oxford University Press, 78–91.

Loveman, M. (1998) "High-Risk Collective Action: Defending Human Rights in Chile, Uruguay, and Argentina," *American Journal of Sociology*, 104, September: 477–525.

Mancur, O. (1965) *The Logic of Collective Action*, Cambridge: Harvard University Press.

March, J. G. (1986) "Bounded Rationality, Ambiguity, and the Engineering of Choice," in Jon Elster, ed., *Rational Choice*, New York: New York University Press, 149.

Mason, T. D. (1984) "Individual Participation in Collective Racial Violence: A Rational Choice Synthesis," *American Political Science Review*, 78: 1040–1056.

Mehdi, A. and Legenhausen, G. (1986) (eds) *Jihad and Shahadat: Struggle and Martyrdom in Islam*, Houston, TX: Institute for Research and Islamic Studies.

Milton-Edwards, B. (1996) *Islamic Politics in Palestine*, London: I. B. Tauris, 1996.

Mishal, S. and Sela, A. (2000) *The Palestinian Hamas*, New York: Columbia University Press.

Moghadam, A. (2003) "Palestinian Suicide Terrorism in the Second Intifada: Motivations and Organizational Aspects," *Studies in Conflict and Terrorism*, 26, March–April: 65–92.

Moore, M. and Anderson, J. W. (2002) "Israel Widens Its Range of Reprisals," *Washington Post*, August 7.

—— (2003) "Top Israeli Officer Says Tactics Are Backfiring," *Washington Post*, October 31.

Morris, P. F. (1996) "*Rational Choice, Empirical Contributions, and the Scientific Enterprise,*" in Jeffrey Friedman, ed., *The Rational Choice Controversy*, New Haven, CT: Yale University Press: 87.

Muller, E. N. and Karl-Dieter Opp. (1986) "Rational Choice and Rebellious Collective Action," *American Political Science Review*, 80, June: 471–487.

Muller, E. N. and Weede, E. (1990) "Cross-National Variation in Political Violence," *Journal of Conflict Resolution*, 34, December: 646.

Muller, E. N., Dietz, H. A., and Finkel, S. E. (1991) "Discontent and the Expected Utility of Rebellion: The Case of Peru," *American Political Science Review*, 85, December: 1261–1282.

Myre, G. (2003) "A Young Man Radicalized by His Months in Jail," *New York Times*, May 30.

Noll, R. G. and Weingast, B. (1991) "Rational Actor Theory, Social Norms, and Policy Implementation," in Kristen R. Monroe, ed., *The Economic Approach to Politics*, New York: HarperCollins, 237–258.

Oberschall, A. (1973) *Social Conflict and Social Movements*, Englewood Cliffs, NJ: Prentice-Hall.

Oliver, P. (1980) "Rewards and Punishments as Selective Incentives for Collective Action," *American Journal of Sociology*, 85: 1356–1375.

Olson, M. (1965) *The Logic of Collective Action*, Cambridge, MA: Harvard University Press.

Pape, R. (2003) "The Strategic Logic of Suicide Terrorism", *American Political Science Review*, 97: 343–361

—— (2005) *Dying to Win: The Strategic Logic of Suicide Terrorism*, New York: Random House.

Pedatzur, R. (2002) "The Wrong Way to Fight Terrorism," *Ha'aretz*, December 11.

Polletta F. and Jasper, J. M. (2001) "Collective Identity and Social Movements," *Annual Review of Sociology*, 27: 283–305.

Robinson, G. E. (1997) *Building a Palestinian State: The Incomplete Revolution*, Bloomington, IN: Indiana University Press.

Ross, M. H. (1993) *The Culture of Conflict: Interpretations and Interests in Comparative Perspectives*, New Haven, CT: Yale University Press.

Roy, S. (2000) "The Transformation of Islamic NGOs in Palestine," *Middle East Report*, Spring: 24–27.

Rubin, E. (2002) "The Most Wanted Palestinian," *New York Times*, June 30.

Rubinstein, D. (2003a) "Palestinians: Israelis 'Deserved' Haifa Bombing," *Ha'aretz*, March 6.

—— (2003a) "The Point of Control," *Ha'aretz*, May 18.

Sandler, T., Tschirhart, J. T., and Cauley, J. (1983) "A Theoretical Analysis of Transnational Terrorism," *American Political Science Review*, 77: 36–54.

Santino, J. (2001) *Signs of War and Peace: Social Conflict and the Use of Public Symbols in Northern Ireland*, New York: Palgrave.

Shadid, M. (1989) *al-Jihad fi al-Islam* [Holy Struggle in Islam], Cairo: Dar al-Tawzia wal-Nashr al-Islamiyya.

Shay, S. (2004) *The Shahids: Islam and Suicide Attacks*, Somerset, NJ: Transaction Publishers.

Speckhard, A. (2005) *Understanding Suicide Terrorism: Countering Human Bombs and Their Senders* (unpublished paper presented at Ideologies of Terrorism workshop, organized by NATO, Brussels, January 31–February 1).

Sprinzak, E. (2000) "Rational Fanatics," *Foreign Policy*, 120, September/October: 66–74.

Swidler, A. (1986) "Culture in Action: Symbols and Strategies," *American Sociological Review*, 51: 273–286.

Tarrow, S. (1998) *Power in Movement: Social Movements and Contentious Politics*, 2nd edn, New York: Cambridge University Press, 118.

Tilly, C. (1978) *From Mobilization to Revolution*, Boston, MA: Addison-Wesley.

Tololyan, K. (2001) "Cultural Narrative and the Motivation of the Terrorist", in David, C. Rapoport, ed., *Inside Terrorist Organizations*, London: Frank Cass, 217–236.

Varshney, A. (2003) "Nationalism, Ethnic Conflict and Rationality," *Perspectives on Politics*, 1, March: 85–86.

Weinberg, L., Pedahzur, A., and Canetti-Nisim, D. (2003) "The Social and Religious Characteristics of Suicide Bombers and Their Victims with Some Additional Comments about the Israeli Public's Reaction," *Terrorism and Political Violence*, 15, Autumn.

Wiktorowicz, Q., ed. (2004) *Islamic Activism: A Social Movement Theory Approach*, Bloomington: Indiana University Press.

Williams, R. H. and Kubal, T. J. (1999) "Movement Frames and the Cultural Environment: Resonance, Failure, and the Boundaries of the Legitimate," *Research in Social Movements, Conflicts and Change*, 21: 225–248.

—— (2002) "From the 'Beloved Community' to 'Family Values': Religious Language, Symbolic Repertoires, and Democratic Culture," in David S. Meyer, Nancy Whittier, and Belinda Robnett, eds, *Social Movements: Identity, Culture, and the State*, New York: Oxford University Press, 264–265.

Wood, R. L. (1999) "Religious Culture and Political Action," *Sociological Theory*, 17: 307–332.

Yassin, Sheikh Ahmed, Interview with in *al-Hayat* (London), May 22, 2002.

Yee, A. S. (1997) "Thick Rationality and the Missing 'Brute Fact': The Limits of Rationalist Incorporations of Norms and Ideas," *The Journal of Politics*, 59, November: 1001–1039.

4

THE ROOTS OF SUICIDE TERRORISM
A multi-causal approach

Assaf Moghadam

Abstract

This study is a theoretical reflection on the causes of suicide terrorism. It is argued that suicide attacks are best understood when analyzed on three levels of analyses: an individual, an organizational, and an environmental level. A framework for analysis is introduced, and its value illustrated using examples from the Palestinian, Chechen, and Sri Lankan suicide bombing campaigns. The model can be redesigned as a framework to gauge risk factors for suicide terrorism, rendering the framework valuable from both a theoretical and practical point of view.

Introduction

On December 15, 1981, a suicide car bombing against the Iraqi embassy in Beirut killed 61 people, including Ambassador Abdul Razzak Lafta, and injured over a 100 others. Together with three more well-known suicide car bombings that took place in the same city in 1983—the April 18 bombing at the US Embassy and the simultaneous October 23 bombings of the US Marine and French Paratroops Barracks—these incidents marked the beginning of the modern phenomenon of suicide attacks. Well over two decades later, suicide attacks have become a modus operandi employed by an increasingly diverse array of terrorist and insurgent groups in a growing number of countries.[1] The 9/11 attacks in particular have highlighted how acts of suicide terrorism have the potential to cause considerable losses of human lives and damage to physical infrastructure, while influencing the course of global events. In order to develop policies vital to national and international security that will meet the challenges posed by suicide attacks—a phenomenon that shows no signs of subsiding in the near future—the need to understand the causes of this tactic appears evident.

The purpose of this chapter is to introduce a multi-causal framework for the analysis of suicide attacks based on three levels of analysis—an individual, an organizational, and an environmental level of analysis. While the more value-neutral terms "suicide attacks," "suicide missions," or "suicide operations" are the author's preferred terms to describe this particular modus operandi (see Chapter 1 on definitions), the term "suicide terrorism" will be used as well because this chapter reflects on the causes of a modus operandi that is an increasingly common (and potent) sub-tactic of terrorism. Suicide attacks are defined here as an operational method in which the very success of the attack is dependent upon the death of the perpetrator (Crenshaw 2002; Ganor 2002; Schweitzer 2002). Such a definition excludes from the present discussion all attacks in which the perpetrator had a high likelihood, yet no certainty, of dying in the course of the attack.[2]

While many students of terrorism and suicide attacks acknowledge the need that terrorism analysis should be conducted on various levels—including the personal, organizational, societal, or structural level—few researchers have systematically analyzed occurrences of terrorism on all levels, and an even smaller number have attempted to develop an integrated framework for the analysis of the causes of terrorism, let alone suicide attacks.

This chapter will introduce preliminary thoughts about a multi-causal framework for the study of suicide terrorism consisting of three levels of analysis: an individual, an organizational, and an environmental level. The argument will be made that suicide terrorism, and terrorism per se, is best understood when dissected on these multiple levels.

If sufficiently adaptive, such a multi-level, integrative framework may shed further insight into the causes and characteristics of suicide attacks, but can also serve as a framework for the assessment of risk for the occurrence of suicide missions in a particular environment. Hence, the contribution of this multi-causal framework is not limited to the realm of theory, but extends to the area of policy-making.

The first section, "A multi-causal approach to the study of suicide terrorism," of this chapter will introduce the multi-causal framework of analysis. It will provide a brief review over current research into the etiology of suicide terrorism, and will also refer to the question of whether there is a need to distinguish between the causes of suicide terrorism on the one hand, and the causes of non-suicidal terrorism on the other. This brief literature review will be followed by a review of the theoretical foundations of a multi-causal approach to the study of terrorism, and the extent to which such an approach is currently applied. It will be argued that although many analysts seem to acknowledge the need for research on terrorism to take place on multiple levels, few researchers have put such a method to systematic use.

This chapter will discuss the individual, organizational, and environmental levels of analysis in greater detail and will describe a number of characteristics recurrent in situations where suicide operations have been adopted. This study makes no particular effort to list likely causal factors that give rise to ordinary, that is, non-suicidal terrorism. Such comprehensive studies already exist (Post *et al.* 2002). The exclusion of variables largely described in such studies shall in no way indicate that factors that may affect the occurrence of terrorism in general do not apply to suicide terrorism as well, and vice versa. On the contrary, since suicide terrorism is defined here as a particular type of terrorist tactic, most factors generally assumed to contribute to the rise of terrorism also apply to suicide terrorism. Hence, the following sections will focus on those factors that are featured prominently in suicide terrorism campaigns. Further, the purpose of the discussion in the following sections is to illustrate the kinds of variables that the respective level of analysis may contain, not to provide a vast list of possible causal factors for suicide terrorism. In those chapters, the cases of Palestinian, Sri Lankan, and Chechen suicide bombers will be used to illustrate the multiple levels in which suicide attacks occur and need to be understood. The use of these examples serves mainly to illustrate the relevance and utility of a multi-causal model for the study of suicide terrorism.

A multi-causal approach to the study of suicide terrorism

A discussion of the causes of suicide terrorism begs one question from the outset, namely that of the relationship between terrorism and suicide terrorism. This study considers suicide terrorism to be closely related to "ordinary" terrorism, that is, terrorism in which the perpetrator's death is not necessary for the attack to occur. This study concurs with the argument put forward by Martha Crenshaw, namely that suicide terrorism should not be considered a *sui generis* phenomenon because ordinary terrorism and suicide terrorism share many characteristics in common—the main exception being the "motive of individual self-sacrifice and martyrdom" (Crenshaw 2002). Hence, the analytical framework designed here will, with minor adaptations, also shed more light about the causes of non-suicidal terrorism. Unlike a model designed to explain the causes of terrorism at large, however, a model that attempts to conceptualize the roots of suicide terrorism must account for an explanation of self-sacrifice and martyrdom.

Existing research into the causes of suicide terrorism, which is still in its developmental phase,[3] can be broadly divided into four categories:[4] individual/ psychological approaches, which stress individual level psychopathology, humiliation, despair, or identity issues as the leading cause of suicide attacks (Volkan 2002; Sarraj 2002; Harrison 2003; Berko 2004; Lester *et al.* 2004); organizational/strategic approaches, according to which suicide terrorism is used mainly because it has proven to be an effective strategy, militarily and/or politically;[5] socio-cultural approaches, where most explanations focus on religion, nationalism, or societal factors as the primary conditions giving rise to the phenomenon of suicide attacks (Israeli 2003; Argo 2004; Dingley 2005); and multi-causal approaches, which emphasize the presence of several causal variables (Moghadam 2002b, 2003; Atran 2003; Kimhi and Even 2003; Taarnby 2003; Hafez 2005).

That "single-factor explanations overlook the fact that terrorist behavior is an interaction between individual psychology and external environment," as David Long (1990) wrote, has gained increasing acceptance within terrorism studies. A number of scholars have stressed the need for a multi-level approach at the etiology of terrorism (Wilkinson 1974; Long 1990; Atran 2003; Hafez 2005b; Victoroff 2005), but few have attempted to conceptualize such an approach in more or less formal models.[6] One exception is Martha Crenshaw, who has noted the need to distinguish between three levels of causations—situational variables (such as broad political, economic, or social conditions), the strategy of the terrorist organization, and "the problem of individual participation"—that together render the likelihood of terrorism higher in some situations than in others (Crenshaw 1981). Other noteworthy attempts to introduce multi-causal frameworks have been conducted, inter alia, by Jacob Rabbie in his "behavioral interaction model";[7] by Jeffrey Ross, who linked structural and psychological causes of terrorism in a complex model (Ross 1999); and Donatella Della Porta, who integrated environmental and group dynamics variables into a model to describe radicalization processes of social revolutionary groups in Germany and Italy (Porta 1995). Perhaps the most elaborate and comprehensive approach to understand terrorist behavior on a number of levels has been designed by Post, Ruby, and Shaw (Post et al. 2002), with the aim of identifying risk of escalation toward political violence. The authors grouped 32 variables into 4 categories: historical, cultural, and contextual factors; key actors affecting the group; characteristics of the group and organization; and the immediate situation. Although the authors have no doubt rendered an impressive service, they recognize the risk that "the number of indicators is so large, some may well object, as to render the framework impractical and unwieldy" (ibid.).

That suicide terrorism, like ordinary terrorism, is a complex phenomenon with various facets is more or less widely accepted among suicide terrorism researchers. Shaul Kimhi and Shemuel Even, for example, have concluded from their broad review of the literature on Palestinian suicide bombers that "most researchers tend to agree...that suicide terror is a multi-factorial phenomenon. The various explanations for suicide terror include personal and group motives, environmental conditions, and their interactions" (Kimhi and Even 2004). That said, studies of the phenomenon of suicide attacks that are systematic in using individual, organizational, and structural levels of examinations are rare, and many multi-level studies confine themselves to only two levels of analysis.[8]

The distinction of three levels of analysis was introduced by Kenneth Waltz in his examination of the causes of war over fifty years ago (Waltz 1954). Waltz's three "images," as he referred to them, consisted of human behavior, the internal structure of states, and the nature of the international system. Waltz deemed these three levels of analysis central to our understanding of politics, and even "a part of nature. So fundamental are man, the state, and the state system in any attempt to understand international relations," he wrote, "that seldom does an analyst, however wedded to one image, entirely overlook the other two" (Waltz 1982: 11).

The multi-causal framework for the analysis of the causes of suicide terrorism adopts Waltz' broad distinction into three images.[9] Rather than using Waltz's second image—the analysis of the state—the present framework understandably focuses on the terrorist or insurgent organization as the unit responsible for the planning and execution of suicide operations. Waltz' third level of analysis, that of the international system, is replaced in the current framework with an environmental level that emphasizes socio-cultural aspects.

The first level of analysis, the individual level of analysis (L1), is designed to identify personal motivations of the various actors involved in suicide attacks. L1 should focus not only on the perpetrator of the suicide attack, but should extend to other actors that are part of the terrorist system. As Davis and Jenkins point out, terrorism can be decomposed in a number of systems—including a system of different classes of actors. Viewing terrorism, among many other possible systems, as a system of actors allows the researcher to distinguish between lieutenants, recruiters, foot soldiers, and the overall population, among other classes of actors (Davis and Jenkins 2002). Applying such a systems approach to the case of suicide terrorism, the relevant actors whose personal motives are to be scrutinized should include: where information is available, the suicide bomber, the dispatcher, the recruiter, the organization's leader, and, where applicable, the spiritual leader or leaders that give religious consent to suicide attacks.

When the system of actors is decomposed, L1 then focuses on the individual motivation of the actor and attempts to identify what reasons led the suicide bomber, the recruiter, the dispatcher, or the organizational and spiritual leader to contribute their particular role to the planning and/or execution of the suicide attack. If sufficient biographical data is available, L1 may also discuss possible psychological motivations of individual bombers—although psychopathologies are not proven to be disproportionately present among terrorists, nor should psychological motivations be considered in isolation (Victoroff 2005).

The second level of analysis (L2) focuses on organizations. Understanding the nature of terrorist organizations is important because the overwhelming majority of suicide attacks are planned and executed by members of more or less identifiable organizations, groups, or cells that form part of a larger network.[10] There is a need to distinguish among individual motives on the one hand and organizational reasons to engage in suicide attacks on the other hand, for a number of reasons. Individuals motivated to carry out a suicide attack are very unlikely to possess the resources, level of operational intelligence, and logistical capacity required to organize a suicide bombing. As stated in a report in *Jane's Intelligence Review*, the organization of suicide attacks "is extremely secretive. The success of the mission depends on a number of elements: level of secrecy; thorough reconnaissance; and thorough rehearsals. Secrecy enables the preservation of the element of surprise, critical for the success of most operations" (JIR 2000). Clearly, most individuals lack these capabilities.

An additional reason for the need to distinguish between individual and organizational motives is that organizations rarely supply suicide bombers from among their own ranks, but will instead opt to recruit individuals from outside of the group (Moghadam 2003). It is certainly uncommon for organizations to send the top leadership and members on the lieutenant levels on suicide missions, and there is no known case in which the leader of an organization that has adopted suicide attacks has himself volunteered to detonate himself in the course of an attack.

Most importantly, a distinct organizational level of analysis is required because organizations have distinct goals and motives—the need to maintain themselves (Barnard 1938: 216; Wilson 1973; Crenshaw 1985), to act in line with ideological prescriptions, or to adopt suicide terrorism tactics out of competition and rivalry with other terrorist groups. Terrorist organizations may also choose to adopt a particular tactic, including suicide operations out of strategic and tactical considerations, as will be described in the section on "The organizational level of analysis."

The purpose of the third level of analysis, the environmental level (L3), is meant to uncover the various socio-cultural factors and conditions that provide the context for the individual and the organizational levels. Addressing larger environmental conditions is key to understanding how individuals and organizations are affected by their political, historical, cultural, societal, religious, and economic context. Individuals and organizations do not act in a vacuum, but are affected by the environment in which they live and operate. In the case of suicide terrorism, the environmental aspects that seem particularly important in understanding why this modus operandi is used in some contexts and not in others seem to be societal, historical, and cultural factors. L3 also includes discussions of such factors as political context, economic conditions, and religious factors. There is, however, a general consensus among terrorism scholars that the political, economic, or religious contexts by themselves cannot explain why terrorism occurs in some situations and not in others.

As stated, environmental factors directly influence the organization and the individual—a situation marked in Figure 4.1 by an arrow leading from L3 to L1 and L2. L1 and L2, meanwhile, also interact with each other. Both L1 and L2

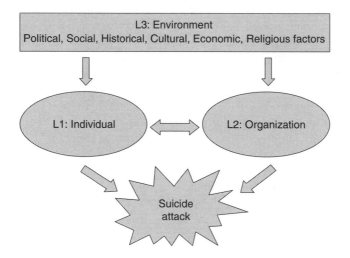

Figure 4.1 The levels of analysis and their interactions.

86

are more proximate to the actual terrorist attack than L3 because planning and execution is conducted by individuals (L1) that are members of more or less identifiable organizations (L2). L1 and L2 are further related to one another for two reasons. First, some of the motivations emanating from the individual and organizational level are identical, because they stem from the same environmental context. A country or region that is known to be very religious, for example, is likely not only to produce many religious individuals, but would also tend to lead many organizations to adopt religious guidelines. Similarly, a certain political context, be it a long-standing conflict or perhaps a nation's struggle for national independence, is also likely to have similar effects on the motivations of individuals as it will on those of organizations. A final reason why the individual and organizational level can at times be closely intertwined is that the terrorist or insurgent organization exerts influence on its members in one way or another. Membership in the group itself provides the terrorist with a sense of belonging, purpose, perceived social status, and empowerment that he would otherwise not enjoy. The individual may join the terrorist group because he views the rewards of joining as highly satisfying. Terrorist organizations can also provide the individual an opportunity for excitement, glamour, and fame, as well as a chance of demonstrating his or her courage.

An additional conclusion that can be drawn from this model is that L1 and L2 serve as intermediate units that channel environmental influences (L3) into the terrorist attack through, on the one hand, individual motivations and, on the other,

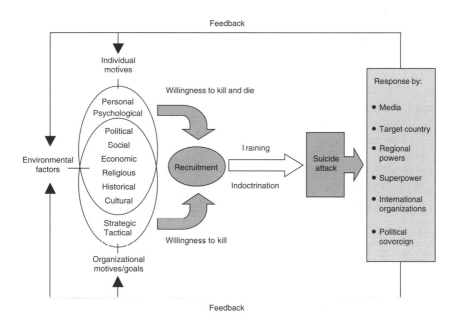

Figure 4.2 The suicide terrorism cycle.

87

organizational goals, motives, and ideological guidelines, as is graphically depicted in Figure 4.2.

Figure 4.2 shows that the three levels of analysis can also be imagined as a feedback system in which the consequences of the suicide terrorist act influence the environment, and thus, through the influence L3 exerts on L1 and L2, individual and organizational motives and decisions of whether or not to engage in suicide attacks.[11]

Figure 4.2, which can be thought of as the "Suicide terrorism cycle," also illustrates the relationship between L3 on the one hand and L1 and L2 on the other. It is noteworthy that the area of overlap between individual and organizational motives is identical to the environmental factors affecting the decision to engage in suicide missions.

Beginning on the left, Figure 4.2 shows the individual and organizational levels and the motives and goals emanating from them. On the individual level, personal motives (such as revenge for the loss of a lost one) and psychological motives are particular to the individual and not shared by the organization. On the organizational level, tactical and political motives and goals affect the organization's decision to embark on suicide attacks. There are several factors in the area of overlap of L1 and L2, and these sociological, religious, cultural, economic, and nationalist motives are the influence exerted by the environment (L3). The organization and the individual must profess a willingness to kill and to die in order for the suicide attack to occur (Merari 1998). The individual and organizational motives, influenced in part by the larger environment, converge at the recruitment stage, whence the suicide bomber comes under the purview of the organization (Moghadam 2003). After the suicide bombing occurs, the political consequences of the attack are likely to affect the environment. Depending on the consequences of the attack—including the nature of the response of the targeted country, international reactions, or the media—the political and/or social atmosphere may change into a situation that will become more or less encouraging of additional attacks. The environment, in turn, will affect the preferences and motivations of individuals and organizations.

One conclusion we can draw from the framework of analysis offered here is thus that L1, L2, and L3 interact with each other, and at times are thoroughly intertwined, resulting in synergetic effects. This model thus helps demonstrate the symbiotic relationship between the individual, the organization, and the environment, thus highlighting the shortcomings of mono-causal explanations of the causes of suicide terrorism.

As a final thought in this theoretical introduction of the framework, the multi-causal framework offered here accepts Harry Eckstein's distinction between preconditions and precipitants developed in his analysis of the causes of internal wars. "Clearly no internal war can occur without precipitant events to set it off; and clearly no precipitants can set off internal war unless the condition of society makes it possible for them to do so," Eckstein wrote in a passage that easily applies to suicide terrorism, a very common strategy used in internal wars today (Eckstein 1972; Crenshaw 1981). Given the relative unpredictability of precipitants, however—specific events that immediately precede the suicide attack—this framework should be considered in large part a framework of the preconditions of suicide attacks.[12]

In the subsequent discussions of the three levels of analysis, no attempt is made to provide a comprehensive list of all possible variables of motivations for suicide attacks on the three levels—an undertaking that would be as time- and space-consuming as it would be impossible. Many causal factors have been described in previous works by terrorism scholars and there is no need to recount them here. The following discussion simply serves to highlight some motivations and causes that appear to exist across several different suicide terrorism campaigns. The main purpose of the subsequent discussion is not to unearth all the motivations of suicide attacks, but rather to support the argument that an adequate analysis of the causes of suicide terrorism requires an analysis across the three levels. To that end, the cases used in the following serve merely as illustrations.

The individual level of analysis (L1)

"According to the first image of international relations," Kenneth Waltz wrote, "the locus of the important causes of war is found in the nature and behavior of man" (Waltz 1982: 9). Similarly, the individual level of analysis into the causes of suicide terrorism offered here is concerned with the attitudes and motives of individuals involved in the planning and execution of suicide attacks. It is important to consider individual motivations because grievances that may give rise to terrorism lead to the use of terrorist violence of only a select few. More commonly, the reasons that lead some individuals to resort to the use of political violence will lead others to react through nonviolent means. Hence, there must be an element of individual decision involved in the genesis of terrorism (Friedland 1992: 88).

Ideally, a comprehensive analysis of suicide attacks on an individual level is conducted upon all actors involved in the support, planning and execution of suicide attacks, including the actual bomber, the dispatcher, the recruiter, the organizational leader, and the religious leader (where applicable) who provides doctrinal justifications for suicide attacks. For reasons of space, however, the current analysis remains limited to the actual suicide bomber.

Individuals who plan, support, or execute suicide attacks are highly unlikely to be influenced by singular motives since "there are probably as many reasons for committing terrorist acts as there are terrorists," as David Long aptly put it (1990: 15). As shown in a study on the motivations of Palestinian suicide bombers, for example, individuals who volunteer for suicide missions are likely to be influenced by several motivations at once. In the Palestinian case, motivations of the suicide bomber have been shown to include any given combination of a number of possible motivations, including the seeking of revenge, the expectation of personal posthumous benefits, the expectation of material or immaterial rewards for family members, religious motives, the struggle for national liberation, or the influence of a widespread culture of martyrdom on the individual (Moghadam 2003: 87). It is also highly unlikely that any two suicide bombers will decide to execute a suicide attack as a result of the same exact combination of these motivations (Ibid.).

Kimhi and Even, who have conducted research on the personalities of Palestinian suicide bombers, have distinguished four prototypes, including that of the exploited suicide bomber—a category that includes adults with personal problems or those seeking to redeem themselves from "sins" such as a love affair outside the family, homosexuality, or collaboration with the Israeli enemy (Kimhi and Even 2003). Kimhi and Even's findings thus also corroborate the argument that research into suicide terrorism on an individual level is important.

Personal problems such as the loss of a husband or financial distress seems to be a common feature among Chechen women suicide bombers. One example is Zarema Muzhakhoyeva, one of only a few Chechen women suicide bombers alive, who now sits in a Russian prison after her bomb failed to detonate. Reports about her life prior to arrest indicate an existence filled with personal hardship. Her home region, Achkoi-Martan, was largely destroyed in the first Chechen war; she left school, pregnant, at age fifteen, and married her boyfriend only to see him killed fighting against Russian troops. Following her husband's death, his family kept her much like a slave. She escaped, later borrowing money from a group of men that demanded from her to pay back with her life. Were she to become a suicide bomber, the group promised, her debts would be repaid and her family would receive some money (Groskop 2004).

Muzhakhoyeva's conundrum may sound similar to the background of an ordinary suicide. Most suicide terrorism analysts, however, reject the notion that suicide bombers are similar to ordinary suicides. Most also insist that there is no such thing as a typical profile of a suicide bomber.[13] The importance of psychological factors among suicide bombers, or other terrorists for that matter, has preoccupied many researchers. Some argue that individual psychological reasons—sometimes generated by the socio-political context—account for the behavior of suicide attackers. Eyad el-Sarraj, for instance, argues that "politically, suicide bombing is an act of absolute despair" (Sarraj 2005: 3). Based on personal interviews, psychiatrist Anne Speckhard believes that deep personal traumatization and bereavement, based on humiliating treatment in part explains the resort of some Chechens and Palestinians to suicide attacks (Speckhard 2005). Going a step further, Vamik Volkan believes that potential suicide bombers have disturbed personal identities based on prior humiliating experiences that hindered the formation of a healthy identity (Volkan 2002).

The broad consensus among psychologists and psychiatrists interested in terrorism is that terrorists are not mentally ill. "This failure of mental illness as an explanation for terrorism," psychiatrist Marc Sageman sums it up, "is consistent with three decades of research that has been unable to detect any significant pattern of mental illness in terrorists" (Sageman 2004: 83). Most researchers agree that terrorists, while clearly highly alienated from society, are sane and relatively "normal," that is, they do not exhibit signs of suffering from a salient psychopathology (McCauley and Segal 1987).

Psychological aspects of the terrorism phenomenon need to be approached with caution, and with a clear understanding of psychology's limitations in illuminating our understanding of terrorism, Jeff Victoroff concludes in a recent review article (Victoroff 2005). None of the psychoanalytical and nonpsychoanalytical theories of terrorism studies conducted has produced any persuasive evidence that terrorists suffer from some of the personality disorders described in them. Psychological theories of terrorism also tend to be subjective and speculative, and all too often make broad generalizations that have not been rigorously proven. No terrorism expert or psychiatrist has been able to conclusively identify a common predisposition for terrorism (Ibid.). Nonetheless, psychological factors of terrorism remain an important area of research, and have contributed much to our understanding of terrorism in particular with regard to theories of group processes (ibid., 30–31). Understanding psychological processes has also proven helpful in describing the process of mental preparation for attacks through mechanisms of moral disengagement, including dehumanization, advantageous comparison, or euphemistic labeling—processes that can also occur, and are in fact reinforced, on a group level (Bandura 1998).

One prevailing motive on the individual level that does seem to recur in situations where suicide attacks are practiced is the seeking of revenge, at times reinforced by perceived humiliation, which also seems to be a key motive for terrorism in general.[14] Kimhi and Even, for instance, identified the individual seeking retribution for suffering as a major prototype of Palestinian suicide bombers (Kimhi and Even 2003). Eyad el-Sarraj, a Palestinian psychiatrist, believes that "the tribal mentality which urges individuals to avenge defeat to the bitter end even across generations is essential to understanding suicide attacks in the Arab world" (Sarraj 2002). Similarly, revenge seems to play a dominant role in the case of Chechen suicide bombers, where retribution is firmly entrenched into the local warrior culture and the ancient code of honor known as *Adat*. There seems to be no shortage of individuals seeking revenge in Grozny and its surroundings where, as Christoph Reuter described it, "one can meet young Chechens every day who will tell you that they have lost a brother, a sister, one of their parents, in the course of the struggle for independence" (Reuter 2004: 49). "Russians have, by many accounts, looted, abducted, tortured, and murdered suspected supporters of Chechnya's independence movement with impunity," he continues. "The young Chechen survivors vow to avenge every one of these murders, until all the Russians have gone" (ibid., 150). One such avenger was Aisa Gazuyeva, who detonated herself in front of Geidar Gadzhiev, the military commandant of Ursus Martan, southwest of Grozny. Four months earlier, Gadzhiev had brutally murdered Gazuyeva's husband in front of her eyes (Langer 2005). Revenge also seems to be a strong motive for young Tamils in Sri Lanka to join the Liberation Tigers of Tamil Eelam, an insurgent organization whose suicide attack squad—the

Black Tigers—are among the most sophisticated and "successful" employers of suicide operations. One young Tamil who lost three brothers in the service of the Tigers, a 22-year old named Mahendran, described his feelings about joining the LTTE's suicide squads thus: "I am thinking of joining [the LTTE]. The harassment that I and my parents have suffered at the hands of the army makes me want to take revenge (Joshi 2000)." The LTTE, meanwhile, exploits the widespread feelings of anger for its own benefit by specifically targeting those families who have lost members to Sinhalese security forces (Hoffman and McCormick 2004: 259).

The expectation of personal benefits in the afterlife that seems to motivate some Palestinian suicide bombers (Ganor 2002: 144–145; Moghadam 2003: 72), such as a guaranteed place in heaven and the eventual reunification with one's family, does not necessarily apply to other cases of suicide attacks. In the case of the secular Black Tigers, for example, there is no expectation of a posthumous compensation. "A Black Tiger is an...'idealist,'" notes Peter Schalk, "whose only satisfaction just before death, during his act of killing, is to have eliminated one obstacle for the realization of [Tamil Eelam]," the aspired homeland (Schalk 1997).

An additional factor for the individual that seems particularly relevant to suicide attacks relates to the notion of identity. Hoffman and McCormick, for instance, believe that individuals choosing to become suicide bombers make decisions based on what the correct course of action is under the circumstances in which they find themselves in, rather than a clear-cut cost-benefit analysis in which they expect returns in the afterlife. This type of rule making, they argue, is connected to one's identity, which provides the template for interpreting and understanding the world, one's place in it, and how one responds to external events (Hoffman and McCormick 2004: 252–253). Mark Harrison believes that suicide bombers act mainly out of a need to enhance their identity, their most valuable asset. Continuing to live, he argues, would be tantamount to abandoning one's identity (Harrison 2003). For Mohammed Hafez, the suicide bomber, by detonating himself, performs "a duty to one's own values, family, friends, community, or religion. Failure to act, consequently, is perceived as a betrayal of one's ideals, loved ones, country, God, or sense of manhood" (Hafez 2005b: 13).

The above discussion of the individual level of analysis of the causes of suicide attacks suggests that individual motives are an important part of the puzzle of suicide attacks that scholars should not ignore. Whenever possible, it has been argued, an L1 analysis should be applied to the various classes of actors in the suicide terrorism system. L1 motivations may include, but are not limited to, personal reasons such as interpersonal relational issues or financial distress, perceived humiliation, and/or the expectation of posthumous benefits or benefits to one's family. Revenge seems to be an important factor in all three cases used as examples in this study. An additional area where further research seems adequate is the relationship between suicide attacks and individual perceptions of identity. Needless to say, the previous discussion is far from comprehensive in listing all possible motivations of individuals engaged in the act of suicide attacks in one way or another. It has served, instead, to highlight some of the reasons that can lead individual suicide bombers to accept suicide missions if approached by organizations, or to volunteer for suicide attacks. Many other factors are clearly at play.

It is also no secret that an individual level of analysis of suicide attacks—or any other level for that matter—does not explain why suicide terrorism occurs in some contexts and not in others—a problem that is at the pivot of terrorism studies and well recognized by many analysts.[15] An awareness that motivations at multiple levels are at play, however, is a useful start into a better grasp of the roots of suicide terrorism. The next section will therefore look at the organizational level of analysis.

The organizational level of analysis (L2)

The organizational level of analysis (L2) for understanding the causes of suicide terrorism is concerned with the reasons that emanate from the terrorist organization to adopt suicide missions as a modus operandi. Analysis on the organizational level is particularly important in the study of terrorism (and suicide terrorism) and its causes because terrorist acts are rarely carried out by individuals acting on their own,[16] but by individuals who are members of organizations, groups, or cells attached to a larger network. Even the most highly motivated potential suicide bomber will, in most cases, lack the wherewithal needed to stage a successful attack. It is for that reason that many analysts regard the role of the group as the most important element in the appeal of suicide terrorism.

Martha Crenshaw, who pioneered the theoretical formulation of the organizational approach to the study of terrorism (Crenshaw 1985), has argued that terrorism can be understood as the result of a deliberate choice by terrorist organizations which believe that violence is the best means to advance their political goals (Crenshaw 1998). In determining when to stage terrorist attacks, and which particular tactic to use, terrorist organizations may be guided by a variety of calculations. The organization may believe that at a particular moment the cost of an attack is low, or the chances of success are high (Crenshaw 1988). The suicide bomber who assassinated President Ranasinghe Premadasa of Sri Lanka, for example, had lived in the capital, Colombo, for three years before carrying out the attack. He was a regular guest at the household of the President, befriending his valet. On May 1, 1993, wearing a suicide belt, the bomber's acquaintance with the valet enabled him to approach the President on his bicycle with no problem. After reportedly being greeted by the valet, the suicide bomber detonated himself, killing the Sri Lankan leader (Gunaratna 2002).

Terrorist or insurgent organizations may also decide to adopt suicide attacks after they have tried a number of other terrorist tactics. Most terrorist groups existed for years or decades before they began executing suicide missions. Some factors connected to the organization may influence the timing of the use of the suicide attack. The organization may possess a rare opportunity to stage a successful suicide attack or it may have a unique opportunity to strike a target of particularly high value, deciding to use a suicide operation to increase the chances of success. This occurred in the case of the Narodnaya Volya's assassination of Tsar Alexander II on March 1, 1881. Following eight previous unsuccessful attempts on the Tsar's life, one of the four Russian revolutionaries who equipped themselves with bombs on that day decided to detonate the bomb in such close proximity to the Tsar that it would ensure not only his target's death but also his own.[17]

An organizational level of analysis must be conducted because organizations have motives and goals that are distinct from those of individuals. Organizational motives to commit acts of suicide terrorism revolve, as argued in the introductory part, first around the need for organizational survival (Barnard 1938: 216; Wilson 1973; Crenshaw 1985). A minimum degree of violent presence is necessary for terrorist groups to remain effective. Failure to maintain such a degree of violence will eventually lead to the group's irrelevance and eventual disappearance as a political force.

The organizational strive to persist and remain relevant is closely related to terrorist organizations' pursuit of political power—a key feature of any terrorist group (Hoffman 1998: 14–15). As part of their struggle for power, most organizations that adopt suicide tactics, like those who do not, vie for the support of the local population.[18] This struggle for market share, Mia Bloom explains, can lead to the adoption of suicide attacks by groups that have not previously used such tactics, especially when various terrorist organizations are engulfed in a struggle to "outbid" themselves. "With several groups in fierce competition," Bloom notes, "violence becomes the litmus test against which the organizations and individuals measure themselves" (Bloom 2004b). The adoption of suicide attacks by organizations for tactical and political reasons has been noted in the Palestinian case of suicide attacks[19] as well as in Sri Lanka, where suicide attacks paved the way for the LTTE to distinguish itself from other militant Tamil groups that challenged the Tigers' aspiration to stand at the helm of the resistance movement (Hoffman and McCormick 2004: 262). Lebanon serves as an additional example where two Shiite groups, Hizballah and Amal, began to outbid themselves in suicide attacks (Kramer 1991).

Bloom adds that

> if the domestic popularity of the organization using suicide terror increases, we observe an increase in bombings. If the domestic environment supports the use of suicide terror and an insurgent group does not use the tactic, they tend to lose market share and popularity.
>
> (2005: 95)

Anat Kurz, meanwhile, suggests that a reduction in the support for suicide attacks can lead to the decline of the use of suicide operations. She cites the case of the LTTE, where the erosion in the support for the LTTE among the Tamil diaspora, including reduced financial contributions, was one among several factors that brought a temporary halt to suicide attacks in 2002 (Kurz 2005).

An additional reason why some groups prefer suicide bombing tactics is that they believe that such a modus operandi will benefit them in various ways. First, even more than ordinary terrorist attacks, suicide operations are likely to draw attention to a group's cause, aided in large part by the extraordinarily high attention such operations enjoy in the media, "the terrorist's best friend" (Laqueur 1979: 160), as Walter Laqueur once described it. In this regard, suicide attacks can be thought of as a form of "strategic signaling," whereby terrorist attacks are used to communicate a group's character and goals to the target audience (Hoffman and McCormick 2004). As pointed out by Hoffman and McCormick, for instance, the LTTE used suicide attacks to signal an image of elitism, professionalism, invincibility, and fanatical single-mindedness to the Sri Lankan government (ibid.: 262). Second, suicide attacks, even more than ordinary terrorist attacks, serve the organization's attempt to create extreme fear in the larger population—a key feature of terrorist attacks. This occurs in part due to the group's demonstration of the inefficacy of the targeted government, and in part due to the demoralization of the public and law enforcement. Suicide attacks create not only a disproportionately intense amount of fear among targeted populations, but their effect may be particularly traumatizing and long-lasting (Joshi 2000; Harel 2003; Richburg 2004). Third, by employing a tactic that involves the death of members of the constituency that the organization purports to represent, the group may believe that it can strengthen support in the international arena.[20] There is some evidence that outside audiences may sympathize with groups who are using martyrdom tactics, assuming that members of a community willing to sacrifice themselves must have been subjected to particularly gruesome treatment by their enemy, thus leaving them with no other option other than to seek death. Indeed, the belief that suicide bombers must act out of desperation if they are willing to sacrifice themselves is at times entertained even by elements of the targeted population.[21] A fourth benefit of suicide attacks occurs if the organization, as is sometimes claimed, intends to provoke a harsh response by the government, hoping that such a response might heighten sympathies and support for the group's cause.[22] Indeed, the high lethality of suicide attacks which, on average, kill four times as many people as do other terrorist attacks (Hoffman 2003), certainly does little to restrain governments in their responses to suicide attacks. Fifth, suicide attacks also serve as an internal moral-booster for the terrorist group. The group member's willingness to die for the benefit of others, Adam Dolnik notes, is "used as evidence of moral superiority of the groups' members over their adversaries, resulting in the perception among the group that an eventual victory is inevitable" (Dolnik 2004: 846). Terrorist organizations, finally, adopt suicide operations because of a number of tactical benefits. These tactical advantages of suicide missions, such as their great accuracy, high lethality, cost efficiency, and the irrelevance of planning a complicated escape route, among others, have been described in greater detail by other authors (Sprinzak 2000: 66–67; Ganor 2002: 143–144; Cronin 2003), and there is no need to enumerate them here in full.

This part of the chapter has examined possible causes of suicide terrorism on an organizational level of analysis. The goals and motives of organizations have been shown to differ significantly from individual motives. Whereas individual motives are personal, organizational motives are generally strategic and tactical. The above discussion of organizational goals and motives is far from complete, and one can safely assume that there are various other reasons why organizations use suicide attacks that have not been mentioned here. An additional area into which an organizational level of analysis of the causes of suicide terrorism should delve is the organization's role in training and indoctrinating its members to become suicide bombers. Training and indoctrination are not causes of suicide attacks per se, but are nonetheless generally necessary to produce suicide bombers (Moghadam 2003). As is true for the other parts of this chapter, the main purpose of this discussion has been to demonstrate the need to engage in various different levels of analysis when examining the etiology of suicide attacks. The next part of the chapter will discuss a third set of conditions, namely environmental factors, which exert influence on both individuals and organizations.

The environmental level of analysis (L3)

The third level of analysis of the causes of suicide terrorism, the environmental level (L3), is concerned with the various socio-cultural factors and conditions that affect the genesis of suicide terrorism.[23] Whereas suicide terrorism is planned and executed by individuals (L1) who are members of organizations, groups, or cells (L2), these two levels are in turn influenced by broader environmental conditions that include the political, social, historical, cultural, economic, and religious context. Clearly, some of these sub-elements of the broader environment are more relevant in some cases than in others. The religious context, for example, is a more important factor to take into account in explaining why some Islamist groups employ suicide attacks than it is in the case of the LTTE, a predominantly nationalist organization. The existence of economic incentives for engaging in suicide terrorism are controversial to begin with, and certainly do not explain why Muhammad Atta and his cohorts, most of whom came from affluent backgrounds, engaged in suicide terrorism.

Like most of the structural conditions discussed in this chapter, economic motives have at best indirect effects on suicide attacks. Recent studies have shown, for instance, that there is no direct connection between poverty or poor education on the one hand, and terrorism on the other (Krueger and Maleckova 2002; Abadie 2004; Piazza 2005). On the other hand, poverty may exert indirect influence on the rise of terrorism: First, poor countries are more likely to serve as or be exploited as safe havens by terrorists; second, poor countries are more likely to undergo ethnic and religious conflict, which in turn may breed "homegrown" terrorism or may attract foreign elements; third, poverty may indirectly affect the rise of terrorism in that the usually more well-to-do leadership levels of terrorist organizations can more easily exploit grievances of economically disadvantaged classes (Moghadam 2006).

Similarly, the political context of a society in which suicide attacks are utilized must be seen as having at best indirect effects. A society under occupation, for example, may have a higher likelihood to employ suicide attacks than a perfectly sovereign, independent state. However, not all societies under occupation have produced suicide bombers, or else we would need to add Tibetans, Kosovars, Cambodians, and other occupied and recently occupied groups to the growing list of suicide bombers. Similarly, governmental repression gives rise to suicide terrorism in some cases—repression exists, in varying degrees, in Russia, Sri Lanka, and Israel—but does not have the same effect in Latin America and Africa, where suicide attacks have remained a rarity despite the many examples of brutal authoritarian and dictatorial regimes found on these continents.

Hence, structural conditions that may give rise to terrorism suffer from the same "fundamental problem of specificity" that Sageman described for psychological explanations of terrorism. In addition, however, environmental factors differ from the individual and organizational levels in that they are not directly affecting the rise of suicide terrorism, but require intervening variables. These variables are the individual and the organization, which do not live and operate in a vacuum. L1 and L2 serve as intermediate units channeling environmental influences (L1) into terrorist attacks by means of personal dynamics of the individual on the one hand, and organizational goals and motives on the other hand.

The following discussion will center around only a few environmental factors that seem particularly relevant to suicide attacks in the Palestinian, Sri Lankan, and Chechen cases. There will be a discussion of the political, social, cultural, and historical context, with a focus on the culture of martyrdom, which seems to be a particularly important phenomenon whenever suicide attacks are systematically used. Due to space limitations, the discussion will appear at times superficial, and the religious and economic context, while clearly important, will be left out altogether.

The political and historical context in Israel/West Bank and Gaza, Sri Lanka, and Chechnya/Russia features, in all three instances, a high level of violence as part of a conflict that has ethnic, nationalist, and religious dimensions. All three cases witness the political and military domination of one group over another. In Sri Lanka, the predominantly Buddhist Sinhalese majority seized power in 1948, after which time it largely refused to share power with the predominantly Hindu Tamils. Civil rights of the Tamils were further curtailed after the proclamation of the republic in 1971, providing a boost to various militant Tamil organizations. After 1983, the Sinhalese army's reprisals against the Tamils increased in their brutality as the LTTE, now at the helm of the Tamil organizations, adopted violent resistance as its tactic. The struggle for a national Tamil homeland is at the center of the conflict, and Sri Lankans oftentimes profess a willingness to die for this cause. Asked why he wanted to become a suicide bomber, one young Sri Lankan, for instance, said that "This is the most supreme sacrifice I can make.

The only way we can get our eelam [homeland] is through arms. That is the only way anybody will listen to us. Even if we die" (Joshi 2000).

Chechnya has historically been subjected to many conquests, in particular by its Russian neighbor. Russia's invasion of Chechnya in 1858 and its aftermath decimated the Chechen population in half (Dunlop 1998). In 1944, ten years after Chechnya became a Soviet Socialist Republic, Stalin accused the Chechens and the Ingush populations of collaboration with the Nazis and deported them to Siberia and Central Asia. Stalin's purges and forced exile killed an estimated one- quarter of the Chechen population and permanently imbued the episode in Chechen collective memory. After 1991, a Russia reluctant to lose control over Chechnya due to the latter's oil resources and strategic importance, invaded its Southern neighbor and former Soviet republic. In the subsequent wars, which have witnessed flagrant human rights violations on both sides, Russian troops destroyed several Chechen cities, culminating in the leveling of the capital Grozny in late 1999.

Within the environmental level of analysis, the cultural context of societies in which suicide operations are used is an additional factor to take into account. The case of Chechnya is especially relevant. There, the traditional Chechen code of honor, *Adat*, permits, even prescribes, retribution for the sake of honor. Chechen cultural history is also replete with legends and myths about the prowess of Chechen warriors who heroically fought countless invaders (Chivers and Myers 2004). This code of conduct has been described by one Chechen mafia boss who stated,

> We Chechens keep our secrets, and none of our people will ever talk about them to an outsider. We are also united. But even more important is the fact that we are disciplined and self-restrained... We only use force when necessary but if we give a warning, everyone knows we mean it and they'd better listen. That is why all the other groups, the Russians, the Azeris, the Georgians, and whoever—they all have to pay rent to us, and respect our territory.
>
> (Lieven 2000)

On the societal level, a phenomenon that is not only present in most conflicts where suicide attacks are widely used, but that also appears to be the distinguishing characteristic between suicide terrorism and ordinary terrorism, is what is known as the culture of martyrdom (Lelyveld 2001; Brooks 2002; Dickey 2002: 26; Moghadam 2002b), well described by Christoph Reuter as a

> network of reimagined and reawakened medieval myths and popular-culture hero worship. This culture combines modern-day marketing techniques like trading-cards, film music, and video-clips, with a "creative" reinterpretation of theology that lends religious legitimacy to the attackers' suicides by characterizing them as the noblest form of fearlessness in the face of death.
>
> (Reuter 2004: 13)

98

The concept of martyrdom, however, is not solely a religious but also a secular phenomenon whose roots can be traced to the concept of the hero (Hoffman and McCormick 2004: 253). Martyrdom, in addition, is not merely an act of self-sacrifice that is done for personal reasons, but the self-conscious creation of a model for future emulation and inspiration. The martyr, Crenshaw writes, "expects to impress an audience and to be remembered. For someone whose life otherwise has little significance, transcendent fame can be a powerful motive."[24]

The culture of martyrdom is particularly pronounced among Palestinians, and manifests itself in various ways, be it a soccer tournament named after a suicide bomber (Eichner 2003) or a popular drama series about the most famous of Palestinian bomb makers, the "Engineer," Yahiye Ayyash (Moghadam 2002b; Kimhi and Even 2003; Abu Toameh 2004). Palestinian groups adopted many practices of this cult of death—including the labeling of suicide attacks as "martyrdom operations"—from the Lebanese Hizballah (Dickey 2002: 26). The radical Shiite group, in turn, copied the culture of the martyr from revolutionary Iran—including such practices as celebrating the death of the martyr as a wedding (Reuter 2004: 48).

That a culture of martyrdom can also be practiced among nationalist groups can be seen in the example of the LTTE, whose fallen heroes, especially the members of the Black Tigers suicide squad, are honored and revered after death. Drawing on the Hindu tradition of heroic self-sacrifice, asceticism, and obligation, which are firmly entrenched within Tamil society, the Sri Lankan version of the culture of martyrdom features such practices as the building of holy shrines for the fallen heroes; the establishment of five occasions on its calendar when martyrs are venerated, including Martyrs Day on July 5, when the first Sri Lankan suicide bomber, Captain Millar, detonated himself (Schalk 1997); radio broadcasts on Martyrs' Day reporting the brave deeds of the Black Tigers; the naming of weapons after the suicide squad (Francis 2000); and the euphemistic labeling of the act of dying as "thatkodai" (to give yourself) rather than "thatkolai" (to kill yourself) (Waldman 2003). The LTTE has even composed songs about the cyanide vial, with which every LTTE fighter is equipped, making even the poisonous capsule a subject of the cult of martyrdom (Schalk 1997).

Conclusion

In his 1972 essay on the etiology of internal war, Harry Eckstein argued that "theoretical reflection can introduce some order into the chaos that internal war studies present. Most important, it can produce useful judgments as to the more economic lines to pursue in empirical inquiry" (Eckstein 1972: 12). The aim of this chapter, to paraphrase Eckstein, was to present some theoretical reflections of suicide attacks with the aim to contribute to more useful scholarly analyses of the phenomenon.

The framework offered here has not uncovered each and every cause of suicide attacks in the cases described here, nor has it attempted to do so. Many crucial variables that play a critical role in understanding the genesis of suicide terrorism have been left out for space limitations. On both the individual and the organizational levels, for example, the role of leadership is a critical variable to examine, as the cases of suicide attacks particularly in the case of the LTTE and the Kurdistan Workers Party (PKK) attest, given the centrality of their respective leaders, Vellupillai Prabhakaran and the imprisoned Abdullah Ocalan. Other important variables on the organizational level largely neglected in this study, but nonetheless critical for improving the analyst's understanding of the terrorist or insurgent organization's contribution to suicide attacks are indoctrination, ideology, training, and organizational decision making. Similarly, variables of the environmental level that have been overlooked in the present study are the role of religion and economic conditions which, as argued, have no direct effects on terrorism, but may contribute to the rise of suicide terrorism through indirect ways.

Rather than providing an exhaustive list of all variables,[25] this study has chosen a few variables for the purpose of illustration. The main goal was to present a multi-causal model as a useful theoretical concept and analytical framework with which to approach the study of the causes of suicide attacks. Clearly, it is not the intention of the author to argue that each study of suicide attacks, or terrorism for that matter, needs to be conducted on multiple levels of analysis. Nor should this study be understood as a criticism of mono-causal approaches, as studies focusing on one causal variable have immensely contributed to our understanding of the causes of suicide attacks. The purpose of the introduction of this model is rather intended to raise the analyst's awareness of the "bigger picture" in which the causes of suicide terrorism should be seen.

Beyond the purpose of raising the analyst's awareness to the multiplicity of causes of suicide terrorism, the current framework of analysis has also practical usefulness. First, it can be extended from the study of the *causes* of suicide attacks to an analysis of the *nature* and *characteristics* of suicide attacks. Conducting an in-depth analysis of the particular characteristics of a certain suicide bombing campaign, or employing a comparative analysis of various campaign using multiple levels of analysis, can help uncover certain trends and characteristics that counter-terrorism specialists can in turn use to develop measures to contain this phenomenon.

In addition, this analysis of the causes of suicide attacks can be redesigned as a framework for conceptualizing processes leading to the adoption of suicide attacks based on variables that fall within the individual, organizational, and environmental levels of analysis. A study that utilizes levels of analysis L1, L2, and L3 can thus serve as an examination of possible risk factors that increase the likelihood that suicide attacks will be used in a particular context—an important undertaking that was beyond the scope of this study. In developing such future analyses of risk factors, the analyst's challenge will be to develop models that allow for the specification of the relative weight of the various variables and levels of analysis across certain regions. In order to embark on such an important study, recognizing the "big picture" of the causes of suicide terrorism is a crucial first step.

Notes

1 These countries and regions include, but are not limited to, Afghanistan, Algeria, Argentina, Croatia, India, Indonesia, Iraq, Israel, Kashmir, Kenya, Kuwait, Lebanon, Morocco, Pakistan, Russia, Saudi Arabia, Sri Lanka, Tanzania, Turkey, the United States, Uzbekistan, and Yemen.

2 For a discussion of why attacks in which the perpetrator runs a high risk, albeit no certainty, to die in the attack, should be excluded from the definition of suicide attacks, see Boaz Ganor, "Suicide Attacks in Israel," 140–143.

3 By June 2005 only about two dozen books have been written on this topic in the English language, although the quantity of publications on this topic has picked up in recent years. In chronological order, the books are International Policy Institute for Counter-Terrorism (ICT), *Countering Suicide Terrorism: An International Conference* (Herzliyya, Israel, ICT, 2001); Joyce M. Davis, *Martyrs: Innocence, Vengeance and Despair 1 the Middle East* (New York: Palgrave Macmillan, 2003); Raphael Israeli, Islamikaze: Manifestations of Islamic Martyrdogy (New York: Frank Cass, 2003); Barbara Victor, *Army of Roses: Inside the World of Palestinian Woman Suicide Bombers* (Emmaus, PA: Rodale, 2003); Christoph Reuter, *MY life is a Weapon: A Modern History of Suicide Bombing* (Princeton, NJ: Princeton University Press, 2004); Shaul Shay, *The Shahids: Islam and Suicide Attacks* (New Brunswick: Transaction Publishers, 2004); Ergün Capan, ed., *An Islamic Perspective: Terror and Suicide Attacks* (Somerset, NJ: The Light, 2004); Anne Marie Oliver and Paul Steinberg, *The Road To Martyr's Square* (Oxford: Oxford University Press, 2005); Farhad Khosrokhavar, Suicide Bombers: Allah's New Martyrs, transl. David Macey (London: Pluto Press, 2005); Diego Gambetta, ed., *Making Sense of Suicide Missions* (Oxford and New York: Oxford University Press, 2005); Mia Bloom, *Dying to kill: The Alure of Suicide terror* (New York: Columbia University Press, 2005); and Robert Pape, *Dying to Win: The strategic Logic of Suicide Terrorism* (New York: Random House, 2005).

4 This categorization is far from perfect. Few of the researchers of suicide terrorism cited in the following footnotes confine their analysis to narrow explanations of the phenomenon. Nevertheless, they tend to emphasize the importance of certain variables over others.

5 See, for example, Ehud Sprinzak, "Rational Fanatics," *Foreign Policy* (September/October 2000); Mia M. Bloom, "Palestinian Suicide Bombing: Public Support, Market Share, and Outbidding," *Political Science Quarterly*, 119, 1 (Spring 2004) and Robert A. Pape, "The Strategic Logic of Suicide Terrorism," *American Political Science Review*, 97, 3 (August 2003). The research conducted by Ariel Merari can also be placed in this category. Although a psychologist, Merari, like Sprinzak, regards suicide terrorism to be an "organizational phenomenon." In Assaf Moghadam, "Fletcher Hosts Ariel Merari, Israeli Expert on Suicide Terrorism," *Fletcher Ledger*, February 4, 2002. Available at http://www.fletcherledger.com/archive/2002-02-04/020402-NfinalSuicideTerrorism.htm, last accessed March 2, 2006.

6 Attempts to create integrative and/or interactive models for analysis of terrorist incidents on at least 2 of the 3 levels described here have been made by Jacob M. Rabbie, "A Behavioral Interaction Model: Toward a Social-Psychological Framework for Studying Terrorism," *Terrorism and Political Violence*, 3, 4 (Winter 1991); Nehemia Friedland, "Becoming a Terrorist: Social and Individual Antecedents," in Lawrence Howard, ed., *Terrorism: Roots, Impact, Responses* (New York: Praeger, 1992); Donatella Della Porta, *Social Movements, Political Violence, and the State: A Comparative Analysis of Italy and Germany* (Cambridge, UK: Cambridge University Press, 1995); Jeffrey Ian Ross, "Beyond the Conceptualization of Terrorism: A Psychological-Structural Model of the Causes of this Activity," in Craig Summers and Eric Markusen, eds, *Collective Violence: Harmful Behavior in Groups and*

Governments (Lanham, MD: Rowman & Littlefield, 1999); Jerrold M. Post, Keven G. Ruby, and Eric D. Shaw, "The Radical Group in Context: 1. An Integrated Framework for the Analysis of Group Risk for Terrorism," *Studies in Conflict and Terrorism*, 25, 2 (March–April 2002); and "The Radical Group in Context: 2. Identification of Critical Elements in the Analysis of Risk for Terrorism by Radical Group Type," *Studies in Conflict and Terrorism*, 25, 2 (March–April 2002); as well as the earlier cited works by Assaf Moghadam and Michael Taarnby. In addition, in a forthcoming textbook, this author has made an attempt to systematically apply a three-level analysis framework to explore the causes of terrorism. Assaf Moghadam, *The Roots of Terrorism* (New York: Chelsea House/Facts on File, 2006 [forthcoming]).

7 Rabbie's model offers a social-psychological framework for examining dynamics of terrorist behavior. Although highly useful, it is questionable whether the average terrorism researcher is able to disaggregate the plethora of psychological orientations described in this model. See Jacob M. Rabbie, "A Behavioral Interaction Model."

8 Two studies, for example, that are primarily focused on the individual and organizational levels only are Assaf Moghadam, "Palestinian Suicide Terrorism in the Second Intifada" and Bruce Hoffman and Gordon H. McCormick, "Terrorism, Signaling, and Suicide Attack," *Studies in Conflict and Terrorism*, 27, 4 (July–August 2004); Meanwhile, Pedahzur *et al.* apply Durkheim's model of altruistic or fatalistic suicide to current suicide bombers, thus utilizing an individual and societal level of analysis in their research. Ami Pedahzur, Arie Perliger, and Leonard Weinberg, "Altruism and Fatalism: The Characteristics of Palestinian Suicide Terrorists," *Deviant Behavior*, 24, 4 (July–August 2003).

9 Elsewhere, the author has adopted and applied the model to discuss the causes of terrorism at large. Assaf Moghadam, *The Roots of Terrorism* (New York: Chelsea House/Facts on File, 2006 [forthcoming]).

10 I thank Marc Sageman for pointing out that many of these organizations are increasingly difficult to identify and more fluid and amorphous than in the past. Ami Pedahzur made the suggestion in this regard to replace the term "organization" with "group" as a more flexible term for the purposes of analysis. Discussion at the Harrington Workshop "A Culture of Death: On Root Causes of Suicide Terrorism," University of Texas at Austin, May 12, 2005.

11 Figure 4.2 is a model expanded from the author's Two-Phase Model of Suicide Terrorism. In Assaf Moghadam, "Palestinian Suicide Terrorism in the Second Intifada," 67–69. For another feedback model on the causes of terrorism, see Jacob M. Rabbie, "A Behavioral Interaction Model," 136.

12 The framework does not entirely fail to take into account specific circumstances, however. On the organizational level, for instance, terrorist organizations sometimes decide to perpetrate an attack when an opportunity presents itself, that is, when the chance of a successful strike is high and/or the cost of failure is low.

13 See, for example, Ariel Merari, "Suicide Terrorism," in Robert I. Yufit and David Lester, eds, *Assessment, Treatment, and Prevention of Suicidal Behavior* (New York: Wiley, 2004), 431–454. Lester, Yang, and Lindsay take exception to both statements, arguing that before establishing that psychological profiles are impossible, extensive biographies of individuals involved need to be constructed, which has not been done to date. David Lester, Bijou Yang, and Mark Lindsay, "Suicide Bombers: Are Psychological Profiles Possible?" *Studies in Conflict and Terrorism*, 27, 4 (July–August 2004): 283–295.

14 For an argument that revenge is a critical area in the study of terrorism, see, for example, Walter Reich, "Understanding Terrorist Behavior: The Limits and Opportunities of Psychological Inquiry," in Walter Reich, ed., *Origins of Terrorism*, 261–279. On humiliation-revenge theory, see especially Mark Juergensmeyer, *Terror in the Mind of*

God: The Global Rise of Religious Violence (Berkeley, CA: University of California Press, 2003); and Jessica Stern, *Terror in the Name of God: Why Religious Militants Kill* (New York: Ecco/Harper Collins, 2003). For a useful summary of humiliation-revenge theory, see Jeff Victoroff, "The Mind of the Terrorist," 29–30.

15 See, for example, Marc Sageman, *Understanding Terror Networks*, 91, 95. Sageman refers to this problem as the "fundamental problem of specificity."

16 Very few exceptions of individuals acting entirely on their own exist, including the "Unabomber," Theodore Kaczynski, as well as 15-year-old Charles Bishop, who crashed a light plane into the 28th floor of the Bank of America Plaza in Tampa, Florida, on January 5, 2002.

17 On the assassination of Tsar Alexander II, see, for example, Bruce Hoffman, *Inside Terrorism*, 17–19. It is not entirely clear whether the assassin of Tsar Alexander II should be considered a suicide bomber.

18 This characteristic applies especially to more traditional campaigns of suicide attacks such as in Lebanon, Israel, or Sri Lanka. This is less obvious in some current suicide bombing campaigns. In Iraq, for example, some insurgent groups have targeted the local population in an apparent effort to intimidate them. It is questionable whether they aim to win the local support by using such methods.

19 Bloom uses the example of the Popular Front for the Liberation of Palestine (PFLP) as a case study to prove this hypothesis. See Mia Bloom, "Palestinian Suicide Bombing: Public Support, Market Share, and Outbidding," *Political Science Quarterly*, 119, 1 (Spring 2004); Ely Karmon similarly argues that the Fatah Al Aqsa Brigades adopted suicide tactics after Hamas threatened its status, in large part due to its use of suicide attacks. Quoted in Christopher Dickey, "Inside Suicide Inc.," *Newsweek*, April 15, 2002, 26.

20 In this regard, Scott Atran convincingly argues that ironically, terrorist organizations regard suicide bombers not necessarily as a loss, but as expendable assets whose loss generates a net gain by expanding public support and pools of potential recruits. Scott Atran, "Genesis of Suicide Terrorism," 1537.

21 Former Israeli chief of staff, Lt. Gen. Amnon Lipkin-Shahak, for instance, declared that "the basic reason for this act [i.e. suicide attacks] is desperation, and the feeling that they have reached a dead end." Amnon Lipkin-Shahak, "Introduction," in ICT, *Countering Suicide Terrorism*, 6.

22 In his "Mini-Manual of the Urban Guerrilla," Carlos Marighella suggested just such a strategy. For a copy of the manual, see the appendix of Robert Moss, *Urban Guerrilla Warfare* (London, International Institute for Strategic Studies, 1971).

23 For a more elaborate discussion of the environmental level of analysis and how it relates to the causes of terrorism at large, see Assaf Moghadam, *The Roots of Terrorism* (New York: Chelsea House/Facts on File, 2006 [forthcoming]).

24 Martha Crenshaw, " 'Suicide Terrorism' in Comparative Perspective," 26. Christoph Reuter calls this emulation effect the "Werther effect."

25 A study that lists a comprehensive list of variables likely to increase the risk of political violence and that can be mostly applied to the risk of suicide terrorism as well, is Jerrold M. Post *et al.* "The Radical Group in Context: 1," and "The Radical Group in Context: 2."

Bibliography

Abadie, A. (2004) *Poverty, Political Freedom, and the Roots of Terrorism*, NBER Working Paper No. 10859, October.

Abu Toameh, K. (2004) "Ramadan Drama Documents Life of Yehya Ayyash," *Jerusalem Post*, October 11.

Argo, N. (2004) *Understanding and Defusing Human Bombs: The Palestinian Case and the Pursuit of the Martyrdom Complex*, Paper presented at the ISA Annual Convention, Montreal, Quebec.

Atran, S. (2003) "Genesis of Suicide Terrorism," *Science*, 299, March 7: 1534–1539.

Bandura, A. (1998) "Mechanisms of Moral Disengagement," in Walter Reich, ed., *Origins of Terrorism: Psychologies, Ideologies, Theologies, States of Mind*, Washington, DC: Woodrow Wilson Center Press, 161–191.

Barnard, C. I. (1938) *The Functions of the Executive*, Cambridge, MA: Harvard University Press.

—— (1973) *The Functions of the Executive*, Cambridge, MA: Harvard University Press, 216.

BBC (2004) *Young Israelis "Traumatized" by Conflict, BBC News Online*, June 2.

Berko, A. (2004) *On the way to the Garden of Eden*, Tel Aviv, Israel: Miskal/*Yediot Ahronot* (Hebrew).

Bloom, M. (2004a) "Palestinian Suicide Bombing: Public Support, Market Share, and Outbidding," *Political Science Quarterly*, March, 61–88.

—— (2004b) *Devising a Theory of Suicide Terror*, Paper submitted at the ISERP Seminar on Contentious Politics, 25.

—— (2005) *Dying to Kill*, Columbia University Press, 95.

Brooks, D. (2002) "The Culture of Martyrdom," *Atlantic Monthly*, June. Available online at http://www.theatlantic.com/doc/prem/200206/brooks, last accessed March 2, 2006.

Capan, E., ed. (2004) *An Islamic Perspective: Terror and Suicide Attacks*, Somerset, NJ: The Light.

Chivers, C. J. and Myers, S. L. (2004) "Chechen Rebels Mainly Driven by Nationalism," *New York Times*, September 12.

Crenshaw, M. (1981) "The Causes of Terrorism," *Comparative Politics*, 13, 4 (July): 379–399.

—— (1985) "An Organizational Approach to the Analysis of Political Terrorism," *Orbis*, Fall.

—— (1988) "Theories of Terrorism: Instrumental and Organizational Approaches," in David C. Rapoport, ed., *Inside Terrorist Organizations*, New York: Frank Cass, 44–62.

—— (1998) "The Logic of Terrorism: Terrorist Behavior as a Product of Strategic Choice," in Walter Reich, ed., *Origins of Terrorism*, 7–24.

—— (2001) " 'Suicide Terrorism' in Comparative Perspective," in *International Policy Institute for Counter-Terrorism (ICT), Countering Suicide Terrorism*, Herzliyya, Israel: International Policy Institute for Counter-Terrorism [ICT], 21–29.

Davis, J. M. (2003) *Martyrs: Innocence, Vengeance and Despair in the Middle East*, New York: Palgrave Macmillan.

Davis, P. K. and Jenkins, B. M. (2002) *Deterrence and Influence in Counterterrorism: A Component in the War on Al Qaeda*, Santa Monica, CA: RAND, 30–32.

Dickey, C. (2002) "Inside Suicide, Inc.," *Newsweek*, April 15: 26.

Dingley, J. (2005) *The Human Body as a Terrorist Weapon: Hunger Strikers and Suicide Bombers*, University of Ulster, Manuscript under Review.

Dolnik, A. (2004) "Critical Commentary on 'Who are the Palestinian Suicide Bombers?' " *Terrorism and Political Violence*, 16, 4 (winter): 846.

Dunlop, J. P. (1998) *Russia Confronts Chechnya: Roots of a Separatist Conflict*, Cambridge, UK: Cambridge University Press, 7.

Eckstein, H. (1972) "On the Etiology of Internal Wars," in Ivo Feierabend eds, *Anger, Violence, and Politics: Theories and Research*, Englewood Cliffs, NJ: Prentice Hall, 12, 13.

Eichner, I. (2003) *"Terror Tournament," Yediot Ahronot*, January 22: 6.

Francis, S. (2000) "The Uniqueness of LTTE's Suicide Bombers," *Institute of Peace & Conflict Studies*, Article No. 321, February 4, Available at http://www.ipcs.org/, last accessed January 10, 2005.

Friedland, N. (1992) "Becoming a Terrorist: Social and Individual Antecedents," in Howard, ed., *Terrorism: Roots, Impact, Responses*, London: Praeger, 88.

Gambetta, D., ed. (2005) *Making Sense of Suicide Missions*, Oxford and New York: Oxford University Press.

Ganor, B. (2002) "Suicide Attacks in Israel," in *International Policy Institute for Counter-Terrorism (ICT), Countering Suicide Terrorism*, Herzliyya, Israel and New York: Anti-Defamation League and ICT, 140–141, 144–145.

Groskop, V. (2004) "Chechnya's Deadly 'Black Widows'," *New Statesman*, September 6.

Gunaratna, R. (2002) "*Suicide Terrorism in Sri Lanka and India*," in *ICT, Countering Suicide Terrorism*, 106–107.

Hafez, M. (2005a) *Strategy, Culture, and Conflict in the Making of Palestinian Suicide Bombers*, Unpublished manuscript, January.

—— (2005b) *Manufacturing Human Bombs: The Making of Palestinian Suicide Bombers*, Washington, DC: United States Institute of Peace, 13.

Harel, A. (2003) "Suicide Attacks Frighten Israelis More Than Scuds," *Haaretz*, February 13.

Harrison, M. (2003) "The Logic of Suicide Terrorism," *Royal United Services Institute Security Monitor*, 2, 1: 11–13.

Hoffman, B. (1998) *Inside Terrorism*, New York: Columbia University Press, 14–15.

—— (2003) "*The Logic of Suicide Terrorism*," *Atlantic Monthly*, June.

Hoffman, B. and McCormick, G. H. (2004) "Terrorism, Signaling, and Suicide Attack," *Studies in Conflict & Terrorism*, 27: 243–281.

International Policy Institute for Counter-Terrorism (ICT) (2001) *Countering Suicide Terrorism*, Herzliyya, Israel: International Policy Institute for Counter-Terrorism [ICT].

Israeli, R. (2003) *Islamikaze: Manifestations of Islamic Martyrology*, New York: Frank Cass.

JIR (2000) "Suicide Terrorism: A Global Threat," *Jane's Intelligence Review*, October 20.

Joshi, C. L. (2000) "Sri Lanka: Suicide Bombers," *Far Eastern Economic Review*, June 1.

Juergensmeyer, M. (2003) *Terror in the Mind of God: The Global Rise of Religious Violence*, Berkeley, CA: University of California Press.

Khosrokhavar, F. (2005) *Suicide Bombers: Allah's New Martyrs*, transl. David Macey, London: Pluto Press.

Kimhi, S. and Even, S. (2003) "Who are the Palestinian Suicide Terrorists?," *Strategic Assessment*, September 2: 6. Available online at http://www.tau.ac.il/jcss/sa/v6n2p5Kim. html, last accessed March 2, 2006.

—— (2004) "Who are the Palestinian Suicide Bombers?," *Terrorism and Political Violence*, 16, 4 (October–December).

Kramer, M. (1991) "Sacrifice and Fratricide in Shiite Lebanon," *Terrorism and Political Violence*, 3, 3 (Winter).

Krueger, A. B. and Maleckova, J. (2002) "Education, Poverty, Political Violence, and Terrorism: Is there a Causal Connection?," *NBER Working Paper No. 9074*, July.

Kurth Cronin, A. (2003) "Terrorism and Suicide Attacks," *CRS Report for Congress*, August 28, 8–12.

Kurz, A. (2005) "Non-Conventional Terrorism: Availability and Motivation," *Strategic Assessment*, 7, 4 (March). Available online at http://www.tau.ac.il/jcss/sa/v7n4p6Kurz.html, last accessed April 16, 2005.

Langer, A. (2005) "Schwarze Witwen: Menschen Töten ist wie Vögel Abschiessen," *Spiegel Online*, March 7.

Laqueur, W. (1979) as quoted in Yonah Alexander, "Terrorism and the Media: Some Considerations," in Alexander, Y. Carlton, D., and Wilkinson, P., eds, *Terrorism: Theory and Practice*, Boulder, CO: West View Press, 160.

Lelyveld, J. (2001) "All Suicide Bombers are Not Alike," *New York Times Magazine*, October 28, 2001. Available online at http://query.nytimes.com/gst/fullpage.html?sec= health&res=9900EFD81F3EF93BA15753C1A9679C8B63, last accessed March 2, 2006.

Lester, D., Yang, B., and Lindsay, M. (2004) "Suicide Bombers: Are Psychological Profiles Possible?," *Studies in Conflict and Terrorism*, 27, 4 (July/August): 283–295.

Lieven, A. (2000) "Nightmare in the Caucasus," *Washington Quarterly*, 23, 1 (Winter): 145.

Long, D. E. (1990) *The Anatomy of Terrorism*, New York: Free Press, 15, 16.

McCauley C. R. and Segal, M. E. (1987) "Social Psychology of Terrorist Groups," in C. Hendrick, ed., *Group Processes and Intergroup Relations, Vol. 9 of Annual Review of Social and Personality Psychology*, Beverly Hills, CA: Sage.

Merari, A. (1998) "The Readiness to Kill and Die: Suicidal Terrorism in the Middle East," in Walter Reich, ed., *Origins of Terrorism: Psychologies, Ideologies, Theologies, States of Mind*, Washington, DC: Woodrow Wilson Center Press, 192–210.

—— (2004) "Suicide Terrorism," in Robert I. Yufit and David Lester, eds., *Assessment, Treatment, and Prevention of Suicidal Behavior*, New York: Wiley, 431–454.

Moghadam, A. (2002a) "Fletcher Hosts Ariel Merari, Israeli Expert on Suicide Terrorism," *Fletcher Ledger*, February 4, 2002. Available at http://www.fletcherledger.com/ archive/2002-02-04/020402-NfinalSuicideTerrorism.htm, last accessed March 2, 2006.

—— (2002b) *Suicide Bombings in the Israeli-Palestinian Conflict: A Conceptual Framework*, Project for the Research of Islamist Movements (PRISM), May, 36–38. Available online at http://www.e-prism.org/, last accessed March 2, 2006.

—— (2003) "Palestinian Suicide Terrorism in Second Intifada: Motivations and Organizational Aspects," *Studies in Conflict and Terrorism*, 26, February/March: 67–69, 72.

—— (2006) *The Roots of Terrorism*, New York, NY: Chelsea House/Facts on File.

Oliver, A. M. and Steinberg, P. (2005) *The Road to Martyr's Square*, Oxford: Oxford University Press.

Pape, R. A. (2003) "The Strategic Logic of Suicide Terrorism," *American Political Science Review*, 97, 3 (August).

—— (2005) *Dying to Win: The Strategic Logic of Suicide Terrorism*, New York: Random House.

Pedahzur, A., Perliger, A., and Weinberg, L. (2003) "Altruism and Fatalism: The Characteristics of Palestinian Suicide Terrorists," *Deviant Behavior*, 24, 4 (July–August).

Piazza, J. (2006) "Rooted in Poverty? Terrorism, Poor Economic Development and Social Cleavages," *Terrorism and Political Violence*, 18, 1: 159–178.

Porta, D. D. (1995) *Social Movements, Political Violence, and the State: A Comparative Analysis of Italy and Germany*, Cambridge: Cambridge University Press.

Post, J. M., Ruby, K. G., and Shaw, E. D. (2002) "The Radical Group in Context: 1. An Integrated Framework for the Analysis of Group Risk for Terrorism," *Studies in Conflict and Terrorism*, 25, 2 (March–April).

—— "The Radical Group in Context: 2. Identification of Critical Elements in the Analysis of Risk for Terrorism by Radical Group Type," *Studies in Conflict and Terrorism*, 25, 2 (March–April).

Rabbie, J. M. (1991) "A Behavioral Interaction Model: Toward a Social-Psychological Framework for Studying Terrorism," *Terrorism and Political Violence*, 3, 4 (Winter).

Reuter, C. (2004) *My Life is a Weapon: A Modern History of Suicide Bombing*, Princeton, NJ: Princeton University Press, 13, 48, 49, 150.

Richburg, K. B. (2004) "Suicide Bomb Survivors Face Worlds Blown Apart," *Washington Post*, January 31: A15.

Ross, J. (1999) "Beyond the Conceptualization of Terrorism: Psychological-Structural Model of the Causes of this Activity," in Craig Summers and Eric Markusen, eds, *Collective Violence: Harmful Behavior in Groups and Governments*, Lanham, MD: Rowman & Littlefield Publishers, 169–192.

Sageman, M. (2004) *Understanding Terror Networks*, Philadelphia, PA: University of Pennsylvania Press, 83.

Sarraj, E. (2002) "Suicide Bombers: Dignity, Despair, and the Need of Hope," *Journal of Palestine Studies*, 31, 4 (Summer): 71–76.

—— (2005) *Paradise Waiting: Palestinian Experience in Suicide Bombing*, Paper distributed at the NATO Advanced Research Workshop: Ideologies of Terrorism, Brussels, Belgium, January 31, 2, 3.

Schalk, P. (1997) *Resistance and Martyrdom in the Process of State Formation of Tamil Eelam*, Available online at http://www.tamilnation.org/ideology/schalkthiyagam.htm, last accessed April 16, 2005.

Schweitzer, Y. (2001) "Suicide Terrorism: Development and Main Characteristics," in *International Policy Institute for Counter-Terrorism (ICT), Countering Suicide Terrorism*, Herzliyya, Israel: International Policy Institute for Counter-Terrorism [ICT], 77–88.

Shay, S. (2004) *The Shahids: Islam and Suicide Attacks*, New Brunswick: Transaction Publishers.

Silke, A. (2003) "The Psychology of Suicide Terrorism," in Silke, A., ed., *Terrorists, Victims, and Society: Psychological perspectives on Terrorism and its Consequences*, New York: Wiley.

Speckhard, A. (2005) *Understanding Suicide Terrorism: Countering Human Bombs and Their Senders*, Unpublished Manuscript, January.

Sprinzak, E. (2000) "Rational Fanatics," *Foreign Policy*, September/October: 66–67.

Stern, J. (2003) *Terror in the Name of God: Why Religious Militants Kill*, New York: Ecco/Harper Collins.

Taarnby, M. (2003) *Motivational Parameters in Islamic Terrorism*, Centre for Cultural Research Working Paper, University of Aarhus, Denmark, August.

Victor, B. (2003) *Army of Roses: Inside the World of Palestinian Women Suicide Bombers*, Emmaus, PA: Rodale.

Victoroff, J. (2005) "The Mind of the Terrorist: A Review and Critique of Psychological Approaches," *Journal of Conflict Resolution*, 49, 1 (February): 3–42.

Volkan, V. (2002) "September 11 and Societal Regression," *Group Analysis*, 35, December: 456–483.

Waldman, A. (2003) "Suicide Bombing Masters: Sri Lankan Rebels," *New York Times*, January 14.

Waltz, K. N. (1954) *Man, the State, and War: A Theoretical Analysis*, New York: Columbia University Press.

—— (1982) "The Origins of War," in John Reichart and Steven Strum, eds, *American Defense Policy*, 5th ed., Baltimore, MD: Johns Hopkins University Press, 9, 11.

Wilkinson, P. (1974) *Political Terrorism*, New York: John Wiley & Sons.

Wilson, J. Q. (1973) *Political Organizations*, New York: Basic Books, Inc., 30–36.

5

SUICIDE TERRORISM FOR SECULAR CAUSES

Leonard Weinberg

This is a chapter about a secular or non-religious campaign of suicidal terrorism that occurred several decades ago and one that has largely gone unnoticed in recent discussions of the subject. These discussions have emphasized the overwhelmingly religious nature of the activity, at least from 1980s to the present. Further, popular as well as academic commentary about suicide terrorism (defined here as "...an operational method in which the very act of the attack is dependent upon the death of the perpetrator") often characterize it as violence carried out by Islamists or Islamic fundamentalists, that is, martyrs and self-sacrificers, against a range of targets, most spectacularly against American, Russian, and Israeli ones (Ganor 2001: 135).

Observers are not imagining things. In a widely read article, Robert Pape identifies Sixteen suicide terrorism campaigns that occurred in various parts of the world between 1980s and 2001 (Pape 2003). We can add another if we include the one presently (2005) underway in Iraq. Of this total, 11 of the 17 campaigns appear to have been driven by religious considerations. And of those that were not, the cause of Chechen separatism and the efforts of the Liberation Tigers in Sri Lanka to carve out a separate country for the Tamils, religion seems to play a role at least. Only the two campaigns (Pape mentions) waged by the nominally Marxist Kurdish Worker's party (PKK) against the Turkish government were motivated by exclusively non-religious considerations.

Recent efforts to trace the history or pre-history of suicide terrorism also stress its religious origins. The histories of the phenomenon usually run from the Assassins and Sicarii through the eighteen-century suicide attacks of Muslim warriors against Western colonial rule in India, Indonesia, and the Philippines through Japan's Second World War Kamikazes to the Iranian children, the Basij, used by Revolutionary Guards to clear out minefields during the Iran/Iraq war (1980–8) (Reuter 2002). The causes for which those involved sacrificed themselves and, usually, as many others as possible, were religious or some mix of religious and nationalist/patriotic objectives. The itinerary of suicide terrorism then passes from the front lines of the Iran/Iraq war to Lebanon in 1982–3 in the period following the Israeli invasion and the arrival of Franco-American peacekeeping forces.

There is an alternative secular pattern to suicide related terrorism we should consider. It is worth pointing out at the beginning that such astute observers of early modern or "first wave" terrorism as Fedor Dostoevski (The Possessed) and Ivan Turgenev (Fathers and Sons) detected a suicidal element in the behavior of many of those who committed acts of terrorist violence on behalf of such ostensibly secular causes as anarchism, nihilism and, later, various Marxist ideas about working-class revolution.

Writing in 1890s the French psychologist Dr Emanuel Regis identified a certain type of regicide:

> ...Proud of his mission and his role, he acts always in daylight and public, and never uses a secret weapon like poison but one that demands personal violence. Afterwards, he does not seek to escape but exhibits pride in his deed and desire for glory and for death, either by suicide or "indirect suicide" as an executed martyr.
>
> (Tuchman 1967: 124)

Albert Camus, writing much later and from a very different perspective notes,

> ...But the extremists...forgot nothing. From their earliest days they were incapable of justifying what they nevertheless found necessary and conceived the idea of offering themselves as a justification and of replying by personal sacrifice to the question they asked themselves. For them...murder was identified with suicide.
>
> (1954: 140)

Camus and Dr Regis' views find support in the expressions of some turn-of-the-century (i.e. nineteenth- to twentieth-century) terrorists themselves. In 1887, on the night before his execution for his involvement in the Haymarket killings the anarchist Louis Lingg blew himself up with a capsule of fulminate of mercury scrawling "Long live anarchy!" in his blood before expiring. Another anarchist convicted for his involvement in the Haymarket affair on the day of his execution proclaimed "this is the happiest day of my life." Five years later another anarchist, Alexander Berkman, attempted to assassinate the Carnegie Steel Company executive Henry Clay Frick in his Pittsburgh Pennsylvania office. The attempt failed and Berkman was arrested. At the police station the authorities discovered that the would-be assassin had two capsules of fulminate of mercury on his person. Evidently, Berkman had planned on following the example set by Lingg (Tuchman 1967: 78, 96). "A life is paid for by another life, and from these two sacrifices springs the promise of a value" (Camus 1954: 141). The Russian revolutionaries were hardly strangers to this line of reasoning. After his arrest in 1881, Already Jeliabov, the man who planned the assassination attempt on Alexander II, demanded to be hanged along with those who actually carried out the attack. In February 1905, a member of the Socialist Revolutionary Party's Combat

Organization, Ivan Kaliev, assassinated the Russian Grand Duke Sergei in St. Petersburg. Before the attack Kaliev had volunteered to kill himself by throwing himself under the horses pulling the Duke's carriage. In fact, he detonated a bomb as Sergei's carriage passed by and then waited at the site to be arrested and, eventually, hanged for this deed (Geifman 1993: 55). Other examples could be brought to bear.

Virtually, all the terrorists involved in these and similar episodes were atheists who did not believe their acts of murder and self-sacrifice would result in eternal life and admission to Paradise, however perceived. Yet the pursuit of martyrdom does not seem too far below the surface. It may require a certain amount of poetic license or conceptual "stretching", but the kind of martyrdom these turn-of-the-century terrorists seem to have pursued was what Robert Jay Lifton describes, in a very different context, as "revolutionary immortality" (Lifton 1968). By killing themselves in the course of an "operation" or structuring the situation in such a way as to guarantee their subsequent execution, as a kind of assisted suicide, these terrorists sought to maintain the hope of revolution alive for future generations. They would die, but their names and, most importantly, their cause would live on. And despite their atheism and the revolutionary nature of the cause, it is not all that hard to see a powerful though distorted Christian imagery behind the conduct. Permitting oneself to be sacrificed on behalf of a broader humanity is certainly a core concept in the history of the Western world even if it is expressed as sacrifice on behalf of a social class (i.e. the proletariat) History has chosen to redeem mankind.

Some will likely object to the foregoing description of turn-of-the-century anarchist and Russian revolutionary "operations" as authentic manifestations of suicide terrorism. Using Boaz Ganor's definition (see page 108), the question becomes: was the very act of their attacks dependent upon the death of the perpetrators? Such an objection is well taken because in the cases cited earlier there is an element of voluntarism involved. Unlike today's martyrs and self-sacrificers, the turn-of-the-century terrorists were confronted not by 1 but by 2 choices in carrying out their attacks. The first, whether or not to do it, is one they share with the current perpetrators. The second choice, whether or not to die or permit themselves to be killed in carrying out the attack, is one that confronted the earlier generations of suicidal terrorists but rarely the contemporary ones. In the former case, the anarchists and Russian revolutionaries retained the option of fleeing after committing their deed. In theory, at least, they could have attempted to evade capture. Their deaths were not totally indispensable in completing the mission. They simply testified to the seriousness of the cause for which the mission had been launched.

But approximately the same observation might be made about some early manifestations of religiously inspired suicide terrorism. The self-sacrificers, members of the Assassin sect in the Middle Ages, exercised similar latitude. Most members of the Sicarii sect sought escape by blending back into the crowd after stabbing their victims in what were, admittedly, high-risk settings.

I

To this point the paper has focused on what amounts to the pre-history or early manifestations of suicide terrorism, both religious and secular. Now it is appropriate to call attention to a campaign of suicide terrorism, one waged on behalf of a clearly secular cause that has largely gone unnoticed by most observers of the current phenomenon. The campaign in question is the one waged by the Viet Cong and their North Vietnamese allies in what was then South Vietnam against the Saigon government and American military and civilian forces from the mid-1960s through the years following the 1968 Tet offensive.

The reasons for the neglect are not hard to come by. Unlike more recent suicide bombing campaigns involving, for example, Hamas or Al Qaeda attacks on Israeli and American targets, the one conducted by the Viet Cong was simply one part of a much larger insurgency, an insurgency that most observers think of as a guerrilla war waged in tropical rain forests and remote hamlets and villages. To the extent that anyone recalls the role of suicide in the struggle over South Vietnam it is the one played by those Buddhist monks who killed themselves by pouring gasoline over their bodies and then lighting themselves on fire on the streets of Saigon and Hue in protest against the anti-Buddhist measures of Ngo Din Diem's dictatorial regime in the period 1962–3, before the latter's ouster by the military, and then sporadically afterward (Karnow 1983). The purpose of these acts of self-immolation was to draw attention, but they were hardly acts of terrorism (Biggs 2004).

Terrorism however did play a significant role in the struggle for Vietnam. Before turning our attention to this role however, it makes sense to briefly review this struggle in a general way so as to both refresh our memories and place the terrorism in context.

Briefly, we should bear in mind there were not one but two struggles for Vietnam in the decades following the Second World War. The first involved an insurrection launched by the Viet Minh under the leadership of Ho Chi Minh against the re-assertion of French rule in the aftermath of Japan's wartime occupation of the country. The French colonial administration, through the instrument of a "play-boy" monarch Bao Dai and his corrupt supporters, dismissed offers of a compromise solution made by Ho and his followers. What followed was an armed insurrection that began in 1946 and culminated with the French defeat at the battle of Dienbienphu. The result of this defeat was the 1954 Geneva Conference. The latter provided the French with an "exit strategy." The newly independent countries adjacent to Vietnam, Laos and Cambodia (both formerly part of French Indo-China), asserted their neutrality. The French and the Viet Minh (identifying itself as the Democratic Republic of Vietnam) agreed upon a temporary division of the country, with the latter withdrawing their forces from the southern part of the country and the former from the north. In other words, a North and South Vietnam were created, at least on a temporary basis, with nationwide elections scheduled for the summer of 1956 (Fall 1966).

The United States, an interested observer, did not sign the agreement; nor did the nominally independent government of the Emperor Bao Dai. (Following Geneva Conference the latter sought to rule this temporary arrangement from a seaside villa in Cannes.) But the effective government of what became the country of South Vietnam came to be ruled by Ngo Dinh Diem, a Catholic in a largely Buddhist country whose strong anti-communism won the backing of the American administration worried about the spread of communism throughout the region. Diem and his government ignored the elections and went about asserting control over the South by repressing various dissident religious groups and criminal gangs. The Communist government in Hanoi under Ho did not suffer from the same bout of amnesia. By 1957 it began supporting the formation of military units among Communist party cadres (the Vietcong) in the South. Hanoi also began supplying these units with weapons. Ho urged caution until these forces were prepared to launch their own insurgency. In 1960 a National Liberation Front (a classic communist popular front organization) proclaimed its intent to liberate the South and began its insurrectionary campaign.

Things did not go well for the Diem government. Its complex military leadership often became more concerned with internal factional disputes than in fighting the Viet Cong. Diem and members of his family, including his sister-in-law, managed to antagonize the country's Buddhist clergy. Corruption was rampant. The Viet Cong managed to plant agents and spies in government offices in Saigon and elsewhere.

In Washington the Kennedy Administration looked at these developments with alarm. It had come to power in 1961 promising to employ a mix of economic development plans and counter-insurgency operations to stop the spread of communism in the Third World of which Southeast Asia was clearly an important part. Fact-finding missions were sent to Saigon to assess the situation and make recommendations about what to do.

The United States supplied economic and military aid (e.g. helicopters) along with some thousands of military advisors. These initiatives failed to stem the tide. Dissatisfaction with Diem grew both in Washington and among South Vietnam's military leaders.

In October 1963, shortly before Kennedy was himself assassinated, the Vietnamese generals staged a coup d'etat, ousted and then executed Diem. His place was taken by General Duong Van Minh "Big Minh," the first of a long line of generals to lead South Vietnam and attempt to defeat the Viet Cong and their North Vietnamese patrons.

Despite serious misgivings, good advice from some of his advisers, and public statements to the contrary during the 1964 presidential election campaign, Lyndon Johnson decided to escalate the American involvement. What occurred from 1965 through the end of Johnson's term of office in January 1969 was the Americanization of the conflict. At the height of the American presence approximately three quarters of a million American military forces were stationed in and around South Vietnam.

There was upbeat talk about "light at the end of the tunnel" despite more realistic, that is pessimistic, assessments of the situation flowing into Washington from various sources. Then there was the January 1968 Tet (A period of religious observance in Vietnam) offensive. Viet Cong forces staged a series of massive and well-planned attacks throughout the country including the holy city of Hue which was occupied for more than a week, the large American airbase at Da Nang, and Saigon itself. These attacks shattered the belief among even the most optimistic observers that the war could be won no matter how substantial the American commitment (Arnold 2004).

The Nixon Administration came into office in January 1969 claiming to have a plan to end the war: an exit strategy in other words. What it did in practice was pursue the "Vietnamization" of the war by training and equipping ARVN (Army of the Republic of Vietnam) forces so that the American presence (including the increasingly unacceptable casualties) on the ground could be reduced and eventually eliminated. The process of turning the fighting on the ground over to the ARVN was accompanied by an extensive air campaign involving the bombing of Hanoi, Haiphong, and other North Vietnamese cities along with various sites in Cambodia. It also meant in the spring of 1970 an American-led ground offensive aimed at interdicting the supply lines running from the North through Cambodia to the Viet Cong fighting in the South.

None of these schemes brought about the desired result, an independent South Vietnam free of the Viet Cong, the National Liberation Front, and from the influence of the Communist regime in Hanoi. But by 1971–2 the situation was sufficiently stalemated to bring about serious negotiations in Paris between the United States and the North Vietnamese. These discussions led eventually to a peace agreement in 1974 which was grudgingly accepted by the Saigon government.

On the basis of this agreement there was a total American withdrawal. The following year the Viet Cong and the North Vietnamese reneged on the peace agreement and resumed waging full-scale war against the ARVN. The latter disintegrated within a matter of weeks and the Saigon government collapsed. Vietnam was united under communist auspices and none of America's war aims was achieved.

Two questions should be addressed next. First, what role did terrorism play in the Viet Minh and Viet Cong campaigns? Second, within this general context, what place did suicide terrorism have in these struggles against the French, the Americans, and their Vietnamese allies?

The fighting over the fate of Vietnam is commonly depicted as guerrilla warfare, along the lines suggested by the theories of Mao Tse-Tung. Only at the very end of the Viet Minh and Viet Cong campaigns do the tactics shift to more conventional army-to-army confrontations as at the end of the successful Chinese

Revolution in 1948–9. To the extent terrorism is mentioned it is usually at the early "agitation-propaganda" phase of the conflict. Stanley Karnow, for example, describes this event that occurred in a suburb of Saigon in 1946:

> ...At dawn, Binh Xuyen terrorists led by Viet Minh agents slipped past...soldiers supposedly guarding the district. Smashing doors and windows, they broke into bedrooms and massacred one hundred fifty French and Eurasian civilians, sparing neither women nor children. They dragged a hundred more away as hostages, mutilating many before freeing them later.
>
> (1983: 149)

In fact, terrorism continued to be employed as a tactic by the Viet Minh throughout the course of their campaign. Along with such disruptive or sabotage tactics as road cutting and the setting of booby-traps (e.g. the planting of Pungi Sticks), including the use of home-made or ad hoc explosive charges (presently identified as "improvised explosive devices" in the fighting over Iraq), Viet Minh forces staged terrorist attacks against both military and civilian targets. Bombs were planted in or hurled at bars, restaurants, cafes, theaters, and brothels known to be occupied by off-duty French troops. These attacks prevented the French from feeling at ease, prevented them from believing there were certain safe rest areas in the cities, no, as it were, "green zones." In the villages French colonists and Vietnamese civilians thought to be loyal to the French presence, for example, village "headmen," school teachers, were systematically killed by Viet Minh cadres, usually during night-time attacks (Lycos 2005). Thousands were killed as the result of this terrorist campaign.

The terrorism was not always perpetrated by the Viet Minh. There were other players as well. Graham Greene's novel, *The Quiet American*, tells the story of an American agent (apparently a fictional treatment of a real person, Colonel Edward Lansdale) who seeks to promote a "third force" between the French and the communist Viet Minh. Leaders of various criminal organizations and religious cults seemed possibilities, at least to the naive American. He provides help to one such gang chieftain who then has bombs detonated in restaurants and bars in Saigon.

The terrorism persisted in the period between the failure to hold national elections in 1956 and the beginning of the Viet Cong insurgency in 1960. For instance, "Bernard Fall [a French-American political scientist] relates that he returned to Vietnam in 1957 after the war had been over for two years and was told by everyone that the situation was fine. He was bothered, however, by the many obituaries in the press of village chiefs who had been killed by 'unknown elements' and 'bandits'. Upon investigation he found these attacks were clustered in certain areas and that there was a purpose behind them (Laqueur 1967: 271)." In fact, the US Mission in Vietnam later estimated that 1,000 Vietnamese were killed by these "unknown elements" and "bandits" in 1958 and 1959 (Hosmer 1970: 42).

The pace and volume of Viet Cong terrorism accelerated dramatically with the launching of the full-scale insurgency in 1960. No systematically gathered statistics are available for terrorist attacks between 1960 through 1965. Nonetheless, the US Mission estimated that the Viet Cong carried out approximately 9,700 assassinations in this period. The report also suggested this estimate was likely on the low side (ibid.). A few event descriptions taken from the US eleventh Cavalry Division's website seem appropriate for illustrative purposes.

23 August 1960: Two school teachers... are preparing lessons at home when communists arrive and force them at gun point to go to their school... in Phong Dinh province. There they find two men tied to the school veranda. The communists read the death order of the two men, named Canh and Van. They are executed, presumably to intimidate the school teachers.

28 September 1960: Father Hoang Ngoc Minh,... priest of Kontum parish, is riding from Tan Canh to Kondela. A communist road block halts his car. A bullet smashes into him. The guerrillas drive bamboo spears into Father Minh's body, then one fires a submachine gun point blank killing him. The driver..., his nephew, is seriously wounded.

6 December 1960: Terrorists dynamite the kitchen at the Saigon Golf Club, killing a Vietnamese kitchen helper and injuring two Vietnamese cooks.

22 March 1961: A truck carrying 20 girls is dynamited on the Saigon-Vung Tau road. The girls are returning from Saigon where they have taken part in a Trung Sisters Day celebration. After the explosion terrorists open fire on the survivors. Two of the girls are killed and ten wounded. The girls are unarmed and traveling without escort.

16 February 1964: Three Americans are killed and 32 injured most of them U.S. dependents, when terrorists bomb the Kinh Do movie theater in Saigon.

(Theavnam 2005)

From the middle of 1966 onward data on terrorist incidents were systematically collected by the US Mission. The Public Safety Division even developed a Terrorist Incident Reporting System (TIRS) beginning in 1968.

Table 5.1 reports terrorist events from the middle of 1966 through 1969, except for terrorist attacks carried out during the month long 1968 Tet offensive. The figures that leap to our attention are the overall number of events, over 40,000, and the number of killings involved, more than 18,000, the majority of which were attacks not directed against public officials or government employees but members of the general Vietnamese public. Further, unlike the various international terrorist event data sets accessible to researchers in more recent times, the Vietnamese collection does not include less serious forms of terrorist violence. It is limited to kidnapping and assassination.

Table 5.1 US mission reports of Viet Cong assassinations and abductions, 1966–9

	Assassinations	*Abductions*
Government officials	1,153	664
Government employees	1,863	381
General populace	15,015	24,862
	18,031	25,907
	Total = 43,938	

Source: Stephen Hosmer, *Viet Cong Repression and Its Implications for the Future* (Lexington, MA: Heath Lexington Books, 1970), 44.

In other words, the overall volume and lethality of Viet Cong terrorism rivals or exceeds all but a handful (e.g. Algeria, Sri Lanka) of terrorist campaigns waged over the last third of the twentieth century. The Viet Cong campaign is obscured by the fact it occurred in the context of a more general conflict, one in which not thousands but hundreds of thousands of people lost their lives. The terrorism was a war within a war. What place did suicide terrorism have in this horrendous conflict?

Two types of Viet Cong units were involved in carrying out acts of suicide terrorism. The first were "suicide cells" or "suicide teams" created beginning in November 1967 in connection with the "General Offensive and General Uprising," that is, the Tet offensive, which aimed to weaken the Saigon government hold on much of the country. By capturing and holding cities, villages, and hamlets previously under the enemy's control the Viet Cong would be presented with a "target rich environment," that is, large numbers of civilians suspected of or known to sympathize (often these individuals were identified through "black lists") with Saigon. The environment was so rich that leaders believed their forces would be stretched thin. According to captured Viet Cong documents, provincial leaders issued a series of directives calling for the formation of "suicide teams." In Binh Dinh Province, for example, villages were ordered to form suicide units of 10–20 members. Each of these units was then to be sub-divided into three-person cells. The instructions emphasized that the recruits should be teenagers but over the age of 15. Girls as well as boys were to participate. The cells or teams were to perform essentially two functions.

A letter attributed to the head of the Ban Me Thuot Province summarizes these purposes:

> ...each hamlet where our agents are available should choose from 2 to 3 persons to activate a hamlet uprising section and 2 to 3 suicide cells (selected from among male and female youths) to keep track of and destroy wicked tyrants in the hamlet.... At present, the conditions are ripe for the implementation of the plan of the Revolution; however the

people are controlled by wicked tyrants and administrative personnel in hamlets and villages. If we are able to guide suicide units to kill these wicked tyrants, the people in villages and hamlets, even though there are no agents present, will rise up to overthrow the enemy government and support and join the Revolution.

(Hosmer 1970)

What the provincial Viet Cong leader is telling his subordinates is that the suicide cells, equipped with grenades and daggers, will help the cause not only by eliminating "wicked tyrants" along with various "spies" and "traitors" (i.e. Special Forces personnel, rural development cadres, enemy commanders, and pacification personnel) but also through their self-sacrifice perform exemplary acts that would win over the peasant masses to the cause of revolution. In effect, they would engage in "propaganda by deed" on behalf of the Viet Cong. The evidence is fragmentary, but the operations of these cells continued at least through August 1968, months after the conclusion of the Tet offensive. (Hosmer 2005).

The second type of Viet Cong and North Vietnamese unit that staged suicide attacks confronts us with a more complex set of circumstances. Instead of suicide cells devoted almost exclusively to the killing of local notables, the Viet Cong (VC) and North Vietnamese (NVA) sapper units were part of their regular armed forces. Further, the sappers were active not only in the villages and hamlets but also in Saigon and other cities, particularly during Tet. Also, suicide operations were simply one of several tasks performed by the sappers. They carried out various high-risk attacks on American and ARVN military forces as well. And while the young people recruited for the suicide cells were essentially adolescent throw-aways, the sappers were regarded as a highly disciplined elite (Scire 2005a). In this regard recruits to the Sapper Corps received special training in the use of explosives and electric wiring along with sophisticated reconnaissance and assault techniques. Sapper training lasted six months, far longer than that provided to members of the conventional Viet Cong and NVA units (Gruntonline 2005).

During Tet Viet Cong sappers were sent on suicide missions against high prestige or high visibility targets. In Saigon, units of the Viet Cong C-10 Battalion consisting of approximately 250 men and women (many of whom had been working undercover as taxi cab drivers to disguise their attentions and also become familiar with the city) not only attacked the American Embassy compound (they evidently hoped to assassinate US Ambassador Ellsworth Bunker) but also the South Vietnamese Joint General Staff headquarters, Navy headquarters, the Presidential Palace (in an attempt to assassinate President Nguyen Van Thieu), the National Broadcasting Station, and Tan Son Nhut Air Base (Pohle and Hosmer). United Press International (UPI) dispatches refer explicitly to "communist suicide squads" in describing these attacks. The journalist Don Oberdorfer provides this account:

The Presidential Palace, which is probably the most heavily defended installation in the downtown [Saigon] area, was attacked by a team of

117

thirteen men and a woman.... In view of the odds against them this was clearly a low-cost attempt at political impact. The sapper team, which arrived in three vehicles, including a truck loaded with TNT, was repelled at the side gate of the palace within a few minutes. The Viet Cong took refuge in an unfinished apartment building across the street and held out for fifteen hours in a running gun battle until nearly all [sic]of the small unit was killed.

(2001: 142)

These missions failed in the sense that the sappers did not succeed in carrying out the assassinations or seizing complete control of the high prestige buildings before those guarding these heavily defended installations killed them, but their suicidal operations certainly helped persuade millions of Americans who watched these events on television that US government claims about a "light at the end of the tunnel" were pipe dreams. If terrorism is about communication and influencing audiences then the attacks were eminently successful.

Sapper units before and after Tet were also launched against conventional American, especially, and ARVN military targets, in the Vietnamese countryside. Sometimes they were used in conjunction with or in support of large-scale Viet Cong and North Vietnamese attacks. Sometimes they were sent on sabotage missions to destroy enemy installations. On other occasions though, particularly following Tet, sappers were sent on what were oftentimes suicide missions. In these attacks sappers often sought to penetrate and destroy local American command headquarters, signal centers, radar stations, and other heavily defended installations through the detonation of explosives carried on their person.

In an email correspondence with this writer, a former US Army officer provides this description:

...In my area of operations, Northern I Corps during the first eight months of 1969, there were no major actions involving Vietcong units as they had been substantially destroyed in Tet of 1968. Instead our enemy was two Divisions of the North Vietnamese Army who were to be found near the Laotian and North Vietnamese borders. Most of our action occurred in the area south of KheSanh down to and across the Laotian border. In most cases we had set up Fire Support Bases on tops of mountains near the Laotian border and those bases were the object of ground assaults involving North Vietnamese soldiers. We were told at the time that the Sappers mode of operation was to place charges to blow up barbed-wire obstructions and to throw satchel charges (bags of plastic explosives) into bunkers and artillery firing pits. We were also told that they were prepared to detonate the charges on themselves if it came to that.... My experience...in Northern I Corps (Quang Tri Province) [was that] suicide acts by sappers were not the norm but a fallback strategy when there was no other way...

(Scire 2005b)

What motivated the youthful members of the village-level suicide cells and the Viet Cong and North Vietnamese sappers? Religion, Buddhist, Confucian, Christian, or otherwise, did not seem to play a role. At least for this study the evidence will have to be adduced from findings about the sources of recruitment for the Viet Cong in general. Unfortunately, a substantial amount of guesswork is involved and it is by no means clear that the same set of motives were at work for members of the suicide teams and the sappers.

In a Rand Corporation report for the Defense Department, John Donnell summarizes the results of a series of interviews with 261 Viet Cong defectors and prisoners of war (Donnell 1967). The interviews were conducted during 1964–5, well before Tet.

Some reasons Donnell found for joining the Viet Cong in general seem less plausible than others as incentives for engaging in suicide operations (although the post-induction results of training, socialization, and "group-think" may make them more plausible). The desire of young men to evade being drafted into the ARVN (when the draft notice was received) as well as the prospect of acquiring more farmland were evidently significant factors in the Viet Cong's recruitment campaigns. But these motives do not seem powerful enough to explain or warrant suicide attacks, among other things they are tangible and fixed on a literally terrestrial future. A stronger candidate explanation involves reactions against air or ground attacks carried out by American or ARVN forces on villages and hamlets. When civilians were killed or injured in these attacks, some survivors unsurprisingly were left with feelings of hatred for the attackers. When the desire for revenge was combined with appeals to patriotism, expelling foreigners, Viet Cong recruiters seem to have had a potent mixture with which to work. The Rand report also mentions "adventurousness." The desire for "action" is, of course, a widely discussed motive for the young joining all types of violent groups, from small terrorist bands to large scale protest movements. There is the matter of Marxism Leninism. Ideology though was rarely mentioned by those interviewed in the Rand study. In fact, as another Rand analyst notes, "Most village youth join the Viet Cong for a variety of personal reasons. These seldom seem inspired by political motives. Speaking of the new recruits, several captured Viet Cong Cadres noted that their 'political understanding is almost nil' " (Goure 1965: 5). What place ideology had in post-induction training regimens carried out by the Viet Cong was no doubt extensive. But the evidence suggests the VC cadres responsible for such training were writing on pretty blank slates.

II

Whatever the motives of those who sacrificed their lives on behalf of the Viet Cong and the North Vietnamese cause, religion does not seem to have been a significant one. Neither by itself nor in conjunction with nationalism, as in Chechnya, Palestine, or Sri Lanka, do spiritual considerations seem to have been at work. Acts of suicide or suicidal terrorism appear to have been carried out in the pursuit of exclusively secular aims. Whether or not members of "suicide teams" and VC sappers hoped to achieve "revolutionary immortality" by their self-sacrifices is a question that will have to remain unanswered based on the evidence presently available to this writer.

Postscript

The United States is presently engaged in an extended military/political campaign in Iraq. Are there any parallels between the experience in Vietnam and the current undertaking? Certainly those opposed to the Iraq initiative find them in abundance: another quagmire. Any extended commentary is well beyond the scope of this chapter, nevertheless a few observations seem appropriate. First, in the struggle over Vietnam suicide terrorism was simply one tactic, and a relatively minor one, in the Viet Cong's "repertoire of contestation." The Viet Cong and the North Vietnamese waged guerrilla war whose aim was the capture of an ever-expanding territory. Terrorism, including suicide terrorism, was a valuable tool in the conflict, but not the predominant form of action. For the insurgents in Iraq however, terrorism and especially suicide terrorism comes close to being the only arrow in their quiver. In Iraq, "liberated zones," even in the Sunni Triangle, are hard to detect. Second, and finally, this being said, the 1968 Tet offensive had precisely the kind of psychological impact on American audiences that Al Qaeda in Iraq is hoping to achieve. And, we should remember that the suicide terrorist attacks staged by Viet Cong sappers helped to achieve this affect.

Bibliography

Arnold, J. (2004) *Tet Offensive 1968: Turning Point in Vietnam*, Westport, CT: Praeger, 85–91.

Biggs, M. (2004) *Dying without Killing: Self-Immolations, 1963–2002*, in Diego Gambetta, ed., *Making Sense of Suicide Missions*, New York: Oxford University Press, 173–208.

Camus, A. (1954) *The Rebel*, New York: Alfred, A. Knopf, 140–141.

Donnell, J. (1967) *Viet Cong Recruitment: Why and How Men Join*, Rand: RM-5486-1-ISA/ARPA, December, 14–138.

Fall, B. (1966) *Viet-Nam Witness*, New York: Frederick Praeger, 69–83.

Ganor, B. (2001) "Suicide Attacks in Israel," in *Countering Suicide Terrorism*, Herzliya, Israel: ICT, 135.

Geifman, A. (1993) *Thou Shalt Kill: Revolutionary Terrorism in Russia, 1894–1917*, Princeton, NJ: Princeton University Press, 55.

Goure, L. (1965) *Some Impressions of the Effects of Military Operations on Viet Cong Behavior*, Santa Monica, CA: Rand RM-4517-1-ISA, 5.

Gruntonline (2005) *NVA Sappers: Introduction, Training and Objectives*, Available at: http://www.gruntonline.com/NVAandVC/nva_sappers1.htm, accessed August 5.

Hosmer, S. (1970) *Viet Cong Repressions and Its Implications for the Future*, Lexington, MA: Heath Lexington Books, 42, 46–47, 55–56.

—— (2005) Communication with Hosmer, R. and Corporation, May 24.

Karnow, S. (1983) *Vietnam: A History*, New York: The Viking Press, 149–150, 279–281.

Laqueur, W. (1967) *Guerrilla*, Boston, MA: Little, Brown, 271.

Lifton, R. J. (1968) *Revolutionary Immortality*, New York: Random House.

Lycos (2005) *Viet Minh Strategy and Tactics, 1945–54*, Available at: http://members.lycos.co.uk/Indochine/vm/tiger.html, accessed August 5.

Oberdorfer, D. (2001) *TET!*, Baltimore, MD: The Johns Hopkins University Press, 142.

Pape, R. (2003) "The Strategic Logic of Suicide Terrorism," *American Political Science Review*, 97, 3: 343–361.

Pohle, V. *The Viet Cong in Saigon: Tactics and Objectives During the Tet Offensive*, Rand RM5799-ISA/ARPA, 8–22.

Reuter, Ch. (2002) *My Life is a Weapon*, Princeton, NJ: Princeton University Press, 1–51.

Scire, J. (2005a) Writer's interview with Capt. (ret.) John Scire, US Army Special Forces, Reno, February.

—— (2005b) E-mail, from Capt. John Scire (US Army ret.), June 21.

Thcavnam (2005) Available at: http://www.11thcavnam.com/education/namterror.htm, accessed August 5.

Tuchman, B. (1967) *The Proud Tower*, New York: Bantam Books, 78, 96, 124.

6

ISLAM AND AL QAEDA

Marc Sageman

One of the explanations for the present wave of global Islamist terrorism blames Islam in general, arguing that there is something inherently violent in Islam, namely jihad, which inevitably leads to confrontation with non-Islamic people. In consequence, fanatic young Muslims, brainwashed by militant Imams, unleash terrorist operations against "infidels" in a "clash of civilizations." The Islamist command to wage a jihad against the West is indeed so strong that these young men are happy to die for their cause. This chapter will empirically test this argument.

A popular tendency is to lump all Muslim terrorists together. However, terrorism is a strategy used by many organizations and social movements. Some of them happen to be Muslim, using this strategy for more traditional goals, such as liberation from occupation or overthrowing their own governments. Mixing these terrorists with those that threaten the West might cause confusion. To try to keep this sample as analytically pure as possible, I have included only those terrorists who use violence against foreign or non-Muslim governments or populations to establish an Islamist state. This means that Muslim terrorists with more national-ist goals, such as Palestinians, Chechens, or Algerians fighting in their respective countries, were excluded from the sample.

The terrorists who flew into the World Trade Center, the Pentagon, and crashed in the fields of Pennsylvania on September 11, 2001 were part of al Qaeda. The term al Qaeda is confusing, because it refers both to a specific organization and to a more diffuse and global social movement at war with the United States. Al Qaeda, the for-mal organization, is the vanguard of this violent Islamist revivalist social movement. The sample in this chapter includes people who belonged to this terrorist social move-ment, which might be called the global Salafi jihad, because many of the terrorists are not formally in al Qaeda, in the sense of swearing an oath of loyalty to Osama bin Laden, its leader, but are nevertheless fellow travelers with them. In order to define who belongs to this social movement, it is important to understand its nature.

The evolution of the global Salafi jihad ideology

This terrorist social movement is held together by a common vision. It arose in the context of gradual Muslim decadence over the past 500 years, during which

122

Islam fell from its dominant position in the world. Because Islam claims to be the last and perfect revelation from God, this decline presents a problem. Many explanations, secular and religious, have tried to deal with this obvious mismatch between claim and reality. One of the more popular religious explanations is simply that Muslims have strayed from the righteous path. The source of strength of the original and righteous Muslim community was its faith and its practices, which pleased God. Recapturing the glory and grandeur of the Golden Age requires a return to the authentic faith of the ancient ones, namely the Prophet Mohammed and his companions, the *salaf*, from the Arabic word for predecessor or ancient one. The revivalist versions of Islam advocating such a return are called Salafi. Their strategy is the creation of a pure Islamist state, which would create the conditions for the reestablishment of such a community.

Most Salafists advocate a peaceful takeover of the state, either through face to face proselytism or the creation of legitimate political parties. Their peaceful strategy was undermined by Egyptian President Nasser's brutal crackdown in the name of a pan-Arabist socialist project. Some Islamists like Sayyid Qutb concluded that Nasser would never give up power peacefully and preached his violent overthrow (Qutb n.d.). He argued that Muslim countries had reached a state of decadence and injustice, which was similar to the state of barbarism, *jahiliyya*, prevailing in the Arabian Peninsula just before the revelations of the Quran. This was due to a "crisis of values," namely greed, corruption, and promiscuity, which could only be redressed from above, by capturing the state. Because their rulers were accused of having abandoned true Islam, they were branded apostates, and the Quranic punishment for apostasy was death. Qutb was executed before he was able to specify how "true Muslims" might create this true Islamist state. Some of this followers, led by Mohammad Abdal Salam Faraj (Faraj 1986), advocated the violent overthrow of these impious Muslim rulers, the "near enemy," and argued that this was the forgotten duty of each Muslim, a sixth pillar of Islam. Other followers, led by Shukri Mustafa, advocated a denunciation of society as infidel (*al Takfir*) and withdrawal from it, as the Prophet withdrew from Mecca (*al Hijra*). The Egyptian press dubbed his Society of Muslims *Al-Takfir wa'l-Hijra*, and the label stuck for the more recent radical Islamist groups, who combine these two versions by violently targeting civil society.

The 1979 Soviet invasion of Afghanistan further galvanized the Islamist militant movement worldwide. Sheikh Abdallah Azzam preached a traditional jihad against the Soviet invaders. Many militants from all over the Muslim world answered his call. As the Soviets withdrew, Azzam extended the defensive jihad into a more global one. He preached that all former Muslim lands dating back to the fifteenth century, from the Philippines to Spain, had to be liberated from the infidels. Militant Muslims from all over the world answered his call to defend their co-religionists in Afghanistan. After the Soviet withdrew, most of these foreigners returned to their country. But those who could not, mostly because of prior terrorist activities at home, stayed behind and became the nucleus of al Qaeda, the organization. After many Middle Eastern countries complained to Pakistan that it was harboring terrorists, Pakistan expelled them. The most militant went to the Sudan, invited by the new militant regime of Hassan al-Turabi.

During this Sudanese exile, the Islamist militants held intense discussions about their failure to capture a core Arab state and transform it into an Islamist one. Some militants argued that this failure was due to the United States propping up the local regimes. The strategy espoused by the most militant was to switch priorities and fight the "far enemy" (the United States and Jews) in order to expel them from the Middle East, so that they could then overthrow the "near enemy," their own regimes. This argument split the Islamist militant community, for many did not want to provoke and take on a powerful enemy like the United States. When the Sudan was forced to expel the militants from their country, the few who advocated fighting the "far enemy" returned to Afghanistan. So the most militant of the most militant of the most militant returned to Afghanistan under the leadership of Osama bin Laden in the summer of 1996, and within two months of their return declared war on the United States (Bin Laden 1996). In February 1998, bin Laden extended his "Jihad against Jews and Crusaders" to include civilians outside the Middle East, ruling that "to kill the Americans and their allies—civilians and military—is an individual duty for every Muslim who can do it in any country in which it is possible to do it" (Bin Laden 1998).

The earlier outline suggests that the ideology of the global Salafi jihad is definitely not part of mainstream Islam. Some of the more obvious differences between the ideology of the global Salafi jihad and more traditional versions of Islam are: a dogmatic, literalist, and rigid interpretation of the scriptures (the *Quran*, the *Sunna*, and the *Hadith*), rejecting fourteen centuries of Quranic interpretations; modeling themselves strictly on the "pious ancestors" (*al-Salaf al Salih*); adoption of the Wahhabi view of Christians and Jews as "unbelievers" (*kuffar*) in contrast to the traditional Islamic attitude of qualified respect for "People of the Book" (*Ahl al-Kitab*); the extension of this rejection of civilian society to Muslims (takfiri); advocacy of the use of violence against non-Muslims and Muslims alike to achieve an Islamist state; and reorientation of takfiri jihadi targets from the "near enemy" (apostate Muslim regimes) to the "far enemy" (the West, especially the United States and France). The full range of these ideas is shared by only a tiny minority of Muslims.

Data

There is a paralyzing assumption in terrorism research that there is no good data for research. First, terrorists would not grant interviews to serious researchers for security reasons. Second, the state would not grant access to captured terrorists for national security reasons. Third, one is never sure whether the terrorists would be honest with the interviewer. This has prevented the emergence of evidence-based terrorism research. However, with the development of the Internet, open source data has become more available even in one's home. All the data collected for this paper came from the public domain. I did not have direct access to the terrorists or to any government's secret reports. Despite the problems listed earlier, there is enough information in open sources to support an empirical analysis of the global Salafi jihad. My sources included the documents and transcripts of legal proceedings involving global Salafi terrorists and their organizations, government documents, press and scholarly articles, and Internet articles. The information was often inconsistent. I considered the source of the information in assessing facts. In decreasing degrees of reliability, I favored transcripts of court proceedings subject to cross examination, followed by government documents such as the 9/11 Commission Report, followed by reports of court proceedings, then corroborated information from people with direct access to the information provided, uncorroborated statements with people with that access, and finally statements from people who had heard information secondhand. "Experts" fall into the last category, for their reliability as sources of information depends on their diligence as historians.

The collected information suffers from several limitations. First, the terrorists selected are hardly representative of the global Salafi jihad as a whole. Journalists and scholars tend to focus on the unusual: leaders, people they can investigate, and unusual cases. This bias toward leaders and unusual cases tends to ignore those who cannot be investigated and downplays the rank and file. Second, reliance on journalistic accounts is fraught with danger. In the rush to publish, the initial information may not be reliable. Lack of direct access to information feeds the wildest rumors, and journalists are born storytellers, who fill in the gaps in knowledge. These initial inaccuracies can be corrected by following the developing stories over time, rather than simply relying on initial reporting. Third, reliance on retrospective accounts from principals and witnesses are subject to the biases of self-report and flawed memory. These accounts were often the only available information, and were very occasionally able to be corroborated with existing contemporaneous documents. Finally, there is a lack of a relevant control group that would allow the generation of statements specific to the terrorists. It is difficult to make specific statements about these terrorists without comparison to a group of Muslims with similar backgrounds and activities who did not participate in terrorism despite having had an opportunity to do so.

Nevertheless, the hope was that even though each piece of information may be of questionable validity, the emerging pattern would be accurate because of the large numbers involved. A description of the whole sample might be able to support or refute the conventional wisdom about al Qaeda terrorism. With the definition of a global Salafi terrorist elaborated in the previous section, there were 394 terrorists, on whom there existed enough background information to include them in empirical generalizations as to age, origin, religious commitment, and education.

The global Salafi jihad and Islam

The "blame Islam" argument would suggest that there is something inherent to "Islam" as a unitary phenomenon, which inspires and motivates Muslims to kill

125

and die in the name of Islam. This implies that Muslims either learn about this "something" either in the midst of their families, at school, or simply living in their hate-filled culture. This exposure brainwashes them to take arms against the West. Some versions of these arguments blame *madrassas*, or Islamic boarding schools, which allegedly fill unsophisticated and naïve young men with hatred of the West. The argument further suggests that it is Islam that mobilizes young Muslims into terrorist organizations and motivates them to carry out atrocities against the West.

The global Salafi jihad is a diaspora phenomenon. By diaspora, I mean 1 of 2 things: people either joined the global jihad in a country where they did not grow up; or they were second or third generation immigrants. In my sample, 84 percent joined the jihad in the diaspora. Robert Leiken of the Nixon Center replicated my study in Western Europe and found that 87 percent belonged to the diaspora. Although some were members of a diaspora in a Muslim country, many joined while living in a non-Muslim country. Nor were they particularly religious at the time they joined. The four Hamburg students who became the leaders of the 9/11 Plot and the Montreal immigrants who plotted to bomb LAX airport as part of a Millennial Plot were living in the West, and were not particularly religious at the time they became radicalized. Indeed, there might have been a dip in their religious devotion at the time for many were experimenting with Western lifestyle. Nor did they come from very religious families. Most came from mildly religious families, who rejected this Salafi jihadi ideology and seemed shocked to learn that one of their own believed it. In terms of madrassas, only 13 percent of my samples were madrassa educated, and they were unique to Southeast Asian mujahedin, who had gone to two Islamist boarding schools: *Pondok Ngruki* in Indonesia and *Pensantren Luqmanul Hakiem* in Malaysia. This specific distribution of the madrassa educated mujahedin comes from the fact that these madrassa heads, Abdullah Sungkar and Abu Bakar Basayir, recruited their best students into their terrorist organization, the Jamaah Islamiyah. So, 87 percent of the members of the global Salafi jihad had a secular education. The entire sample from the North African region and the second generation Europeans went to secular schools. Madrassas might constitute a threat to local governments, such as Pakistan, but they do not constitute a threat to the United States because there is little evidence that madrassa educated mujahedin would be able to operate in the West.

In terms of extent of education, about 60 percent of global Salafi terrorists had some form of college education in contrast with their peers from their respective countries where higher education is relatively rare. Most were in the technical fields, such as engineering, architecture, computers, medicine, and business. Most of the terrorists have some occupational skills. Three-fourths are either professional (physicians, lawyers, architects, engineers, or teachers) or semi-professionals (businessmen, craftsmen, or computer specialists). Surprisingly, very few were formally educated in religion. So, almost paradoxically, the future terrorists were very well educated, but lacked any religious education. It was not ignorance *per se* but this combination of technical education and lack of religious sophistication that made them vulnerable to an extreme interpretation of Islam. I suspect a traditional religious Islamic education might have protected them against this form of interpretation.

In terms of the cultural variant of the "blame Islam" argument, many joined the jihad in a non-Muslim country in Western Europe or North America. Indeed, about 10 percent of the samples are Christian converts to Islam, who could not have been brainwashed into this ideology as young people by either their family, school, or "culture". In order to understand the specific relationship between Islam and this new wave of terrorism, let us examine the way people joined the jihad.

Joining the jihad

From the data, there were seven major trajectories of joining the jihad. The first was the path followed by the leadership group, which met in Afghanistan during the Afghan-Soviet War of the 1980s and progressively took control over this violent social movement in the 1990s. The majority of this group is Egyptian, which is consistent with its ideology, also mostly of Egyptian origin. This group is al Qaeda proper and has been operationally neutralized after the post 9/11 US offensive against this social movement. It is an extremely well-educated group of people and about 20 percent have a degree equivalent to a doctorate. The second trajectory to join this terrorist social movement is the one followed by the Southeast Asian faction. They are the students of Baasyir and Sungkar and have stayed loyal to their former teachers. The people comprising these two trajectories were already very religious by the time they joined the global jihad. Together, they constitute about a quarter of the sample.

The third trajectory consists of the "best and brightest" of Middle Eastern countries, who went to study in the West, because that is where the best schools are. They came from upper middle class caring and mildly religious families, who grew up with strong positive values of religion, spirituality, and concern for their communities. Abroad, they were truly global citizens, conversant in 3 to 6 languages, and skilled in computer technology. They became homesick, and drifted to places where other Muslims aggregated: mosques. There, they met others like them, became friends, and often moved in together in communal apartments. The fourth trajectory is that of young upwardly mobile economic immigrants coming to the West, legally or illegally, for economic opportunities. In the new host country, they had difficulty finding good jobs. They met other immigrants like them and organized themselves into petty crime to make ends meet. The fifth trajectory is that of excluded second or third generation Maghreb Arab Muslims in Western Europe. They usually dropped out of school and organized themselves into gangs of petty criminals to survive economically. They collectively drifted to religion as a group, often to escape their petty criminal lifestyle. This second group of trajectories constitutes about 60 percent of the sample. They clustered around very few extremely militant mosques, who were preaching jihad. Indeed, about twelve mosques worldwide generated about half the sample. So, this movement was very narrowly distributed around specific Salafi mosques, suggesting that it was not Islam in general, but the specific message preached at these mosques that radicalized these young men.

The third group of trajectories includes young Muslims, who joined the jihad in their home country in the Middle East. Often they were gifted young people, who were excluded from the rewards of society and became attracted to an ideology that provided an explanation for their circumstances. The last trajectory is of course the puzzling one of Christian converts, who joined the jihad. They had become close friends to people already in the jihad and simply joined their friends or married into the jihad.

The common themes in these trajectories were loneliness, alienation, marginalization, underemployment, and exclusion from the highest status in the new or original society. Although the future terrorists were not religious, they drifted to mosques for companionship. There, they met friends or relatives, with whom they moved in together often for dietary reasons. As their friendship intensified, they became a "bunch of guys," resenting society at large which excluded them, developing a common religious collective identity, egging each other on into greater extremism. By the time they joined the jihad, there was a dramatic shift in devotion to their faith. About two-thirds of those who joined the jihad did so collectively with their friends or had a long-time childhood friend already in the jihad. Another fifth had close relatives already in the jihad. These friendship or kinship bonds predated any ideological commitment. Once inside the social movement, they cemented their mutual bonds by marrying sisters and daughters of other terrorists. There was no evidence of "brainwashing": the future terrorists simply acquired the beliefs of their friends.

Joining this violent social movement was a bottom-up activity. Al Qaeda had no top-down formal recruitment program. There was no central committee with a dedicated budget for recruitment or any general campaign of recruitment. There was no need for them. There were plenty of volunteers who wanted to join the jihad. Al Qaeda's problem was never recruitment but selection. It was akin to applying to a very selective college. Many apply but few are accepted. Likewise, al Qaeda was able to assess and evaluate potential candidates who showed desire to join by coming to Afghanistan for training. It invited only about 15 to 25 percent of that group to join the jihad.

The process just described is grounded in social relations and dynamics. To look at it through individual lenses, as a Robinson Crusoe on a deserted island narrative, is to miss the fundamental social nature of this process. And this is where women play a critical role. So far, the account of the global Salafi jihad seems to be a pure male story of heroic warriors fighting the evil West. Yet, women also play a critical role in this process. They may provide the invisible infrastructure of the jihad. As influential parts of the social environment, they often encourage their relatives and friends to join the jihad. Many Christian converts or secular Muslims joined because of marriage to a committed wife.

Indeed, invitation to join the Indonesian *Jemaah Islamiyah* depends on the background of the spouse of the applicant. And once in the jihad, single members often solidify their participation by marrying the sisters of other members. This further separates the new recruit from the rest of society and increases his loyalty to the social movement.

Motivating terrorist operations

So far, the evidence points to mobilization into this terrorist social movement as a social process based on pre-existing friendship and kinship. But the most troubling aspect of this group of terrorists is their willingness to kill innocent civilians and themselves in the process. How does this process take place? This is where the role of this specific version of Islam comes into play.

Salafi ideology promotes new values, centered on personal commitment to Islam and the Islamic community. It preaches a new activist conception of Islam, where it is a personal duty incumbent on every Muslim to participate in the building of an Islamist society and state. New adherents usually welcome this new activist mandate despite considerable personal cost because it replaces the malaise of their passivity in the face of their marginality in society with a new sense of purpose and efficacy born from action. It also rewards them with feelings of solidarity with small cliques of like minded militants transcending their alienation from society and its values.

This transformation starts innocuously with the lifelong struggle to become a good Muslim. In Salafi doctrine, it implies an imitation of the utopian Salaf through a process of self-purification or struggle within oneself for the sake of God (greater jihad). His behavior must set a personal and vivid example to promote Islam as a worldview and a way of life. The novice must battle his own desires and temptation and reject material and sensual pleasures in his quest. Self-denial is difficult for life is full of temptations. This may explain the hostility at tempting and suggestive sexual images, making such self-control all the more difficult.

Although this personal jihad is presented as an individual struggle against one's temptations, in reality, it is a social one. Faith and commitment are grounded and sustained in intense small group dynamics as friends and peers provide support and strength to help cope with any potential hardship. These born-again believers welcome struggles in this life as a test of their faith. Over time, "authentic" Islamic spirituality and religious growth replace dominant "Western" values of career advancement and material wealth, which had contributed to their original feelings of exclusion, frustration, unfairness, and injustice. The jihadists embrace Qutb's diagnosis that society faces a "crisis of values" for its main problems are not material but spiritual. The progressive detachment from the pursuit of material needs allows them to transcend their frustrated realistic aspirations and promotes satisfaction with spiritual goals. These goals are more consistent with their limited resources and opportunities, and relieve the malaise arising from their exclusion and marginalized status. Their sacrifices and participation in this Islamist vanguard provide them with a sense of moral superiority, optimism, and faith in a collective future. Their activism and firm belief in the righteousness of their mission generate a sense of efficacy that enables them to overcome the apathy and fear that would otherwise inhibit high-risk terrorist operations.

Over time, there is a general shift in values: from the secular to the religious; from the material to the spiritual; from short-term opportunity to long-term vision; from individual concerns to communitarian sacrifice; from apathy to active engagement; from traditional morality to specific group morality; and from worldly gains to otherworldly rewards. This transformation is possible only within intense small group face-to-face interactions. The values and fellowship of these groups not only forge intense bonds of loyalty and a collective identity but also give a glimpse of what a righteous Islamist society could be like. The small size of these cliques and the mutual dedication of their members allow them to spontaneously resolve their problems among themselves. The quality of these small and dense networks promotes in-group love, transforming self-interest into self-sacrifice for the cause and comrades. The militants' experience in these groups deludes them into believing that social problems would also be spontaneously resolved in a righteous Islamist society, accounting for their curious lack of concern about what this ideal society would actually look like or how it might function politically or economically.

So far, this description of the transformation from a newly mobilized recruit into a motivated militant has stressed the positive and idealistic dimension of the process, much as militants report or subjectively experience it. However, there is a darker and more negative part of this process that insiders rarely talk about but outsiders clearly pick up, namely the out-group hate displayed by these groups. Such hate is loud and clear in their private speech captured in the wiretaps of the Hamburg, Montreal, and Milan al Qaeda cells recorded in the late 1990s and all too visible on websites sympathetic to al Qaeda. A top-down focus on the refined abstractions of the Quran and Hadith or al Qaeda official proclamations cannot explain the unleashed hatred and passion. Only a bottom-up examination of the concrete interactions of the militants and their circumstances can account for this hatred. It is grounded in their everyday experience of humiliating exclusion from society at large and promoted within the group by a vicious process of one-upmanship in mutual complaints about the alienating society. This "bunch of guys" phenomenon escalates resentment into a hatred and rejection of the ambient society itself. They expressed their hatred by cursing its symbols and legitimizing myths and by endorsing a conspiracy theory of Jews corrupting a now totally degenerate and unredeemable society. The wiretaps give a hint of this visceral hatred that seeks to destroy society even at the cost of their own lives. This virulent rejection of society finds a home in the doctrine of *takfir* or excommunication of society, which is popular in militant circles and sanctions the commission of crimes against infidels in the pursuit of the jihad.

This trajectory from low-risk participation with an increasingly closer set of friends, to medium-risk proselytism for an ideal way of life, and to high-risk terrorist activities is a progressive and insidious one. This progression embraces an ideology that frames activism as a moral obligation demanding self-sacrifice and unflinching commitment to the jihad. This particular interpretation of Islam stands apart and challenges mainstream Islamic faith and practices. It isolates the new adherents to this doctrine from the rest of the Muslim community. Their self-sacrifice is again grounded in group dynamics. The terrorist is ready to show his devotion to his now exclusive friends, their group, and their cause by seeking death as a way to show his devotion to all of them. In-group love combined with out-group hate, under this violent and extreme ideology, is a strong incentive for committing mass murder and suicide.

Conclusion

The terrorism of the global Salafi jihad is grounded in group dynamics under a violent interpretation of Islam, inspiring and guiding the terrorists. Once a participant in this violent social movement, it is difficult for an individual to abandon it without betraying his closest friends and family. The violent global Salafi ideology feeds on this natural and intense loyalty to the group and transforms alienated young Muslims into fanatical terrorists.

Bibliography

Bin Laden, O. (1996) *Declaration of War against the Americans Occupying the Land of the Two Holy Places*, Published in al-Quds al-Arabi (London), August 23, Available at: http://www.pbs.org/newshour/terrrism/international/fatwa_1996.html

—— (1998) *Jihad Against Jews and Crusaders*, February 23, Available at: http://www.fas.org/irp/world/para/docs/980223-fatwa.htm

Faraj, M. Abd al-Salam. (1986) "Al-Faridah al Ghaibah," in Johannes Jansen, ed., *The Neglected Duty: The Creed of Sadat's Assassins and Islamic Resurgence in the Middle East*, New York: Macmillan, 159–234.

Qutb, S. (n.d.) *Milestones*, Cedar Rapids, IA: Mother Mosque Foundation.

7

AL-QAEDA AND THE GLOBAL EPIDEMIC OF SUICIDE ATTACKS

Yoram Schweitzer

Introduction

In recent years suicide terrorism has become the most dominant tactic among the various modus operandi utilized by terror organizations. It has captured the attention of the media and consequently the entire world. Al-Qaeda's role in this trend has been crucial both in conceptualizing self-sacrifice for the sake of God (Istishad) as its supreme organizational value and its horrifying implementation.

This chapter will present Al-Qaeda's unique contribution to the spread of the epidemic around the world through its position as a role model mainly for its affiliates, Islamic terror groups, and networks. It will argue that one of the most urgent and neglected elements in order to effectively counter the spread of this phenomenon should be the consolidation of a united Islamic authoritative voice led by Islamic scholars and highly esteemed leaders, intended to distance new cadres from the extreme interpretation of Al-Qaeda and its like minded disciples to the imperatives of Islam.

While the willingness of terrorists to extremely risk or even sacrifice their lives during terrorist attacks is not a new phenomenon in human history, still modern suicide terrorism is nonetheless a unique phenomenon. Its most common trait is the fact that it almost exclusively involves explosives being carried either on a person's body or in a vehicle being driven by one or more people, with an aim to detonate oneself at or near a chosen target. Thus a suicide attack is defined here as

> a politically motivated violent operation carried out consciously, actively, and with the premeditated intention of an individual (or a number of individuals) to kill himself or herself during the operation, along with a chosen target. The planned and certain death of the perpetrator by such an act is a necessary precondition for the success of the operation.
> (Schweitzer and Shay 2002: 150)

However, it should be noted that this definition does not include many cases of self-sacrifice where the perpetrator's chance of survival is extremely low or even where the perpetrator had no intention of remaining alive.

The inclusion of such cases in this category would have resulted in much higher numbers of suicide attacks than those appearing here. However, last minute interceptions of suicide bombers who failed to successfully execute their planned attacks due to technical failures or to their arrest by security forces are included in the data.

Modern suicide terrorism is both an individual and very personal act, and at the same time it is a group phenomenon. The major role played by organizations in preparing the suicide action and exploiting it for their own purposes after it is carried out is noteworthy. Terrorist groups sending men, and sometimes women, to carry out suicide attacks have used sophisticated means of "production" in the aftermath of the attack to provide videotaped wills, announcements to the press, and interviews with the perpetrators. This exalts the act, mystifies the character of the suicide bombers, and glorifies the idea for which suicide attacks are carried out. In this way, the act of suicide terrorism is at once both a personal and collective process (Schweitzer and Ferber 2005). On the one hand, the person committing suicide undergoes a deep, complex personal and psychological process leading him or her from a state of conscious awareness to a state of consciousness similar to an operator-dependant hypnotic reaction, from the preparatory stages until the moment s/he actually carries out the act of self-sacrifice combined with murder. On the other hand, it is the outcome of organizational activity. From the moment an individual consciously decides to volunteer for such an operation, the process is closely supervised by an organizational framework which links itself to the personal process, preserves it, and intensifies it, both to make sure that volunteers do not change their mind about carrying out the task and to facilitate execution. In this process, one component cannot exist without the other—the suicide bomber

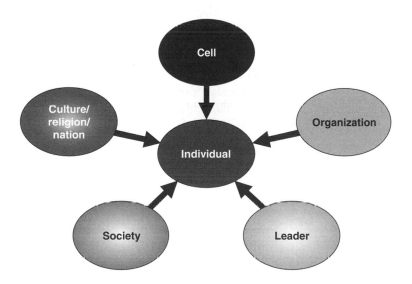

Figure 7.1 Factors influencing a suicide bomber.

133

needs the organizational production, and the organization is ineffective without the individual perpetrator. Convincing the individual to volunteer for the task, to stay committed, and to actually carry it out is usually done without threats, but rather through temptation, persuasion, and indoctrination, according to the personality of the volunteer and the cultural-social-organizational-group context of the volunteer's group of belonging[1] (see Figure 7.1).

Al-Qaeda and Istishad

Modern suicide terrorism emerged as an ongoing and familiar phenomenon at the beginning of the 1980s (the fact that it was also used in Vietnam in the mid-1960 was not widely published until recently (see Chapter 5). The ability of suicide bombers to inflict mass casualties and immense destruction upon their opponents endowed their operators with an image of power that far exceeded their actual strength. This was true in the case of Hizbollah, which was the first to introduce suicide attacks as a continuous and effective tool, and the other, primarily secular, terrorist groups in Lebanon that followed in its footsteps. Thus, Hizbollah served as a role model to local groups in other countries throughout the world, such as Sri Lanka, Israel, and Turkey, which adopted this modus operandi. Later, through the influence of Al-Qaeda the tactic spread to many more countries.

To date, the phenomenon of suicide terrorism has spread out across twenty-eight countries (and 4 more if we also count interceptions)[2] in five continents around the world and has been carried out by a large number of secular and religious terrorist groups and networks. More than 1,300 male and female suicide terrorists have taken part in the suicide attacks carried out between 1983 and July 2005 (see Figure 7.2[3]).

Al-Qaeda under Bin Laden's leadership was a latecomer which joined the list of groups carrying out suicide attacks only in 1998, about fifteen years after Hizbollah started its suicide operations. Yet Al-Qaeda has become the dominant force in suicide terrorism and the group directly responsible for its globalization by turning the concept of Istishhad as the organizational symbol and practice for the whole global Jihad camp. Al-Qaeda's involvement has led to escalating levels of death and destruction that reached heights that were hitherto unknown.

The organizational structure of Al-Qaeda's top leadership is based on the legacy which was consolidated during the war in Afghanistan, according to

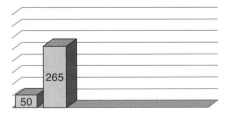

Figure 7.2 Graph of worldwide suicide terrorism (as of July 31, 2005).

the Islamic model of a leader working alongside of an advisory council (*shura*). Decisions of the supreme leader—supported by his interpretation of the correct path according to the Koran, the oral tradition, and consultations with religious teachers—demarcate the path of the organization. Bin Laden emerged as the supreme and irrefutable leader of Al-Qaeda after 'Abdallah 'Azam, the primary ideologue of the "Afghanistan War Volunteers" and Bin Laden's partner and spiritual guide, was killed in a mysterious explosion in 1989. Thereafter, Bin Laden was regarded as the leader of the group, and all those who joined the ranks of Al-Qaeda under his leadership declared their loyalty to him. This personal declaration of loyalty obligated organization members to carry out Bin Laden's orders with strict obedience.

Bin Laden always worked with a dominant figure by his side for consultation, sharing the burden of decision making, and sharing responsibility for Al-Qaeda policy. After the death of his guide 'Abdallah 'Azam, Muhammad 'Atef (Abu Hafez al-Masri), Al-Qaeda's military commander, served as his closest associate and advisor, until he was killed by American shelling in Afghanistan in November 2001. During the past few years, this position has been filled by Bin Laden's new deputy, the Egyptian Dr Ayman al-Zawahiri.

From the beginning of his activity, Bin Laden's working environment and working patterns were shaped during the war in Afghanistan, which he joined in 1979. The multi-national involvement in Afghanistan during the ten years of war required the development of one ideological framework that would serve to unify all the fighters. The unifying idea was the concept of Jihad in the name of Allah (fi sabil allah) against the enemy, which was depicted as a Christian empire of conquest attempting to force its control over Muslim lands and local Muslim inhabitants. The fighters and their chief ideologue, 'Abdallah 'Azam, regarded this land and its population as a microcosm of the Islamic nation.

With the conclusion of the war, Bin Laden, who had acquired the reputation of a contributor, an organizer, and also as a fighter, decided to maintain this force for the upcoming future. This resulted in the evolution of a mode of operation based on a large number of fighters of different nationalities with common experiences and a strong emotional and ideological common denominator. These fighters could be distributed around the world and used to recruit new cadres to strengthen this force into a tight fist, working to advance the idea of global Jihad.

Based on his multi-national experience in Afghanistan, Bin Laden established a decentralized organization that could accommodate and respect differences between organizations and people. This structure enabled participants—fighters and commanders alike—to retain their freedom of action, as long as the organization's unifying principle of self-sacrifice (Istishad) was zealously maintained as a leading principle. Bin Laden understood that, in a decentralized structure, this principle would guide the leadership and function as a unifying force wherever it was disseminated and greatly increase the intensity of the struggle for global Jihad.

The concept of Istishad as a means of warfare is part of an overall worldview that sees active Jihad against the perceived enemies of Islam as a central pillar and an organizational ideal. According to Al-Qaeda's worldview, one's willingness to sacrifice his or her life for Allah and "in the path of Allah" ($fi\ sabil\ allah$) is an expression of the Muslim fighter's advantage over the opponent. In Al-Qaeda, the sacrifice of life became a supreme value, the symbolic importance of which was equal to, if not greater than its practical importance. The organization adopted suicide as a symbol of global Jihad and raised Islamic martyrdom ($al\text{-}shehada$) to the status of a principle of faith. Al-Qaeda leaders worked on the spirit of the organization, constructing its ethos around the readiness to volunteer for self-sacrifice and the implementation of this idea through suicide attacks. They worked hard to imbue veteran members and new recruits with this ethos. Readiness for self-sacrifice was one of the most important characteristics the organization looked for in its new recruits (9/11 Commission Report 2004).

Al-Qaeda's worldview regards the sacrifice of life in the name of Allah as the main aim of a Jihad warrior. This sacrifice is described in terms of enjoyment: "we are asking you to undertake the pleasure of looking at your face and we long to meet you, not in a time of distress ... take us to you ..." (Aziz 2004). The organization's idea of suicide in the name of Allah, which repeats itself regularly in statements of its leaders, is contained in what has become its motto: "we love death more than you, our opponents love life." This motto is meant to express Al-Qaeda fighters' lack of fear of losing temporary life in this world, in exchange for an eternal life of purity in heaven. It is meant to express the depth of pure Muslims in face of the weak spirit, hedonism, and lack of values of their enemies. Sacrifice in the name of Allah, according to Al-Qaeda, is what will ensure Islam's certain victory over the infidels, the victory of spirit over material, soul over body, the afterlife over the reality of day to day life, and, most importantly, good over evil.

Suicide expresses the feeling of moral justification and emotional completion in the eyes of the perpetrators and the organization. An echo of Bin Laden's call for the young members of Islam to actualize the path of God through Istishad was echoed in the will of one of the perpetrators of an attack in Saudi Arabia in May 2003, in which he repeats the passage promising the pleasantries of the Garden of Eden:

> Young members of Islam hurry and set out on Jihad, hurry to the Garden of Eden which holds what the eye has never seen, the ear has never heard, and the human heart has never desired! Do not forget the reward that has been prepared by Allah for a martyr. The messenger of Allah, may peace and prayer be upon him, said: "The martyr is granted seven gifts from Allah: he is forgiven at the first drop of his blood; he sees his status in Paradise; he is dressed in the clothes of Imam; he is safe from the punishment of the grave; he will be safe from the great fear of the judgment; a crown of honor, with a gem that is greater than the entire world and the contamination in it, will be placed on his head; he will marry 72 dark eyed maidens; and he will intercede on behalf of 70 members of his family."
>
> (Wahab al-Muqit 2003)

The organization's success in inculcating the ethos of Istishad among many members was reflected also in the words of one of Al-Qaeda's senior commanders, who was responsible for dispatching a large number of suicide terrorists: "We never lacked potential suicide operators," he explained, "we have a department called 'the suicide operators department'." When asked if the department was still active, he answered, "yes, and it will continue to be active as long as we are fighting a Jihad against the Zionist infidels" (Fouda and Fielding 2003: 114). In one of his interviews, Bin Laden himself clearly expressed the organizational ethos he instilled in his followers: "I do not fear death. Sacred death is my desire. My sacred death will result in the birth of thousands of Osamas" (Ausaf 1998).

Al-Qaeda's entrance into the arena of suicide terrorism had profound influence on the manner in which this mode of operation was employed by its affiliates around the world. Al-Qaeda sees itself as the representative of all the world's Muslims, which, in its view, constitute one indivisible entity (Islamic *uma*).

The group's operations introduced a new paradigm of a "cross-nation" Muslim community (Interview 2004a) dispersed all over the globe, employing extreme violence against those perceived as being opposed to its worldview. The group worked to disseminate an Islamic fundamentalist ideology that regards the entire world as a legitimate arena in which to wage Jihad by means of terrorism in general, and suicide attacks in particular. It is interesting to note that despite the great operational reputation that Al-Qaeda earned for itself over the years, it has only actually independently carried out seven terrorist attacks, all of which were suicide attacks. All the other many suicide attacks which were usually attributed to Al-Qaeda were actually carried out by its affiliates, without its direct involvement.

Al-Qaeda's continuous links with established Islamic terrorist groups and networks operating around the world were based on their shared experiences and mutual identification of the commanders of many of these groups and networks with Al-Qaeda, from the period during which they fought side by side in Afghanistan or from the period of training they got in the camps in Afghanistan after the war already ended in the early 1990s. They maintained their connections with Al-Qaeda commanders and even more so with the doctrine of global Jihad and the concept of Istishad which were instilled in them. The grim consequences later appeared in the suicide campaigns launched in Europe, America, Asia, the Persian Gulf, and the Middle East.

Al-Qaeda has emerged over the years as an organization with global activity and a flexible and dynamic structure. It has undergone changes in membership, leadership, and command locations since its establishment. The globalization of Al-Qaeda (see Figure 7.3) is reflected in the following ways: (1) the dispersal of "alumni" of Al-Qaeda training camps to locations around the world, (2) the organization's aspiration to serve as a model for mode of operations for emulation by other groups, (3) the use of psychological warfare, (4) the use of modern communication media and the internet.

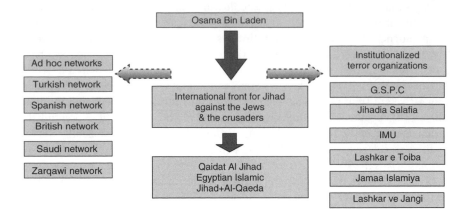

Figure 7.3 The globalization of suicide attack.

1 The Dispersal of the "Afghan Alumni"—Al-Qaeda's central objective was to promote this mode of operation among as many Islamic organizations as possible, primarily those identifying with the concept of global Jihad. Al-Qaeda's policy with regard to suicide attacks also appears to have been of special symbolic importance. Until the second half of the 1990s, the phenomenon of Muslim suicide terrorists sacrificing themselves in the name of Allah has been associated with the Shiite stream of Islam. This stream was responsible for the initial introduction of this mode of operation during the 1980s. Thus, from the perspective of Al-Qaeda leaders, the organization's entrance into the arena of suicide terrorist operators had to dwarf the suicide attacks that had already been carried out by other groups both in scope and in damage, in order to increase the prestige of Sunni Islam and the prestige of the group and its leader.

2 A Role Model for Operations for Emulation—Al-Qaeda worked toward achieving mass death on as high a level as possible. To this end, the group and its partners used especially large groups of suicide terrorists, numbering in certain circumstances 12, 14, 19, or, in the case of Chechnya, 30. And, in fact, these attacks were unprecedented in the number of casualties. The number of terrorists was also unusual in comparison to most other terrorist organizations that had carried out suicide attacks in the past (with the exception of the Tamil Tigers, who operated in Sri Lanka, at times using cells with a larger number of members, numbering as many as a dozen participants in one operation).

3 Having a Psychological Effect on the Enemy—Al-Qaeda saw the suicide weapon as an effective tool for deterring the West—first and foremost, the United States and other prominent European countries—from aggression and for instilling fear in attacked populations around the globe. According to his perception of Western culture, Bin Laden has tried to send clear signals that suicide terrorism is a weapon of defiance challenging the western way of life. By creating a psychological effect stemming from mass indiscriminate killing, he is trying to force public opinion in western countries into pressuring their governments to change their policies to be more in line with his worldview and to give into his various demands. He also uses techniques of propaganda and psychology warfare that intensify the physical effects of harm done to innocents. In this way, Al-Qaeda and its partners tend to issue press releases or videotapes shortly after attacks, reiterating each attack's background and threatening to repeat and intensify attacks if the attacked countries do not change their policies. Sometimes, group leaders aim propaganda directly at public opinion in order to encourage civilians to exert pressure on their governments.

For example, following the attacks carried out in Bali by Al-Jama'ah al-Islamiya with the assistance of Al-Qaeda (October 2002), which claimed 202 casualties, Bin Laden released a cassette in which he threatened to attack Australia a second time, claiming that Australia was cooperating with the United States and harming Muslims with its policy in East Timor (Al-Jazeera 2002). In a similar manner, shortly after attacks in Madrid (March 11, 2004) which killed 191 people, Bin Laden issued a manifest accusing the Spanish government of being responsible for the attack, due to its support for the United States and the presence of its troops in Iraq. In this manifest, he also called for the citizens of Europe to pressure their governments to withdraw their forces from Iraq, in exchange for which they would receive a "*hudna*" (a temporary cease-fire). This generous offer, he threatened, would be removed from the table in three months, after which the attacks in Europe would be renewed (Memri 2004a). Taking advantage of the shocking events, Bin Laden attempted to transfer responsibility for the horrific attacks carried out by those working according to his ideas to the Spanish government, and to send a threatening message to Europe: that failure to comply with his demands within a given period of time would lead to more serious attacks.

4 The Electronic Media and the Internet—There is no doubt that Al-Qaeda uses communications media both for the dissemination of the constitutive concepts of the organization, the most important of which is the principle of self-sacrifice in the name of Allah, and for strategic direction toward preferred targets of operation for supporters of global Jihad. It would not be an overstatement to say that the Arab and Western mass media has been a primary tool of Al-Qaeda commanders in increasing the organization's strength in areas not under their direct control.

The great importance that Al-Qaeda attributes to the media is reflected in its establishment of a communications committee, which was headed for a long period by Khaled Sheikh Muhammad before he became one of the organization's top operational commanders. At the same time, Bin Laden created a company called Al-Sihab, which produced the professional tapes and "image" films disseminated throughout the Arab and Western world, primarily by means of the Qatari television station Al-Jazeera. The preferred status that Bin Laden granted Al-Jazeera and selected sympathetic journalists such as Yusri Fouda (the journalist given the first exclusive with Khaled Sheikh Muhammad and his close colleague Ramzi Bin Al-Shibh just before the first anniversary of the September 11 attacks) and Ahmed Zeidan (the Al-Jazeera correspondent in Pakistan who was allowed to interview Bin Laden in Afghanistan a number of times before the American invasion of the country) was part of Bin Laden's deliberate media policy. This policy was aimed at increasing the prestige of the Arab communications media, which had always been considered inferior and of little interest compared to the western media (Zeidan 2003).

The focus of Al-Qaeda's psychological warfare was divided between satellite television stations and the internet. Whereas television stations throughout the Arab world, and primarily the popular Al-Jazeera network, served Al-Qaeda by publicizing its messages by broadcasting videos produced by the organization, the past few years have witnessed increased use of the internet by Al-Qaeda and its partners. Out of the approximately 4,000 Islamic websites that exist on the internet, about 300 are connected to radical Islamic groups that support Al-Qaeda. These websites disseminate the organization's messages and encourage the recruitment of new suicide volunteers to join the ranks of the global Jihad. Some even provide their readers with instructions for carrying out attacks and making explosive devices. Due to efforts by western forces to close or damage these sites, they regularly change their internet addresses. Sometimes, new addresses appear as messages for previous users, and in some cases addresses are maintained for chat rooms only, where it is passed on by chat participants. All terrorist groups maintain more than one website in more than one language. Two internet newsletters are directly associated with Al-Qaeda: Saut al-Jihad and Mua'askar al-Batar (Interview 2004b). These two websites provide explanations on how to kidnap, poison, and murder people, as well as a list of targets that should be attacked.

Both the terrorists who carried out the attack in Madrid in March 2004 and those who participated in the attacks of September 11 made regular use of the internet for communication. The anonymity of the web facilitates communication on controversial issues without being exposed and without yielding to the pressure of governments. In Europe, the internet provides young Muslims with a virtual community that serves primarily to ease the emotional strain on Muslim immigrants experiencing the difficulties of adapting to a new environment and feeling a need to maintain their religious identity. The internet provides support on a psychological level, enabling them to overcome the alienation felt by Muslims living in Europe in a foreign religious environment, and to dull the sense of crisis that characterizes all acts of immigration. The internet actualizes the ideal of the Islamic "Uma" by making it real and tangible and enabling Muslims to create super-national, cross-border communities. With cyberspace, internet users can quell personal misgivings by receiving militant messages, and even instructions regarding religious activities in the form of verses from the Koran or oral law. As already noted, the internet also offers specific instructions for carrying out terrorist attacks for anyone interested in playing an active part in the Jihad. Sometimes, those responsible for maintaining Al-Qaeda websites include people involved with Al-Qaeda operational activity, as in the case of the Al-Qaeda website editor who was apprehended in Saudi Arabia at the location where authorities recovered the body of Paul Johnson, a Martin Lockheed employee who was kidnapped and then killed by his abductors on January 18, 2004 (Wright 2004). Al-Qaeda has made sure to utilize all channels of the media to take full advantage of its own terrorist attacks, and, more significantly, the attacks carried out by its partner groups. In doing this, the organization has attributed operational successes to the organization and to the idea of global Jihad, and has strengthened the image of power of the message of Istishad.

We can identify a change in Al-Qaeda's policy of claiming responsibility for terrorist attacks after September 11. Until these attacks, Al-Qaeda had refrained from explicit claims of responsibility for attacks carried out by Al-Qaeda. This policy stemmed from his desire to remain unexposed to reprisal attacks, and, more importantly, to prevent the leader of the Taliban from issuing an explicit order to refrain from causing trouble for the regime. This regime was already under international pressure due to its role in the drug trade and terrorism, and had been told to turn Bin Laden over to the United States and to close the terrorist training camps within its borders. At first, Bin Laden did not claim direct responsibility for September 11 either. Despite the fact that his hints and innuendos on the subject were clear to everyone listening, they left him room to maneuver and to enjoy the fruits of his achievement, without actually providing legal proof of his guilt. After the American attack on Afghanistan and the American-led international coalition's declaration of war, a process began in December 2001, through which Bin Laden indirectly admitted that he had been responsible for the attack. Eventually, Al-Qaeda took responsibility for the attacks in the United States in an unequivocal public declaration. This declaration was released in the form of a three-part series of one-hour long segments of an Al-Jazeera program called "It Was Top-Secret," directed by Al-Jazeera correspondent Yusri Fouda. This series was initiated by Al-Qaeda. The broadcast of the segments was timed to take place on the one-year anniversary of the attacks of September 11.

Al-Qaeda's view of the role of the media, and the role of the correspondent it chose to announce its responsibility for the attack, is clearly reflected in a letter from Ramzi Bin Al-Shibh, assistant to the commander of the US attacks, to Yusri Fouda:

As you work in a field that has the ability to influence people's opinion, you are obligated to, and it is expected of you to work for the sake of Allah, and not in order to satisfy people or your personal need for material things or glory. You must place the present confrontation between Muslims and Christians and between the west and the various Islamic countries in historical and religious context—it is important that people understand the overall picture. This is an historic responsibility, in contrast to media coverage until now which has portrayed the struggle inaccurately—that is, as a limited struggle between America and Al-Qaeda.

(Fouda and Fielding 2003: 153)

Bin Laden's personal concern for all aspects of the media, including the quality and angles of filming, was demonstrated when he asked Ahmed Zeidan, the Al-Jazeera correspondent in Pakistan who had come to Afghanistan to interview him, to film him from a flattering angle and to disregard previous footage in which, in his opinion, he did not look good enough. Bin Laden also directed Zeidan to re-film a ballad that he played before an audience of listeners because there had not been a sufficient audience in the original filming (Zeidan 2003: 65). Zeidan makes explicit notes of his impression of Bin Laden as someone who distinguishes clearly between body language and spoken language, and keenly takes both into consideration. Bin Laden stressed to Zeidan his view of the role of the media, and, most importantly, the role of satellite television stations

> that the public and the people really like, that transmit body language before spoken language. This is often the most important thing for activating the Arab street and creating pressure on governments to limit their reliance on the United States.
>
> (Ibid.: 25)

Bin Laden attempted to use Ahmed Zeidan to refute the words of the son-in-law of 'Abdallah 'Azam in the newspaper *Al-Sharq Al-Awsat*, which could be construed to indicate conflicts between Bin Laden and his colleague 'Azam and which hinted that Bin Laden was behind the assassination of his spiritual guide. Bin Laden even admitted to Zeidan that "Al-Qaeda selects [sympathetic] journalists and initiates granting them interviews." The organization's close attention to its appearance in the media is reflected in a fax from Al-Qaeda to Fouda, which explained how, in the view of the sender, the three-part program should be organized (Fouda and Fielding 2003: 145) and who should be interviewed, and noted the prohibition of any musical accompaniment for quotes from the Koran and the Hadith (Ibid.). The fax said that Fouda would be expected to prepare the segments with an understanding of his mission (as a Muslim journalist, of course) for Islam.

During the past few years as well, when Bin Laden and his deputy have been the target of intensive pursuit, the two still make sure to appear from time to time in audio and video tapes that they have produced meticulously, in order to prove that they are still alive and active.

The suicide attacks of Al-Qaeda—an implementation of the concept of Istishad

Al-Qaeda has served as an avant-garde and implemented the concept of Jihad in practice by carrying out seven suicide attacks by the cadres exclusively commanded by Bin Laden's own group. The most spectacular attacks were intended to serve as a role model for its partners in terms of tactics, targets, and of the level of destruction and fatalities they caused.

Al-Qaeda started with the attack on the American Embassies in Kenya and Tanzania (August 1998) which were perceived as the outstretched long arms of

American foreign policy. These attacks resulted in the death of 224 and the injury of more than 4,000 people. The ensuing attack focused on what was perceived by Bin Laden as the long stretched military arm of the American global policy. On October 12, 2000, a boat-bomb disguised as a service vessel, exploded alongside an American destroyer, the U.S.S. Cole, killing 17 American sailors. On September 9, 2001, two days before the attack in the United States, suicide bombers posing as a TV crew assassinated Masoud Shah, the commander of the Northern Front in Afghanistan, in order to defunct the main opposition group to the Taliban—Al-Qaeda's hosts and patrons.

The most significant and lethal suicide operation was carried out by Al-Qaeda in the United States on September 11, 2001 which caused the death of more than 3,000 people. Following the atrocity in the United States, Al-Qaeda was the target of a massive global manhunt. Yet, on December 22, 2001, Al-Qaeda attempted to blow up an American Airlines flight by detonating explosives that were hidden in the suicide bomber's shoe. Due to a technical-operational failure, as well as the awareness of a flight attendant, this attack was prevented only 3 months after the 9/11 attack and demonstrated Al-Qaeda's determination to activate suicide bombers from its European recruits. The same line of "production" of volunteers for suicide operations was repeated in the attack on the ancient synagogue in Djerba, Tunisia on April 11, 2002, when a French citizen from Tunisian immigrant family blew himself up while killing 21 people, mostly German tourists who were visiting the site.

On November 28, 2002, two simultaneous attacks were executed by an Al-Qaeda cell against Israeli targets in Mombassa, one of which was executed by means of a suicide operative. The first attack involved the launch of two missiles at an Arkia flight carrying 261 passengers and crew but due to a technical-operational mishap, the missiles missed their target and no one was injured. Twenty minutes later, a car-bomb driven by a suicide terrorist was detonated at a hotel, 10 Kenyans and 3 Israelis were killed in the attack, and about 80 others were injured.

Al-Qaeda's partners internalized the Al-Qaeda model and used suicide attacks as their symbolic and most effective weapon worldwide but usually added their own unique style and nuances (see Table 7.1).

Al-Qaeda's affiliates' suicide attacks

South East Asia

The regional South East Asian organization of the Jemaa Islamia started using suicide bombers in its operations following its strengthening relationships with Al-Qaeda. These relationships were based on personal knowledge and trust between the senior leaders in both organizations emanated from their previous cooperation in Afghanistan. Thus Jemma Islamiya which never before used suicide bombers started its campaign which was financed by Al-Qaeda's money since 2001.

Table 7.1 Comparison between aspects of Al-Qaeda suicide terrorists and the suicide terrorists of Al-Qaeda partner groups

	Al-Qaeda	*Partner groups*
Planning	Precise and extended, sometimes lasting a number of years	Short-term, usually up to one year (9–12 months)
Management and command	Overall command by a senior member of Al-Qaeda central command, and supervision by an operational commander in the target country	Supervised by the commander of the local terrorist network
Number of attackers	Usually two or more attackers	From individual attackers to groups
Nature of attack	Usually simultaneous	Integrated with other modes of attack
Targets	Focus on symbolic targets and movement toward "soft" targets	"Soft" targets
Claiming responsibility	No direct claim of responsibility until September 11. After September 11, move to direct claim of responsibility	Always claimed responsibility, usually under different names clearly associated with Al-Qaeda and the idea of global Jihad

The first suicide operation was intended to use 7 trucks filled with explosives driven by suicide bombers into buildings of foreign countries and local economic sites in Singapore but it was foiled due to intelligence information (December 2001). The second suicide attack was carried out by suicide bombers in nightclubs in Bali on October 2002 that resulted in 202 fatalities.

Europe

Al-Qaeda-affiliated independent local networks carried out a chain of suicide attacks after several attempts which they planned in the past were intercepted. However on November 15, 2003 two suicide attacks were carried out by a local Turkish network against synagogues in Istanbul which caused the death of twenty-three people and the injuries of few hundreds. On November 20 another simultaneous suicide attacks hit British targets killing 38 and injuring 500 people. The network was established by some local Turkish operatives who went to Afghanistan, met Bin Laden, and later led the attacks by their own infrastructure and members but with Al-Qaeda's financial assistance.

The next attack in Europe by an Al-Qaeda-affiliated network which occurred in Madrid on March 11, 2004 when ten explosive devices were detonated within a short span of time in trains and train stations in the capital was not a suicide attack. Approximately 1,400 were injured, and 191 people were killed in these attacks. Although the attacks against crowded trains and train stations were not performed as suicide operations, when some of the fugitives were surrounded by the Spanish police they chose to kill themselves with explosives they collected in their safe house, and by that practicing the value of Istishad they were brought up to adhere. The explosive belt that was in their possession and the rhetoric they used in their video cassettes they left behind indicated that they probably planned suicide attack if they hadn't been killed.

In July, two waves of attacks were carried out against transportation targets in the British capital. During the first wave, which took place on July 7, 4 suicide terrorists, 3 of them of British nationality and Pakistani descent, detonated explosive devices they were carrying in bags on three trains and a bus killing 52 people. During the second wave, which occurred exactly two weeks later, an attack was again attempted on transportation targets. However, this time the explosive devices were smaller and, presumably due to a technical mishap, no one was killed and only one person sustained minor injuries. Although still early in the investigation, the London attacks appear to have been carried out by a terrorist network based in Britain that relies on an infrastructure located in various cities around the country (Leeds and London). A number of the suicide terrorists communicated with elements outside of the country. Some of the attackers recently visited Pakistan, where they studied and apparently underwent training and perhaps even received guidance and instructions for their mission. The attackers on July 21 were mostly from African origin residing in the United Kingdom. The connection between the two attacks is still under investigation which wasn't made public knowledge yet. However, the social and close affiliation (friendship, some time kinship and discipleship) as the common traits among Al-Qaeda's affiliates operating around the world have also appeared to prevail in these cases too (Sageman 2004: 107).

In Russia, Al-Qaeda's Istishad perception inspired and influenced the Chechens fighting the Russians in what their leaders declared to be part of the global Jihad. The violent dispute in Chechnya served as a pretext for recruitments by Al-Qaeda and its affiliates utilizing video cassettes and CDs showing horrors from the battles there to incite young Muslims and lure them to join the ranks of the global Jihad in general and to Chechnya in particular.

Since June 2000, 103 men and women took part in the suicide campaign (see Table 7.2[4]). This trend reached its peak in two of the most notorious incidents in Moscow and in Beslan. The first incident took place in Moscow in October 2002, when about 40 Chechens, among them 19 women, wearing explosive belts took over a theatre in Moscow, taking hundreds of hostages. Following a rescue operation, 129 of the hostages were killed. The second incident took place during September 1–3, 2004 in northern Ossetia. Thirty-two terrorists carrying large quantities of explosives and weapons, including some explosive belt, took hundreds of hostages in a school in Beslan. The incident, which began as a barricade and hostage situation ended as a mass casualty suicide attack, which claimed the lives of over 300 people.

Arab countries

The Arab countries, especially those who were designated by Al-Qaeda as its most bitter enemies due to what they called their treason of Islamic values, have

Table 7.2 Suicide attacks in Russia

Casualties	Gender	Number of bombers	Date
2	Male	1	00/06/07
2	Male	1	00/06/12
60	Male	5	00/07/03–02
1	Female	1	01/01/29
129	19 were female	41	02/10/22
72	2 male, female	3	02/12/27
59	2 male, female	3	03/05/12
18	Female	2	03/05/14
17	Female	1	03/06/05
0	Female	1	03/06/20
16	Female	2	03/07/05
1	Female	1	03/07/09
0	Female	1	03/07/27
35	Male	1	03/08/01
6	Male + Female	2	03/09/15
44	Male	1	03/12/05
5	Female	1	03/12/09
41	Male	1	04/02/06
2	Male	1	04/02/06
88	Female	2	04/08/25
0	Male	1	04/08/29
10	Female	1	04/08/31
355	Male + Female	33	01/09/04–04/09/03

become in recent years part of the areas where Al-Qaeda's partners used suicide bombers. It started in Morocco when on May 15, 2003, 4 cells containing a total of 13 suicide bombers attacked a number of targets in the Moroccan capital of Casablanca which ended with 45 people dead and additional 100 wounded.

Saudi Arabia, whose nationals have been the dominant component of Al-Qaeda's cadre and its main financial source, has also become one of Al-Qaeda's most hated foes (see Figure 7.4). The suicide attacks in Saudi Arabia were carried out by local cells led by Afghan Alumni; some of them like Ueyeri and Abd el Aziz Muqrin served in Al-Qaeda camos, served as agents of influence, and later delegated the concept of Istishad to the new recruits in the Saudi kingdom who operated under their command. The suicide campaign in Saudi Arabia in the last two years forced its government to take aggressive counter measures and to face the problem of terror in the name of Islam to which they have contributed for many years.

Egypt has just recently joined the Arab countries which witnessed suicide attacks in their territory. On April 2005 two separate suicide attacks were carried out in Cairo, again on tourists, and on July 2005 the most devastating suicide attacks occurred again in the resort area of Sharm al Sheikh causing about ninety fatalities.

Iraq has definitely become the most prominent arena for suicide attacks enduring the most vicious and largest quantity of bombers in the world, even though the relative short time since its start. Since March 2003 and up till the end of

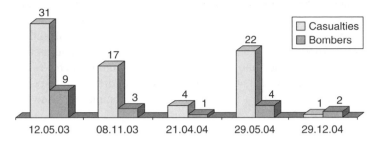

Figure 7.4 Number of casualties and bombers in Saudi Arabia.

Source: Statistical data included in this article is a database compiled by Yoram Schweitzer at the Jaffe Center for Strategic Studies and is based on reports from the media.

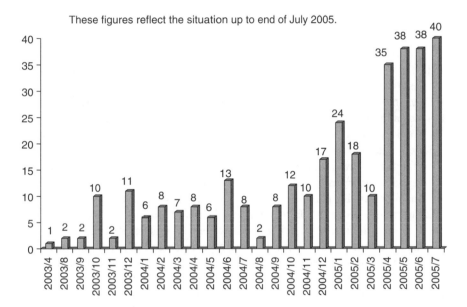

Figure 7.5 Number of suicide attacks by months.

July 2005, hundreds of suicide bombing were carried out by both local Iraqis and foreign perpetrators most of them apparently belonging to the global Jihadist (see Figure 7.5)[5]. The suicide campaign in Iraq is led by Abu Musaab al Zarqawi's own networks and his associates among the Iraqi Islamists like Ansar al Islam and Ansar al Sunna. At the end of 2004 Bin Laden publicly declared that Zarqawi's enterprise in Iraq is officially embraced by Al-Qaeda and he endowed him with the title Al-Qaeda of Mesopotamia (Ibid.). The suicide campaign in Iraq is not expected to subside any time soon and instead it might escalate, unless its leaders, first and foremost Zarqawi, are captured or killed and a stable government system is established in Iraq. However, if the situation remains as it is at the moment, the Iraqi context is likely to continue to serve international Jihad activists as a pretext for promoting the movement's supreme unifying principle—the willingness for self-sacrifice in the name of Allah—in order to expand its application throughout the world. Thus Iraq may become the new training camp for the future where the new bombers may attain valuable first-hand fighting experience that will prove useful when they return to their own countries or to new ones (Hoffman 2004: 426).

Conclusion

This chapter examined the contribution Al-Qaeda has made to the escalation and globalization of suicide terrorism by transforming the concept of self-sacrifice in the path of God (Istishad), into its main unifying principle and value. Al-Qaeda's leaders interpreted the reality of the entire Muslim community as one of deprivation and humiliation, explicitly identified the oppressors, and introduced the venue of suicide attacks as the sole and ultimate venue for true Muslims to rebel against their weak position and to prevail. The close links of Bin Laden's Al-Qaeda with members of terrorist groups and networks possessing radical Islamic worldviews have been based on the heritage of the war in Afghanistan, as well as common experiences in Al-Qaeda training camps after the end of the war. These links enabled Al-Qaeda to instill its partners with the idea of Istishad and to disseminate it around the world.

Although Al-Qaeda joined the ranks of users of suicide terrorism relatively late in the game, the organization quickly emerged as the main force transforming it into an international phenomenon, and increased the death tolls it claimed to hitherto unknown heights. In this way, Al-Qaeda attempted to serve as a model for other terrorist organizations to emulate. For Al-Qaeda, suicide attacks were both an operational mode of operation and a propaganda tool. Their psychological effect was greatly intensified by the widespread use of a broad spectrum of communications media, which helped highlight its determination to actualize its cross-border ideology. Bin Laden stressed the concept of Istishad as the heart and soul of the idea of Jihad, promoting it through the decentralized and empowering management style that he both employed in Al-Qaeda and instilled in other partner groups. This transformed the phenomenon of suicide terrorism, which had hitherto been regarded as a local problem created by local terrorist groups, into an international issue, transforming millions of citizens around the world from spectators into participants in, and victims of, acts of terrorism.

It seems that at this stage, the cross-border paradigm of suicide attacks that Bin Laden presented and implemented only attracts individuals from the population of Muslim countries and the population of Muslim immigrants in non-Muslim countries. That is, it has not become a model of ideological identification for large groups within these populations. Still, there is a danger that this dynamic of empowerment and self-actualization which Al-Qaeda uses to promote the idea of suicide operations around the world could be adopted by socially frustrated Muslim populations in the west, resulting in the evolution of a more popular culture of suicide.

Beyond the clear operative and practical need to thwart the terrorist attacks of Al-Qaeda and its partner groups in general, and "retain focus and maintain vigilance and keep up pressure on terrorists by adapting and adjusting rapidly and efficiently" (Hoffman 2005: 556) the major conclusion of this study is that there is an urgent need to provide an ideological answer to the suicide challenge put forward by Al-Qaeda. Supporters of extremist Islam must be offered an ideological Islamic alternative offering moderate and pragmatic interpretation of the commandments of the Koran, in contrast to the unequivocal extremist interpretation offered by Bin Laden and his associates. Such messages have a slim chance of being accepted if they are disseminated by parties that are not seen as possessing primary Islamic religious and moral authority. Thus, such an alternative can be provided only by prominent Muslim clerics and leaders with wide support in Arab and Muslim countries and recognized Islamic institutions whose opinions are regarded as carrying religious, cultural, and moral weight. Countries in which extremist and reputable religious clerics issue religious rulings supporting religiously sanctioned murder, under the slogan of self-sacrifice in the name of Allah while taking the lives of others, must restrain this activity much more aggressively and not give these individuals the freedom to incite. Non-Muslim forces must play the role of offering encouragement to the leaders of Arab and Muslim countries and of pressuring them to undertake such actions if need be.

At the same time, it is important that countries with large Muslim minority populations—for example, the countries of Europe—begin encouraging leading religious figures to put all of their social and moral weight behind efforts to prevent the spread of radicalizing trends influencing young Muslims today. Increased violence and terrorism coming from extremist Muslim forces may result in counter-extremism among peripheral groups in the west, who could exploit the situation in order to incite a racially based confrontation, plunging the continent into a bloody cycle of religious and racial violence.

Many circles in the Arab and Muslim world have severely criticized the methods of operation of Al-Qaeda and its partners. This criticism has increased in light of the suicide attacks in Iraq, which primarily hurt Iraqi citizens. There has been especially harsh criticism of the kidnapping and execution of hostages in Iraq (such as the murder of twelve Nepalese citizens, the beheading of American hostages, and the kidnapping of French citizens, Italian citizens, and nationals of other countries). Muslim journalists, religious leaders, and spiritual leaders were also shocked by the massacre at the school in Beslan, sparking their condemnation of these methods by which Al-Qaeda and its partners, through such sinful behavior, soil all of Islam and give the religion a bad image (Memri September 8, 10 2004b). The serious consequences that will result from failing to take practical steps to address the trends of radicalization influencing wide circles of Muslims is what creates a necessity to cause pragmatic forces in the Muslim world to take concrete and effective action to defend their religion's good name. They are also what create the chance for success.

It also shows that the potential reserves of suicide terrorists are part of the civilian population which must therefore be addressed ideologically, religiously, and socially, in addition to the security oriented activity involved with thwarting attacks. Part of Al-Qaeda's achievement to date has been its success in instilling the supremacy of the concept of Istishad above the leadership itself, including that of Bin Laden. The Muslim world therefore must, at its own initiative and with the encouragement of the west, generate an ideological alternative as an important component of struggling against this concept. In conclusion, it is important to distinguish between Al-Qaeda's "hard-core" and its partners, all of which are identified by the international media as "Al-Qaeda." This distinction facilitates a better understanding of the nature of the threat and the manner in which it is managed and actualized, and allows us to accurately assess Al-Qaeda's real size and strength. Al-Qaeda and its partner groups cannot be understood as a homogenous body operating under a unified command making centralized decisions about carrying out a wave of terrorist attacks around the world. Clearly, failure to distinguish between the activities of Al-Qaeda and the activities of its partner groups strengthens the image of power that Bin Laden strives to maintain for the Al-Qaeda brand-name, in order to advance his interests and emerge victoriously from the struggle of consciousness that he and his colleagues have been waging in a determined and skillful manner for more than a century.

Notes

1 Interviews with suicide terrorists who survived, undertaken by Yoram Schweitzer in Israeli jails during 2004 and 2005.
2 Morocco, Tunisia, Israel, Argentine, India, Sri Lanka, Kuwait, Lebanon, Iraq, Indonesia, Tanzania, Kenya, Croatia, Turkey, Pakistan, Thailand, China, Saudi Arabia, United States, Afghanistan, Yemen, Russia, Spain, Egypt, Uzbekistan, Colombia, Qatar, United Kingdom. In France, Belgium, Singapore, Australia, suicide attacks were intercepted.
3 The source of the statistical data included in this article is a database compiled by Yoram Schweitzer at the Jaffe Center for Strategic Studies. The numbers may vary in different data mainly concerning Iraq as some American sources counted more than 500 suicide bombers in Iraq.
4 The source of the statistical data included in this figure is a database built and maintained by Yoram Schweitzer at the Jaffe Center for Strategic Studies.
5 The source of the statistical data included in this figure is a database maintained by Yoram Schweitzer at the Jaffe Center for Strategic Studies.

Bibliography

9/11 Commission Report (2004) National Commission on Terrorist Attacks upon the United States, Washington, 234.
Al-Jazeera (2002) November 12.
Ausaf (1998) "Osama says Taliban Rejected US Billions for Arrest," December 28, 1, 7.
Aziz al-Muqrin, A. (2004) *Saut al-Jihad* (The Voice of Jihad) 18, June 3.

Fouda, Y. and Fielding, N. (2003) *Masterminds of Terror*, New York: Arcade Publishing, 114, 145, 153.

Hoffman, B. (2004) "Al-Qaeda and the War on Terrorism: An Update," *Current History*, December: 426.

—— (2005) *Defending Against Suicide Terrorism*, Paper presented to the Austin conference, 556.

Interview (2004a) with Professor Emanuel Sivan, undertaken by Yoram Schweitzer and Sari Goldstein Ferber, Jerusalem, July 23.

Interview (2004b) with Reuven Paz, undertaken by Yoram Schweitzer, September 19.

Memri (2004a) *Osama Bin Laden Speech Offers Peace Treaty with Europe, Says Al-Qaeda Will Persist in Fighting the U.S*, Available at: www.memri.org, no. 695, April 15.

—— (2004b) *Arab and Muslim Reaction to Terrorist Attack in Beslan, Russia*, Available at: *www.memri.org*, no. 780, September 8; *Former Kuwaiti Information Minister: "Not a Single Fatwa has been Issued Calling for the Killing of Bin Laden*," Available at: www.memri.org, no. 781, September 10.

Sageman, M. (2004) *Understanding Terror Networks*, Philadelphia, PA: University of Pennsylvania Press, 107.

Schweitzer, Y. and Goldstein, Ferber, S. (2005) *Al-Qaeda and the Globalization of Suicide Terrorism*, JCSS Memorandum, no. 76, p. 11, Tel Aviv: Jaffee Center for Strategic Studies at Tel Aviv University.

Schweitzer, Y. and Shay, S. (2002) *An Expected Surprise: The September 11th Attacks and their Ramifications* Herzliya: Mifalot Publishing, 150.

Wahab al-Muqit, bin-'Abdul, (2003) Excerpt from the will of Muhammad bin-'Abdul Wahab al-Muqit, Available at: www.cybcity.com/faroq, October 20, 2003.

Wright, L. (2004) "The Terror Web," *The New Yorker*, August.

Zeidan, A. (2003) *Bin Laden Unmasked: Meetings whose Publication were Prohibited by the Taliban*, Beirut: The World Book Company, 15, 25, 65 fn. 12.

8

BEING BIN LADEN

An Applied Decision Analysis procedure for analyzing and predicting terrorists decisions

Alex Mintz, J. Tyson Chatagnier, and
David J. Brulé

Introduction

This chapter presents an analytic procedure for aiding policy analysts in analyzing past decisions made by terrorist groups as well as predicting future decisions. First, we define and operationalize suicide attacks. Then, we describe the procedure—Applied Decision Analysis—generally as a framework for developing descriptive (and predictive) decision profiles of terrorists on the basis of a decision model or a set of processing characteristics. Next, we discuss a decision model—the Poliheuristic Theory—which we argue is a useful tool for forecasting and analyzing decisions. Then, we illustrate the Applied Decision Analysis procedure with two case studies. The first examines al-Qaeda's decision to carry out a suicide attack on the USS *Cole*. The second case study concerns Osama bin Laden's decision to merge his al-Qaeda organization with the Egyptian Islamic Jihad. We conclude by assessing the usefulness of the Applied Decision Analysis procedure for explaining and predicting terrorists decisions.

Defining and operationalizing suicide attacks

Ganor, Schweitzer, and Shay provide a useful definition of a suicide attack: "an operational method in which the very act of the attack is dependent upon the death of the perpetrator" (Ganor 2000: 135). They also point out that in a "true suicide attack, the terrorist knows full well that the attack will not be executed if he is not killed in the process." This definition is widely used in the literature on suicide terrorism. However, different scholars have operationalized and coded suicide attacks in different ways.

Several cases in which suicide attacks were foiled or occurred are not covered by these definitions. For example, on May 16, 2005, the Associated Press has reported that three Jewish militants were interrogated for plotting to blow up the

Dome of the Rock in Jerusalem. According to the AP, "the suspects said they planned to commit suicide after firing an anti-tank missile at the holy site in Jerusalem and throwing grenades at police who would try to arrest them." Such an attack (if carried out) would not have been considered a suicide attack based on conventional definitions, even though the militants planned (a priori) to commit suicide as part of their mission.

To cover such attacks, we expand the definition of suicide attacks to: *any attack where the suicide act of the terrorist was an a priori objective of the mission.* Operational definitions of suicide attacks based on our expanded definition include: (1) instances in which the very act of the attack "is dependent upon the death of the perpetrator" (the conventional way of defining suicide attacks (Ganor 2000)), or (2) instances in which the attacker commits suicide in the course of the attack although the very act of the attack is not dependent upon his or her death.

In addition, to avoid selection bias, *intercepted* suicide attacks should also be coded and analyzed. These intercepted suicide attackers are identified as such if (1) the attacker was intercepted en route to the target and confessed to a plan to commit a suicide attack; or (2) the attacker was intercepted on the way to the target and was subsequently convicted by authorities of attempting to carry out a suicide mission.

Applied Decision Analysis

Applied Decision Analysis (Mintz 2005) is a procedure for developing descriptive (and predictive) decision profiles of individual decision makers on the basis of a decision model and/or a set of processing characteristics. The procedure consists of two key steps. First, the analyst must identify the decision matrix of the decision maker. A decision matrix consists of the alternatives, dimensions, and implications of the alternatives corresponding to each dimension. The second step involves the analysis of the decision through the use of the Poliheuristic Theory of decision making (Mintz *et al.* 1997; Mintz 2004), a fruitful analytic tool for explaining and predicting terrorists decisions.

Identify the decision matrix

A decision matrix consists of a set of alternatives, the dimensions (or criteria) for selecting among these alternatives, and an assessment of the implications of each dimension for each alternative. Weights (levels of importance) can optionally be assigned to each dimension, if the analyst observes that dimensions should receive unequal weight in the analysis.

The Decision Board 4.0 software can be used as a tool for (a) organizing the information relevant to individuals' decisions via the construction of decision matrixes, and (b) for tracing and identifying the decision rule and profile of the terrorist. Once the researcher has chosen the number of dimensions and alternatives relevant to the decision, the Decision Board displays a generic matrix, which can be tailored to the specific policy or research problem.

Alternatives

The set of alternatives includes the likely courses of action a terrorist (or a terrorist group) may reasonably consider when faced with some problem or decision scenario. For example, when involved in negotiations with a state, a terrorist organization's leader may consider the following: "Continue with Attacks," "Temporarily Halt Attacks," or "Stop Attacks." In another example applicable to state leaders when faced with an international crisis, the leader may consider the following alternatives: "Do Nothing," "Apply Sanctions," "Containment," or "Use Force."

Dimensions

A dimension is an organizing theme for related information and variables relevant in evaluating alternatives (Mintz *et al.* 1997). Thus if the leader of a terrorist organization is concerned with the political consequences of a decision while in negotiations with a state, then inter-group rivalry, public sympathy, personal honor, and other variables related to this general organizing theme may be used to evaluate the alternatives "Continue with Attacks," "Temporarily Halt Attacks," or "Stop Attacks." If the leader desires a choice that satisfies such criteria on the political dimension as "increase positive public perception of the group" and "maintain status within group," he or she evaluates the alternatives in light of these criteria. Other dimensions that may be relevant to the alternatives in the terrorist leader's case are "Operational success" and "Support of other countries."

Implications

The implications consist of a description of the likely consequences of an alternative for a given dimension. Each alternative has implications corresponding to each dimension. For example, in the case of the terrorist leader, the "Stop Attacks" alternative has implications for the organization's political standing, relations with other countries, and operational success of the organization— which are all relevant dimensions.

Ratings

Implications can be rated by the analyst, for example, from -10 (very bad) to $+10$ (very good), although assigning *numerical* ratings to implications is optional. For example, if choosing the alternative "Stop Attacks" is likely to result in a loss of domestic support, the analyst should assign a negative rating (very bad, -8 or -9) to the political implications of "Stop Attacks." In contrast, if "Continue Attacks" is likely to lead to an outpouring of public sympathy and increasing recruitment levels, then this alternative should receive a positive rating (e.g. very good, $+8$, or $+9$).

Weights

Weights indicate the importance level of each dimension, for example, from 0 (not important at all) to 10 (very important). Thus, in the terrorist leader example, the analyst assigns different weights to the political, diplomatic, and operational dimensions, unless he or she considers each dimension to have equal weight in the decision.

Poliheuristic decision analysis model

The second step in the Applied Decision Analysis procedure is the analysis of the decision using the Poliheuristic Theory (Mintz *et al*. 1997; Mintz 2004). Much of the current scholarship on terrorist decision making (McCormick *et al*. 2003; Pape 2003; Wintrobe 2002) suggests that terrorist decision making can be largely understood as the product of rational calculations. In other words, choices made by terrorist organizations are the result of goal-oriented, value-maximizing behavior in which terrorists choose the alternative that produces the best of all possible expected outcomes across all relevant dimensions. But terrorist decision makers may choose among alternatives primarily on the basis of a single dimension. Similarly, terrorists may disregard large amounts of relevant information and ultimately choose alternatives that are not the "best" available.

That rational decision making is cognitively demanding is not a new suggestion (Simon 1957). The process by which individuals arrive at decisions may vary in a number of ways, including, for example, alternative-based versus dimension-based information search (Billings and Scherer 1988); compensatory versus non-compensatory information search (Payne *et al*. 1993); maximizing versus satisficing decision rules; and holistic versus non-holistic search (Sage 1990). Moreover, these decision processes may critically affect the choice of the decision maker (Mintz *et al*. 1997).

A useful approach for explicitly taking into account the role of cognitive short cuts in individuals' decisions is the Poliheuristic Theory. The theory postulates a two-stage decision-making process. In the first stage, the decision maker employs a non-compensatory decision-making strategy, which reduces the menu of alternatives through the elimination of options that are unacceptable on a critical decision-making dimension. A high score on a less critical dimension cannot compensate for a low score on the key dimension. In the second stage, the decision maker chooses among the remaining alternatives by using analytic decision rules (Mintz 1993, 2004; Payne *et al*. 1993).

Unlike other decision-making approaches (Friedman 1953; Steinbruner 1974; Kahneman and Tversky 1979), the Poliheuristic Theory identifies a key dimension that must be satisfied in order for an alternative to be accepted. Specifically, crucial dimensions are often non-compensatory. Alternatives are not evaluated simultaneously. Instead, individuals reduce the set of alternatives in the first stage by rejecting those options that fail to breach a minimum threshold

155

on the key decision dimension. For example, if an individual's key decision dimension is "personal safety"—the decision maker seeks to minimize personal risk—he or she is likely to eliminate alternatives that are likely to result in death or injury, despite other potential benefits of choosing those options.

In the second stage, a choice is selected from the remaining alternatives based on its ability to maximize expected benefits on other relevant dimensions (Mintz *et al.* 1997). In other words, decision makers choose from the remaining options based on an alternative's ability to maximize expected net benefits. The theory suggests that decisions are non-compensatory, non-holistic, dimension-based, and order-sensitive in the first stage of the decision-making process and maximizing in the second stage. Moreover, in contrast to rational models of decision making that assume a maximizing principle in which the "best" alternative (the one with the highest benefit-cost ratio) is selected, Poliheuristic Theory postulates that individuals do not necessarily maximize in the first stage of the decision process but do maximize in the second stage of the process, resulting in a satisficing process.

The two-stage, multi-dimensional decision-making strategy posited by the Poliheuristic Theory does not privilege process validity over outcome validity, or vice versa (Mintz 2004). Indeed, it mirrors the manner in which decisions are often made as demonstrated by supportive evidence obtained across a range of diverse methodologies (DeRouen 2000, 2003; Redd 2002; Sathasivam 2003).

In the following pages, we illustrate the utility of the Applied Decision Analysis procedure by examining two decisions by Osama bin Laden—one is organizational, the decision to merge al-Qaeda with Egyptian Islamic Jihad, the other is operational, the decision to carry out a suicide bombing attack against the USS *Cole*.

The suicide attack on the USS *Cole*

On October 12, 2000, an explosion rocked the US Navy destroyer *Cole*, tearing a gaping hole in its side, killing 17 members of the ship's crew, and wounding 39 others. The *Cole* had been refueling in the Yemeni port of Aden, when two suicide attackers drew close to the *Cole* in a small harbor boat and detonated a large quantity of explosives aboard their vessel. Although no one immediately claimed responsibility for the attack, the blast that crippled the *Cole* was the result of a year's worth of planning by al-Qaeda operatives in Yemen and supervised directly by Osama bin Laden (National Commission 2004). The al-Qaeda leader was deeply involved in the terrorist operation. From the selection of the location and type of target to the provision of financial resources for purchasing the explosives used in the attack, bin Laden was the ultimate overseer of the strike in Yemen (ibid.; Mandel 2002).

Before the *Cole* bombing, suicide attacks against military targets were typically the hallmark of desperation. For example, *kamikaze* pilots of the Second World War began sacrificing themselves only when the Japanese cause became desperate

(Berman and Laitin forthcoming; Rosenthal forthcoming). In light of bin Laden's extensive resources and consequent range of potential terrorist operations, why did the terror mastermind choose to carry out a suicide attack on a US destroyer?

The 1998 merger

In 1998, Osama bin Laden orchestrated the fusion of his al-Qaeda terror network with Ayman al-Zawahiri's Egyptian Islamic Jihad. Throughout the late 1990s, bin Laden was concerned with creating a "global Salafi jihad" (Sageman 2004: 46), which would target not only the secular dictatorships in the Middle East, but also—indeed, primarily—the United States and its allies throughout the world (Karmon 1998; Williams 2002; Ressa 2003; Schweitzer and Shay 2003; Whittaker 2004). In order to succeed in this endeavor, it was necessary for bin Laden to increase his network and to acquire greater religious backing for his *fatwas* (Gunaratna 2002). To this end, he attempted to curry favor with several organizations, chief among them Ayman al-Zawahiri's Egyptian Islamic Jihad (EIJ).

After suffering a series of setbacks at the hands of Egyptian security officials, the Egyptian Islamic Jihad (as well as other militant Egyptian Islamist groups) acceded to a process of "progressive integration" into al-Qaeda (Williams 2002; Napoleoni 2003: 110; Sageman 2004). The integration came to a head in February 1998, when bin Laden met with al-Zawahiri and the heads of several other groups, including the Egyptian Islamic Group (EIG), Jamiat-ul-Ulema-e-Pakistan, and the Jihad Movement of Bangladesh (Gunaratna 2002). These groups formed an umbrella organization, with the intent to target Americans and Jews worldwide, both military and civilian, and issued a joint *fatwa* declaring this intent.

While the acquisition of control over each of these groups would be beneficial to bin Laden, it is clear that al-Zawahiri was the most important among them (Scheuer 2002; National Commission 2004; ICT 2005), and the signatory whom bin Laden most desired to keep within the new organization. This is evident not only from his initial attempts at wooing al-Zawahiri into the group—overtures which were not made toward any of the other signatories—but also through his attempts to aid al-Zawahiri when some members of EIJ objected to the shift from "the 'near enemy'...Egypt, toward the 'far enemy,' the United States" (Schanzer 2005: 42). When the leader of EIG found himself in similar circumstances, leading him to retract his signature, bin Laden simply had him replaced (Sageman 2004). These circumstances demonstrate the importance of incorporating al-Zawahiri and his structure into al-Qaeda, and his leadership potential. As a well-respected cleric and a vital partner, al-Zawahiri had the potential to assume the mantle of leadership (or co-leadership) within al-Qaeda, were bin Laden to concede it.

Constructing bin Laden's decision matrix

The first stage in the utilization of Applied Decision Analysis is to identify the decision matrix employed by a decision maker, which in this case is Osama bin

Laden, acting as head of al-Qaeda. Across different decisions, the alternatives will change, but the dimensions and their relative weights should remain reasonably stable. Thus, different decisions can generally be analyzed using the same matrix, and replacing only the alternatives. We first identify the general criteria with which bin Laden seems to be concerned across decisions, and then we identify the alternatives implicit specifically in each decision.

The political dimension

Because traditional decision analysis tends to focus on political leaders, the political dimension is often one of greater importance. It represents an alternative's effects upon the leader's political survival, or potential to stay in office (Mintz *et al.* 1997; Mintz 2004; Kinne 2005). In the case of personalist autocrats, Kinne (2005) suggests that threats to the leader's power may arise from within his country or organization, or from without. Thus, the political dimension for bin Laden is a measure of his personal honor and status among his colleagues and the radical Islamic world.

The political dimension is often—including in this case—the dimension of paramount importance. Leaders place their political survival above other concerns not simply because of an inherent desire to be in office, but because their other goals are not achievable without the position—if they do not lead their countries or organizations, they will have no effect upon future decisions concerning these countries and organizations. According to his own statements, bin Laden sought to expel Americans and non-Muslims from the Middle East, overthrow the secular Arab governments (ICT 2005)—whom he believes to be allied with the United States (Scheuer 2002)—and ultimately re-establish the Caliphate, ostensibly under his own control (Gunaratna 2002; Schweitzer and Shay 2003). For bin Laden to achieve his ultimate goals, he would need to maintain leadership of the al-Qaeda organization.

Through his actions, bin Laden has indeed shown a propensity to concern himself with his personal status. He has been described as an adept manipulator of media and propaganda, who is "careful to tailor his statements carefully for the selected audience," using "selective Qur'anic references" and playing upon the particular feelings of those at whom his statement is directed (Burke 2003: 158). When his mentor, Abdullah Azzam, died, bin Laden "chose selectively" among Azzam's writings and words "to lend credence to his narrow political vision" (Gunaratna 2002: 86). Furthermore, there is evidence that he plotted against Azzam, in order to gain political status and "reconfigure ... the nascent Al Qaeda in his own image" (Gunaratna 2002: 23). Finally, he is not above full denial of fairly obvious facts. Despite the fact that the CIA funding of *mujahideen* during the Soviet invasion of Afghanistan is well-documented common knowledge, bin Laden as a "self-styled champion of Islam" understands that he "cannot afford ... to be seen as owing anything to America" (Corbin 2002: 24). Thus, to increase his status and serve his political goals, he described the CIA as a burden, and claimed that the funding came not from the United States, but from the Arab states.

Because of its inherent primacy among bin Laden's goals (i.e. because his other goals cannot be accomplished without it), the personal political dimension shall be assigned the greatest weight. If bin Laden is a non-compensatory decision maker, he should reject alternatives that score negatively on this dimension. In other words, alternatives that overtly and credibly threaten bin Laden's leadership of al-Qaeda should be eliminated immediately. On the other hand, if bin Laden is a compensatory decision maker, this dimension should function in the same way as the other dimensions, and should only impart a greater influence upon the outcome, as its weight suggests.

It should be further noted that the political dimension can be broken down into bin Laden's standing with the mass public, and bin Laden's standing within his organization. Thus, there is an organizational political dimension and a mass political dimension. These remain the most important of dimensions. The former signifies the amount of power that bin Laden holds within al-Qaeda. If this were to collapse, then so would his leadership and any potential to realize his goals. Within the organization, his personal honor is highly important. For bin Laden, the organizational political dimension is the slightly more important of the two because it has a direct effect upon his leadership, whereas the mass public dimension has an indirect effect.

The mass public political dimension signifies the amount of support that bin Laden has from the public as a whole. To the mass public, it is not bin Laden's personal honor that is important but his reasoning behind his actions and whether he follows through on what he says. Around the world, many Muslims support him not because they condone terrorism but because they are "pleased...that bin Laden is taking a stand and feel a profound...identification with his cause" (Burke 2003: 35). As long as they support him, there is some legitimacy to his rule within the terrorist world.

The religious dimension

Al-Qaeda is first and foremost a religious organization, with more religious motivation than any of the previous major terrorist groups (Scheuer 2002). Its ultimate goal is to be at the vanguard of an Islamic revolution that re-establishes the old Caliphate (Gunaratna 2002; Burke 2003; Schweitzer and Shay 2003). The Caliphate is meant to be an "Islamic utopia," for which the Taliban's Afghanistan was the model (AbuKhalil 2002: 75). Bin Laden himself has frequently (and, again, selectively) cited religious texts in defining the goals and strategies of al-Qaeda, directing his words toward the Islamic world (Gunaratna 2002; Schweitzer and Shay 2003).

The religious dimension is critically important because, despite his intensely religious focus and the fact that he couches goals and tactics in religious terms, bin Laden has no formal religious training and no clerical authority (Gunaratna 2002;

Burke 2003; Schweitzer and Shay 2003). Because he has intensely studied and taught himself Islamic law, bin Laden can and does issue *fatwas* (Burke 2003). However, clerics with formal religious authority could potentially overturn these decrees, and thus bin Laden has been forced to gain and maintain the support of "known, radical Islamic religious clerics who adopted his ideology" in order to give greater influence to his decrees (Schweitzer and Shay 2003: 24).

The religiously oriented goals of al-Qaeda, combined with the importance of maintaining good relations with radical clerics, suggest that the religious dimension is one of great importance to bin Laden. Indeed, it should have a weight just below that of his personal political dimension. It is not the most important because bin Laden can still seek his goals without the support and influence that he has in the religious community. His own knowledge and slight authority on religious matters, along with his ability to couch his goals in nationalistic terms if necessary (AbuKhalil 2002), would mean that a loss of support in the radical Muslim world only make his work more difficult, though not impossible. Nonetheless, it is clear that gaining and maintaining support among Muslims— especially among Muslim leaders—is highly important and incredibly helpful to bin Laden in seeking his goals.

The strategic dimension

"Defeating the United States" is the most important "strategic goal" for Osama bin Laden (Scheuer 2002: 55). While bin Laden ultimately wants to establish an Islamic utopia, his most important immediate goal is the defeat of the United States. In the *fatwas* and declarations of war that he has issued—as well as in interviews he has given—he has repeatedly called on "good" Muslims to direct their fighting against the United States, and has declared every American citizen to be an enemy combatant (AbuKhalil 2002; Gunaratna 2002; Piszkiewicz 2003; Schweitzer and Shay 2003; ICT 2005).

Based on bin Laden's worldview, defeating the United States is a necessary step on the path to achieving his ultimate goals. His primary concern with the United States is its effect upon Muslim countries and the Islamic world in general (AbuKhalil 2002; Gunaratna 2002; Burke 2003). The United States' presence in what is to bin Laden a holy area (i.e. Saudi Arabia) alone is intolerable (AbuKhalil 2002), but he also believes America to be propping up regimes hostile to the idea of an Islamist society.

In striking out at American targets, bin Laden hopes to convince the United States to leave the Middle East and to end all support for Israel (Piszkiewicz 2003). This fits into bin Laden's short-term plan. However, in the long run, he hopes not only to eliminate the influence of the United States, but to destroy it and its allies altogether (Gunaratna 2002).

Alternatives that cause damage to the United States or shift the strategic balance in the direction of bin Laden and al-Qaeda even slightly should be helpful in these endeavors, and should be rated highly along the strategic dimension.

Because this dimension represents the main portion of bin Laden's goals, but not all of them, its weight should be below those of the political and religious dimensions, but still weighted relatively heavily.

The military dimension

Any armed struggle requires soldiers to fight against the enemy. The military dimension represents an alternative's implications with regard to al-Qaeda's ability to fight against the United States and its allies. The measure is fairly straightforward: positive implications would increase the number or the abilities of al-Qaeda's recruits or the amount and power of its weapons; negative implications would lessen the number or abilities of recruits or potential to receive weapons.

Bin Laden has certainly shown concern over recruitment, making a "special appeal to Muslim youths" to join his *jihad* (Scheuer 2002: 58). From al-Qaeda's beginnings, it needed to focus largely on recruiting new young men (Gunaratna 2002). Bin Laden clearly recognizes the need to maintain sufficient numbers of fighters, and would not be so profligate as to send his men to their death without purpose. However, his use of suicide tactics (most obviously in the September 11 attacks that took the lives of nineteen members of al-Qaeda) demonstrates that he is not unwilling to sacrifice warriors to achieve his goals.

Bin Laden has also attempted to acquire biological, chemical, and nuclear weapons (Gunaratna 2002; Schweitzer and Shay 2003), saying of them in 1999 "it would be a sin for Muslims not to try and possess weapons that would prevent the infidel from inflicting harm on Muslims" (Burke 2003: 187). Interestingly, in 2003, an associate of bin Laden and one of Saudi Arabia's senior clerics, Sheikh Nasser bin Hamd al-Fahad, issued a *fatwa* that proclaimed the use of weapons of mass destruction against the United States and Britain to be legitimate (Fighel and Marzouk 2003).

The recruitment of manpower and acquisition of weapons are important to the pursuit of bin Laden's goals. It is likely that he will seek both as often as possible, as long as the search does not interfere with other goals. It is unlikely, for example, that he would choose to sacrifice a member of al-Qaeda in an attack unless it were clear that such a sacrifice would increase enemy casualties or in some other way bring the group closer to its goal. In such a case, the slight decrease in military might from a suicide attack might lead to the alternative being rejected. On the other hand, it is unlikely that he would choose to acquire weapons that were not sanctioned in some form by a religious authority—although this is unlikely since bin Laden has several leading clerics, such as al-Fahad, in his pocket. Thus, the military criterion is relevant; however it is substantially less weighty than the other three dimensions.

Having described the dimensions relevant to bin Laden's decision-making processes, we turn to two decisions carried out by bin Laden—the decision to attack the USS *Cole* and the decision to merge with Egyptian Islamic Jihad. The dimensions described in this section are used to construct the matrixes for these decisions.

Analysis: attack on the *Cole*

Although Osama bin Laden's hatred for the United States seems to have begun in earnest with the staging of American troops in Saudi Arabia in the early 1990s (AbuKhalil 2002), he did not "call for *jihad* against America" for several more years (Corbin 2002: 69). This *fatwa* was driven in large part by his desire to see this American intrusion reversed. The call-to-arms and bin Laden's subsequent actions were also influenced by America's response to him and by his attempts to gain prestige. Here, we explore how the combination of these factors and bin Laden's underlying goals led to the attack of the USS *Cole* warship in 2000. Despite varied long-term and immediate aims, we assert—consistent with Poliheuristic Theory—that bin Laden's decision-making process was dramatically influenced by personal political considerations, which led him to employ a two-stage decision process.

Alternatives considered

In the wake of the failed attack on *The Sullivans*, bin Laden was left with four options, as depicted in Table 8.1. He could continue the plan by approving an operation highly similar to the earlier failed attack. This option would involve targeting another US warship in the same area (i.e. off the coast of Yemen). Alternatively, he could modify the plan by approving an attack with a slightly different focus—non-governmental US target or attack a non-maritime US government target. Finally, in light of the recent failed attack, he could choose to abort the plan, and reject any plans for further attacks.

Bin Laden's options were: (1) attack a US warship, (2) attack a non-governmental US target, (3) attack a non-maritime US governmental target, and (4) do nothing.

1 Attack a US warship. Choosing to continue the plan would involve staging another attack in Yemen against a US warship. Bin Laden's original instructions to the al-Qaeda team in Yemen had been to seek out a warship and destroy it (Gunaratna 2002; National Commission 2004). Continuing the plan would involve a retooling in order to increase the chances of success, but the general target would remain the same.

2 Attack a non-governmental US target. Bin Laden could also choose to retarget the attack slightly. Originally, the al-Qaeda coordinators in Yemen had intended to target "a commercial vessel, specifically an oil tanker" (National Commission 2004: 190). Changing targets in this manner would involve a relatively smooth transition (the planning would be essentially the same), and, as it had been their

Table 8.1 Bin Laden's decision matrix—*Cole* bombing

Dimensions	Alternatives				Weight
	Carry out an attack against a US warship	*Approve an attack upon a non-governmental US target*	*Approve an attack upon a non-maritime US government target*	*Reject the idea of an attack altogether and do nothing*	
Organizational political	Because bin Laden held a personal grudge against the US military warships that hit his camps, an attack would give him personal vengeance, and would demonstrate his ability to strike back Rating: 7	Attacking the Americans at all would likely be beneficial to bin Laden; however, those within his organization were aware of his need to exact revenge upon the US government and so his organizational standing also had the potential to decrease Rating: 0	An attack against the US government would certainly have a positive effect upon bin Laden's organizational prestige. Additionally, this would satisfy the criterion of allowing him to take revenge upon the US government, if not the particular US warships that attacked him Rating: 5	Failing to attack the Americans at all, after the 1998 missile strikes, would make bin Laden appear weak or incompetent, lowering his personal status and value to the organization Rating: −4	10
Mass political	Though it is unlikely that the mass public knew of bin Laden's grudge, they would be pleased that he was following through on his promises with his attack against what they see to be an inappropriate incursion by the US military Rating: 7	The mass public would be pleased that bin Laden was following through on his vow to attack the infidels in the Middle East. They would likely be unaware of his personal grudge against the American government and its warships Rating: 7	The mass public would be pleased that bin Laden was following through on his vow to attack the infidels in the Middle East and that he was going after the US government Rating: 7	If bin Laden did not strike out at the US military in the Middle East, he would not be following through on his word. His support would likely begin to evaporate Rating: −4	9

(continued)

Table 8.1 Continued

Dimensions	Alternatives				Weight
	Carry out an attack against a US warship	*Approve an attack upon a non-governmental US target*	*Approve an attack upon a non-maritime US government target*	*Reject the idea of an attack altogether and do nothing*	
Religious	Because the *Cole* attack would take place in a Yemeni port, this should play well with radical Muslims, as a defensive action against "Crusaders." Furthermore, by framing it as a blow against Zionism, al-Qaeda gains even more Rating: 9	Attacking an American ship, especially one seen as a symbol of American capitalism, would likely still benefit bin Laden, as it would be seen as a symbol of American hegemony within the Holy Land Rating: 7	By hitting an embassy or other American target within the Middle East, bin Laden would be seen as defending the Holy Land from the Crusaders Rating: 7	Bin Laden's appeal to Militant religious fanatics lies in his calls to remove the infidels from the Holy Land By not making good on his threats, he would lose cachet with these groups Rating: −4	8
Strategic	Attacking an American warship	This attack would do little to undermine	This attack would do little to undermine America's	Failure to attack the United States would not	7

				4
	is both symbolically and realistically damaging to the United States and its military power Rating: 10	America's strategic power; its impact would be primarily psychological and economic Rating: 3	strategic power; its impact would be primarily psychological or economic Rating: 3	alter the strategic dimension Rating: 0
Military	There is little reason to believe there would be a military response from the United States. Though there would be some al-Qaeda deaths from the bombing, its use in recruitment videos would attract a greater number of new recruits. This would be further assisted by the fact that it is a military target Rating: 8	There is little reason to believe there would be a military response from the United States. Though there would be some al-Qaeda deaths from the bombing, its use in recruitment videos would attract a greater number of new recruits Rating: 5	There is little reason to believe there would be a military response from the United States. Though there would be some al-Qaeda deaths from the bombing, its use in recruitment videos would attract a greater number of new recruits Rating: 5	The only benefit from not carrying out the attack is that the potential bombers would not be killed in the explosion Rating: 2
Weighted total	30.7	16	21	−10

idea in the first place, it would not be difficult to persuade the team to undertake the mission. However, it would not allow bin Laden to seek the revenge against the US military that he so desired (Gunaratna 2002).

3 Attack a non-maritime US governmental target. To change the plan more significantly, bin Laden could shift to an attack on a non-maritime representation of the US presence. In 1998, al-Qaeda had struck US embassies in Kenya and Tanzania, "rival[ing] the worst attacks in memory" (National Commission 2004: 118), and killing over 200 people in two countries (Robinson 2002; Williams 2004). The attacks were highly successful not only in the amount of damage that they did, but also in bringing al-Qaeda (as well as Osama bin Laden personally) to the attention of the world (Robinson 2002). This would stand out as a potential option, especially in light of its past successes when juxtaposed with the failure against *The Sullivans*. However, like the previous option, it would not have the symbolic revenge aspect to it.

4 Call off the attack/do nothing. There was, of course, the option to back out of the plan after the botched attack on the first ship. In so doing, bin Laden could rescind the orders to the Yemeni cell, advising them instead to do nothing. At a later date, a different attack could be planned. This was especially viable because bin Laden was personally highly involved in the attack and its planning, greatly impinging upon the cell's autonomy (National Commission 2004).

Analysis

Poliheuristic Theory posits that actors engage in a two-stage decision process, using a non-compensatory decision heuristic in the first stage and a rational, maximizing technique in the second (Mintz *et al.* 1997). In the case of Osama bin Laden, the mass and organizational political dimensions are non-compensatory. A significant portion of these dimensions involved a personal revenge criterion. When bin Laden's camps in Afghanistan were struck by US missiles in 1998, he made it clear that he wanted vengeance (Corbin 2002; Gunaratna 2002). Additionally, in 1998, Yemen was an al-Qaeda and bin Laden stronghold (Corbin 2002; Williams 2002; Burke 2003). The uncontested, strengthening US presence was a blow both to the organization and to bin Laden himself. Attacks that did not fulfill the personal revenge criterion would not only fail to meet his desires, but would have a damaging effect upon his image within the organization. As a consequence, 2 of the 4 alternatives—those that did *not* involve the direct targeting of representatives of the US government—were rejected in the first stage of the decision-making process, after which the remaining alternatives were evaluated using a utility maximizing strategy in the second stage.

As evidenced by Table 8.1, aborting the attack was the only option that would be wholly detrimental to bin Laden's political standing. Failure to carry out an attack would have affected him on multiple levels. In addition to appearing ineffectual to the masses by not striking back after being hit by cruise missile strikes (see Gunaratna 2002; Burke 2003), bin Laden would also appear to be backing out of plans well known within the organization (i.e. strike against the United States in Yemen). This option was the worst of those available to bin Laden, as it carried no real advantages politically and would negatively affect his image.

Choosing to attack a non-governmental US target, such as a commercial tanker, would not have been as disadvantageous as the "do nothing" alternative. A non-governmental target would be less guarded than a warship or an embassy, and thus less risky to strike. Moreover, such an attack would have generated publicity for al-Qaeda, boosting bin Laden's favor with the masses, and delivering an economic blow to the United States. But the chief drawback for this alternative would be that it did not involve a direct strike against representatives of the US government who had attacked bin Laden. Although the masses would have been enthusiastic about a strike against a US commercial interest, many al-Qaeda members were aware of bin Laden's interests in Yemen, which were compromised by the US military presence there (Burke 2003). They were also aware both of the strikes against the camps and of bin Laden's reaction (Corbin 2002; Gunaratna 2002). To change the plan such that a non-US governmental interest would be targeted would have failed to fulfill either of bin Laden's objectives, and carried with it the potential to diminish his standing and the organizational view of his willingness to fight the United States. Thus, targeting a non-governmental US target was rejected in the first stage of the decision-making process largely because this alternative failed to directly avenge the 1998 missile strikes against bin Laden's camps in Afghanistan.

It is unsurprising, then, that bin Laden rejected the options that did not allow him to strike back at the United States for its attack against him. Despite the fact that other options were presented to him, bin Laden chose immediately to reject any options that did not allow him to avenge his personal honor, which determines how he is viewed by his colleagues and subordinates in the organization. That is, he rejected those options that could potentially harm him along his organizational political dimension. This rejection marks the end of the first stage of bin Laden's decision-making process. The clear demarcation exists in bin Laden's refusal to consider non-government targets due to their inability to satisfy his noncompensatory dimension and to plan attacks specifically against US government sites in the Persian Gulf (Corbin 2002).

After rejecting the alternatives to call off the attack or to strike targets that were not representative of the US government, bin Laden proceeded to the second stage of Poliheuristic decision-making process. In this phase of the process, bin Laden assessed the remaining alternatives—attack a US warship and attack a non-maritime US governmental target—according to each option's ability to maximize benefits on the subsequent dimensions. In other words, bin Laden would choose the surviving alternative which promised the most net benefits with respect to his religious, strategic, and military goals.

The religious dimension concerns the response that an al-Qaeda action is likely to invoke from the radical Muslim community, as well as its effects upon al-Qaeda's religious status. Bin Laden's ultimate goals, like those of many other radical Muslim leaders, include the expulsion of Americans and non-Muslims from the Middle East (and Saudi Arabia in particular) and the overthrow of the secular Arab governments (ICT 2005), which they believe to be allied with the United States (Scheuer 2002). However, these problems ultimately have their roots in the continuing US military presence in the Holy Land (AbuKhalil 2002; Burke 2003). A US warship is both a symbol and a physical manifestation of this very "armed infidel" presence (Robinson 2002: 132). Thus, while both targets would have resulted in damage to the United States and its interests in the Middle East, as well as the death of Americans, attacking a warship would result in more military deaths. This would in turn be a step toward ending the so-called desecration of the Holy Land by eliminating part of the military presence. He would receive a greater advantage on the religious dimension by attacking a warship than an embassy.

The strategic dimension includes bin Laden's ultimate goal of destroying the United States (Gunaratna 2002; Scheuer 2002), as well as his more immediate goal of driving it out of the Middle East (AbuKhalil 2002; Pape 2003). On the strategic dimension, striking a US warship appears to have been more advantageous than attacking an embassy or consulate. An attack on a US warship would inflict real damage upon the US military, reducing its strength at least slightly. Additionally, it would compel the US government to reassess the utility of its naval presence in the Middle East, which served troops in Saudi Arabia and Egypt (Perl and O'Rourke 2001). On the other hand, striking an embassy or consulate would, at best, kill civilians, damage infrastructure, and lead to the withdrawal of US government civilian personnel and have little bearing on the US military presence on the Arabian Peninsula. This would be similar to the Hezbollah bombings of the US embassy and later the Marine barracks in Beirut in 1983. While the former evoked little response from the United States, the latter led to a US withdrawal from Lebanon (Davies 2003; Pape 2003). Forcing the United States to consider using other logistical bases for refueling and re-supplying ships—as well as killing American military personnel—would further bin Laden's strategic goal of driving the US military out of the areas in and around Saudi Arabia. Thus, an attack on a US warship was superior to an attack on a US embassy or other civilian installation on the strategic dimension.

The military dimension primarily concerns bin Laden's efforts to recruit members to his al-Qaeda organization. Both of the potential alternatives involved daring strikes against the US presence in the Middle East. Provided that bin Laden planned to create a recruitment video from either attack as he ultimately decided to do in the *Cole* bombing (Corbin 2002; National Commission 2004), both of these options would likely generate good recruitment propaganda. However, military targets are inherently "harder" targets than are civilian centers (Berman *et al.* forthcoming). By choosing to attack the better defended target, bin Laden would be better able to showcase his organization's skills, setting his organization apart from those with whom he was competing for mass sympathy and resources, such as Hezbollah and Hamas (National Commission 2004: 191). The strike against the US military also inspired a bin Laden poem ridiculing the United States' "false power," and lauding al-Qaeda's ability to strike at a target whom "even the brave fear" (Burke 2003: 191). Ultimately, an attack on the American military presence was a more difficult task, and as such it better demonstrated al-Qaeda's talents. Its ability to cripple a symbol of US military hegemony made clear that al-Qaeda was one of the world's premier terrorist organizations: "a far cry from what had gone before" (Robinson 2002: 259). An attack on an embassy would simply have been a repetition of the group's previous acts. Although an attack on a non-governmental US target may have helped recruiting efforts, it probably would not have provided the benefits of an attack on a warship, which ultimately did spur an increase in recruitment (National Commission 2004)—perhaps because of the fact that it led growing numbers of disaffected Muslims to believe that it was possible to humble the most powerful military in the world.

In the decision that resulted in the suicide attack on the USS *Cole*, bin Laden rejected alternatives that threatened his personal honor and organizational standing in the first stage of the decision-making process. It is clear that he used a non-compensatory decision rule and refused to consider those alternatives that did not involve the targeting of US government forces in the Persian Gulf. Evidence indicates that despite the existence and even presentation of such options (Corbin 2002; National Commission 2004), bin Laden refused to consider them, demanding that the attack be focused against the US government. In the second stage, bin Laden selected an alternative on the basis of that option's ability to maximize expected net benefits across the remaining dimensions. In this stage, he dealt with those remaining options and chose the target that was most beneficial to his and his organization's goals. His use of a more rational, utility-maximizing process in the second stage is further apparent in his attempt to videotape the bombing and use it as recruitment propaganda (Corbin 2002; Gunaratna 2002; National Commission 2004).

It is important to note that while bin Laden chose the alternative with the highest cumulative score in this decision, such is not always the case in Poliheuristic decision making. In this particular case, an expected utility approach might have allowed for the same predictions. However, this is merely coincidental. Poliheuristic Theory does not maintain (or even suggest) that the alternative with the highest cumulative score ought to be selected. Rather, decisions are made through a non-linear (and non-compensatory) aggregation of values. That is, alternatives with greater overall scores may be rejected in favor of alternatives with lower cumulative scores, but with greater scores on the critical dimension (Mintz 2004). Even if a strike on a commercial tanker had provided a greater overall net benefit to bin Laden, as a Poliheuristic decision maker, he still would have eliminated it in favor of the *Cole*, as it did not meet his political threshold. We now turn to a discussion and analysis of bin Laden's decision to merge his al-Qaeda organization with Egyptian Islamic Jihad.

169

Analysis: merger with EIJ

The analysis of the attack on the *Cole* illustrates that bin Laden's decision-making process appears to follow the two-step procedure we describe. During the decade preceding this attack, bin Laden sought to broaden his organization's infrastructure and add weight to and respect for his religious *fatwas* (Gunaratna 2002). In order to satisfy these objectives, bin Laden embarked upon an effort to unite his al-Qaeda organization with several other organizations, primarily Ayman al-Zawahiri's Egyptian Islamic Jihad (EIJ). As a respected cleric and religious leader, Al-Zawahiri in particular would contribute to al-Qaeda's international prominence. But given bin Laden's proclivity for enhancing his own personal prestige, why did he choose to align himself with someone who may be seen as more important than himself in the organization?

Alternatives considered

The decision to form a terrorist umbrella organization is not unlike any corporate merger. Indeed, it has even been couched in corporate terms, with bin Laden being described as "the Chairman of 'Terror Incorporated'." (Corbin 2002: 67) Ultimately, in any such merger, it must be decided how power will be shared. The options open to bin Laden and their respective implications are represented in Table 8.2. In this case, there were inherently four options: (1) Bin Laden could assume full command of the new group, (2) bin Laden could turn power over to al-Zawahiri, (3) bin Laden and al-Zawahiri could share power, or (4) the status quo could be maintained with no merger.

1 Assume Full Command. By assuming full command, bin Laden would act as emir of the new organization in much the same way he had previously (Corbin 2002; Burke 2003). Al-Zawahiri would serve as bin Laden's deputy, lending weight to his religious legitimacy and providing counsel and "crucial, practical, know how" to bin Laden (Gunaratna 2002: 26). Under this option, al-Zawahiri would have a great deal of influence (Burke 2003), but would ultimately be answerable to bin Laden.

2 Become al-Zawahiri's Deputy. Alternatively, bin Laden could have sworn allegiance to al-Zawahiri as emir. Ostensibly, bin Laden would serve as his deputy, providing his own advice. Al-Zawahiri would not only bring greater religious credentials to the highest echelon of the organizational leadership, but also greater experience, as he had been involved in terrorism longer than bin Laden.

3 Assume co-equal leadership with al-Zawahiri. In the third option—merging as partners and "co-chairs" of "Terror Incorporated"—both men would be co-equal leaders of the new organization. While such an arrangement would, to some extent, bring the benefits of both of the previous options, it is important to note that it would also mean that neither man would retain full control over his organization.

4 Maintain the status quo. Finally, bin Laden could choose to reject the merger altogether. This would mean that al-Qaeda and EIJ would continue as separate entities. It would not necessarily rule out any future collaboration, but there would be no fusion of the two groups.

Analysis

As in the case of the *Cole* bombing, bin Laden's main concern seems to have been with his own personal political standing. However, unlike the decision to attack the *Cole*, the options bin Laden considered prior to the merger with EIJ exerted a far more direct effect upon his political prestige. For bin Laden, to accept an arrangement under which he did not have full leadership (i.e. to hand the reins of power to al-Zawahiri or to merge on equal terms) would have been an obvious blow to his personal status. It would not only have resulted in a demotion in rank—the primary component of his organizational political dimension, which is foundational to other goals—but would ultimately also have frustrated some of his goals and lessened his political clout.

It is well known that bin Laden's strategic goal is to attack the United States and its allies all over the world, with the goals of first eliminating the US military presence in the Middle East and ultimately destroying the United States itself (Karmon 1998; Williams 2002; Ressa 2003; Schweitzer and Shay 2003; Whittaker 2004). EIJ and its leadership, however, had an Egypt-first strategy, with the intent of establishing an Islamic state in Egypt (Karmon 1998; Scheuer 2002). If bin Laden were to enter into any type of arrangement in which he was not the undisputed leader, the international status of al-Qaeda would have dropped, as its attacks would have been forced to focus more on Egypt and regional targets, the preferred targets of the Egyptian groups (Schweitzer 1999). This would further cause a decline in bin Laden's *personal* status as a terrorist leader and would discourage the achievement of his ultimate goals.

Because of the problems inherent in 2 of the 4 alternatives—namely, merging with EIJ with bin Laden as al-Zawahiri's deputy, as well as merging and serving as co-equals—bin Laden only seems to have considered the remaining two seriously: to merge EIJ into al-Qaeda, if al-Zawahiri would accept bin Laden's leadership and the America-first focus, or not to merge at all (Scheuer 2002). Indeed, many reports of the merger indicate very little negotiation and simply state that al-Zawahiri merged EIJ into al-Qaeda (Corbin 2002; Gunaratna 2002; Williams 2002; Burke 2003). This indicates that—as Poliheuristic Theory would predict—options which had a directly adverse affect upon bin Laden's political standing were immediately rejected in the first stage. While al-Zawahiri likely was concerned with his own political dimension, it would not have been non-compensatory in this instance. This is because EIJ had recently been near-fatally weakened through an Egyptian crackdown against terrorists operating within the

Table 8.2 Bin Laden's decision matrix—EIJ merger

Dimensions	Alternatives				Weight
	Maintain the status quo	*Merge with EIJ, but assume full command of the new group, with al-Zawahiri as deputy*	*Merge with EIJ, and defer to al-Zawahiri, becoming his deputy*	*Merge with al-Zawahiri on equal grounds, assuming co-leadership of the new organization*	
Organizational political	Bin Laden retains full leadership of his group. His status is relatively unaffected Rating: 0	The organizations under bin Laden's command would increase in number, thus improving his personal status Rating: 8	Bin Laden loses control of his organization, though he retains importance. This decreases his status slightly Rating: −2	Sharing power with al-Zawahiri diminishes bin Laden's status somewhat, though this is mitigated to an extent by the increased number of organizations he controls Rating: −4	10
Mass political	Not merging would have little effect upon the public's perception of bin Laden Rating: 0	As leader of an umbrella organization, bin Laden would be seen as a more important figure Rating: 4	Because he would no longer be in command of his organization, bin Laden's status would decrease Rating: −1	Being co-equal with al-Zawahiri would not diminish bin Laden in the eyes of the public Rating: 3	9

				8
Religious	By declining to be associated with a well-known Muslim cleric, it is likely that bin Laden's religious status would decline slightly
Rating: -2	Bin Laden associates himself with a well-known cleric, adding religious backing to his decrees
Rating: 6	The organization would now be headed by a prominent Muslim cleric. This would be a tremendous religious boon
Rating: 10	With al-Zawahiri as spiritual head and co-leader, the organization would have much greater religious authority
Rating: 8
Strategic	Because the merger is vital for EIJ's survival, failing to merge could contribute to the downfall of an enemy of the United States
Rating: -3	The merger would augment the power of the US enemies, and by maintaining control, bin Laden could direct them against his primary targets
Rating: 8	Although al-Zawahiri's EIJ did not focus only on the United States, the merger would substantially empower its enemies
Rating: 7	As one of the leaders, bin Laden could direct his more powerful terror machine against the United States with the full cooperation of his co-leader
Rating: 8	7
Military	This would have no immediate effect on the number of al-Qaeda members
Rating: 0	The soldiers from EIJ and other organizations would add to al-Qaeda's numbers
Rating: 8	The soldiers from EIJ and other organizations would add to al-Qaeda's numbers
Rating: 8	The soldiers from EIJ and other organizations would add to al-Qaeda's numbers
Rating: 8	4
Weighted total	-3.7	25.2	13.2	13.9	

country (Williams 2002; Burke 2003). To refuse a merger on any grounds would probably have doomed the organization and cost al-Zawahiri his political power anyway.

The benefits that al-Zawahiri brought to al-Qaeda could not compensate for the potential political loss that bin Laden would suffer if he did not retain full command of the group. However, his religious influence and practical knowledge was a clear asset to al-Qaeda (Gunaratna 2002). As is clear from Table 8.2, there would be no benefit at all from refusing to merge with al-Zawahiri. On every dimension, the merger would be superior, provided bin Laden kept control.

The two-stage process of Poliheuristic Theory comports well with the evidence regarding bin Laden's decision. Initially, half of the alternatives were eliminated because they failed to meet the political threshold, as in the first stage of the Poliheuristic Theory. Evidence suggests that despite their availability as potential choices, these eliminated options were not seriously considered by bin Laden at either time, leading us to infer that they were immediately rejected (Williams 2002; Burke 2003). In the second stage, bin Laden was left with the decision to merge under his leadership or not to merge at all. Because there was no benefit in not merging, bin Laden chose the superior alternative, and employed a more rational strategy to choose between the two options, which are consistent both with Poliheuristic Theory and with the decision pattern in the *Cole* bombing.

As in the *Cole* bombing, bin Laden once again chose the alternative with the highest cumulative score in the decision to merge with EIJ. Once again, the outcome of this decision might have been predicted through a cumulative summation of expected values. However, it is the process involved in decision making that determines the strategy used. In this case, even if bin Laden had received greater overall utility from sharing power with al-Zawahiri, as a Poliheuristic decision maker, he still would have eliminated the option in order to maintain his political power.

Conclusion

In order to "nullify the threat posed by Osama bin Laden . . . we, in the West, must first understand the man" (Scheuer 2002: 3). A thorough understanding of terrorists and their actions is imperative for stopping them. By thinking like the terrorists, analysts can anticipate their moves and potentially prevent them from striking. Learning how terrorists and leaders of terrorist organizations make their decisions is the first step in understanding their thought processes.

Using the Applied Decision Analysis procedure, we have analyzed why Osama bin Laden arrived at certain decisions when faced with multiple alternatives. The procedure's guidance in terms of identifying and organizing relevant information facilitates the analysis of decisions. It allows us to examine the available evidence surrounding an individual's decision, analyze their behavior, and ultimately to infer what kind of process they utilized. When we can determine both the set of available alternatives and those that were seriously considered, it is possible to delineate the stages in the decision process. Accomplishing this task is difficult without making use of Applied Decision Analysis. In analyzing bin Laden's decisions here, we employed this strategy successfully.

Through the Applied Decisions Analysis procedure, we have shown that bin Laden can be thought of as a Poliheuristic decision maker: his decision making follows a two-stage process. In the two decisions that we analyzed, bin Laden placed particular emphasis on personal prestige, honor, and informal political standing among the mass public. Whatever the case, bin Laden does not consider seriously those options that will affect him adversely upon key decision dimensions, rejecting them immediately and rationally selecting an ultimate choice among the surviving alternatives.

For example, in choosing to merge with Ayman al-Zawahiri and his Egyptian Islamic Jihad in 1998, it was demonstrated that bin Laden's organizational standing, control and personal prestige were the driving forces in rejecting any option in which he did not emerge as head of the terror conglomerate. In his decision to attack the USS *Cole* after the failed attack on *The Sullivans*, bin Laden chose to attack that specific target for reasons of personal honor and revenge, rejecting those alternatives that did not allow him to strike back at the United States for its attacks on Afghanistan. During the second phase of each decision, he sought to maximize net benefits across subsequent dimensions.

While these two decisions provide us with some understanding of bin Laden's decision-making process, they are by no means the sole decisions to be analyzed. Indeed, it is important that many other al-Qaeda decisions (as well as those of other terrorist organizations) be analyzed. By utilizing Applied Decision Analysis upon multiple choices of a single decision maker, it might be possible to construct a "decision DNA" (or decision profile) of terrorists and terrorist groups, which can be used to map potential future choices.

Constructing an individual's decision DNA consists of using pattern recognition upon an N number of decisions. This involves an understanding of the individual's decision matrix, what dimensions are non-compensatory, and the individual's decision rule(s). The individual's decision-processing characteristics also play an important role. With a thorough understanding of the decision DNA of an individual—Osama bin Laden, in this case—we can create potential scenarios and predict their likely outcomes, further refining its accuracy with each analysis.

Applied Decision Analysis is a uniquely essential part of discerning the decision DNA of terrorists and their leaders. It provides a comprehensive technique of process tracing and pattern recognition, and a highly useful and flexible analytical tool for understanding why the decisions take place. Further, it allows for evolutionary understandings of decision processes. As additional decisions are analyzed, and we gain more knowledge about terrorists such as bin Laden, we will be able to refine our decision-making model, and track other consistencies among decisions. This will result in a useful knowledge-based system of the terrorist's decision processes and rules. The combination of tools in Applied Decision Analysis—process tracing, pattern recognition, software such as the Decision Board, and an analytical tool such as Poliheuristic Theory—is necessary for creating decision profiles of terrorist leaders, and ultimately for predicting what they will do in the future.

Bibliography

AbuKhalil, A. (2002) *Bin Laden, Islam and America's New "War on Terrorism,"* New York: Seven Stories Press.

Berman, E. and Laitin, D. (forthcoming) "Rational Martyrs vs. Hard Targets: Evidence on the Tactical Use of Suicide Attacks," in Eva Meyersson Milgrom, ed., *Suicide Bombing from an Interdisciplinary Perspective*, Princeton, NJ: Princeton University Press.

Billings, R. S. and Scherer, L. L. (1988) "The Effects of Response Mode and Importance on Decision-making Strategies: Judgment versus Choice," *Organizational Behavior and Human Decision Processes*, 41: 1–19.

Burke, J. (2003) *Al-Qaeda: Casting a Shadow of Terror*, New York: I. B. Taurus & Co. Ltd.

Burns, J. F. and Myers, S. L. (2000) "The Warship Explosion: The Overview; Blast Kills Sailors on U.S. Ship in Yemen," *New York Times*, A1, October 13.

Corbin, J. (2002) *Al-Qaeda: In Search of the Terror Network that Threatens the World*, New York: Thunder's Mouth Press.

Davies, B. (2003) *Terrorism: Inside a World Phenomenon*, London: Virgin Books.

DeRouen, K. (2000) "Presidents and the Diversionary Use of Force," *International Studies Quarterly*, 44: 317–328.

—— (2003) "The Decision Not to Use Force at Dien Bien Phu: A Poliheuristic Perspective," in Mintz, A. ed., *Integrating Cognitive and Rational Theories of Foreign Policy Decision Making*, New York: Palgrave Macmillan, 11–28.

Fighel, Y. and Marzouk, M. (2003) *Saudi Cleric Issues Fatwah on the Use of Weapons of Mass Destruction*, International Policy Institute for Counterterrorism *(ICT)*, July 5, Available at: http://www.ict.org.il/articles/articledet.cfm?articleid =491.

Friedman, M. (1953), *Essays in Positive Economics*, Chicago, IL: University of Chicago Press.

Ganor, B. (2000) *Suicide Attacks in Israel*, in *Countering Suicide Terrorism*, Herzliyya, Israel: The International Policy Institute for Counter-Terrorism, 140–252.

Gunaratna, R. (2002) *Inside Al Qaeda*, New York: Columbia University Press.

Institute for Counter-Terrorism (ICT) (2005) *Al-Qa'ida (The Base)*, Available at: http://www.ict.org.il/organizations/org_frame.cfm?orgid = 74, accessed on March 3, 2006.

Kahneman, D. and Tversky, A. (1979) "Prospect Theory: An Analysis of Decision under Risk," *Econometrica*, 47: 263–291.

Karmon, E. (1998) *Bin Ladin is out to get America!*, Available at: http://www.ict.org.il/articles/articledet.cfm?articleid = 53, accessed on March 3, 2006.

Kinne, B. J. (2005) "Decision Making in Autocratic Regimes: A Poliheuristic Perspective," *International Studies Perspectives*, 6: 114–128.

McCormick, G. H. (2003) "Terrorist Decision Making," *Annual Review of Political Science*, 6: 473–507.

Mandel, D. (2002) "Dissecting Terrorism", *The Review*, August.

Mintz, A. (1993) "The Decision to Attack Iraq: A Noncompensatory Theory of Decision Making," *Journal of Conflict Resolution*, 37, 4: 595–618.

—— (2004) "How Do Leaders Make Decisions?: A Poliheuristic Perspective," *Journal of Conflict Resolution*, 48: 3–13.

—— (2005) "Applied Decision Analysis: Utilizing Poliheuristic Theory to Explain and Predict Foreign Policy and National Security Decisions," *International Studies Perspectives*, 6: 94–98.

Mintz, A. and Geva, N. (1997) "The Poliheuristic Theory of Foreign Policy Decisionmaking," in Nehemia Geva and Alex Mintz, eds, *Decisionmaking on War and Peace: The Cognitive-Rational Debate*, Boulder, CO: Lynne Rienner Publishers.

Mintz, A., Geva, N., Redd, S., and Carnes, A. (1997) "The Effect of Dynamic and Static Choice Sets on Political Decision Making: An Analysis Using the Decision Board Platform," *American Political Science Review*, 91: 533–566.

Napoleoni, L. (2003) *Modern Jihad: Tracing the Dollars Behind the Terror Networks*, Sterling, VA: Pluto Press.

National Commission on Terrorist Attacks upon the United States (2004) *The 9/11 Commission Report*, Washington, DC: United States Government Printing Office.

Pape, R. (2003) "The Strategic Logic of Suicide Terrorism", *American Political Science Review*, 97: 1–19.

Payne, J. W., Bettman, J. R., and Johnson, E. J. (1993) *The Adaptive Decision Maker*, Cambridge: Cambridge University Press.

Perl, R. and O'Rourke, R. (2001) *Terrorist Attack on USS Cole: Background and Issues for Congress*, Washington, DC: Congressional Research Service Report.

Piskiewicz, D. (2003) *Terrorism's War with America: A History*, Westport, CT: Praeger.

Redd, S. B. (2002) "The Influence of Advisers on Foreign Policy Decision Making: An Experimental Study," *Journal of Conflict Resolution*, 46 (3): 335–364.

Ressa, M. A. (2003) *Seeds of Terror: An Eyewitness Account of Al-Qaeda's Newest Center of Operations in Southeast Asia*, New York: Free Press.

Robinson, A. (2002) *Bin Laden: Behind the Mask of the Terrorist*, New York: Arcade Publishing.

Rosenthal, H. (forthcoming) "Suicide Bombing: What is the Answer?," in Eva Meyersson Milgrom, ed., *Suicide Bombing from an Interdisciplinary Perspective*, Princeton, NJ: Princeton University Press.

Sage, A. P. (1990) "Human Judgment and Decision Rules," in Sage, A. P., ed., *Concise Encyclopedia of Information Processing in Systems and Organizations*, New York: Pergamon Press, 232–244.

Sageman, M. (2004) *Understanding Terror Networks*, Philadelphia, PA: University of Pennsylvania Press.

Sathasivam, K. (2003) "No Other Choice: Pakistan's Decision to Test the Bomb," in A. Mintz, ed., *Integrating Cognitive and Rational Theories of Foreign Policy Decision Making*, New York: Palgrave Macmillan, 55–76.

Schanzer, J. (2005) *Al-Qaeda's Armies: Middle East Affiliate Groups and the Next Generation of Terror*, New York: Specialist Press International

Scheuer, M. (as Anonymous) (2002) *Through Our Enemies' Eyes*, Washington, DC: Brassey's, Inc.

Schweitzer, Y. and Shay, S. (2003) *The Globalization of Terror: The Challenge of Al-Qaida and the Response of the International Community*, New Brunswick, NJ: Transaction Publishers.

Simon, H. (1957) *Models of Man*, New York: John Wiley.

Steinbruner, J. (1974) *The Cybernetic Theory of Decision: New Dimensions of Political Analysis*, Princeton, NJ: Princeton University Press.

Whittaker, D. J. (2004) *Terrorists and Terrorism in the Contemporary World*, New York: Routledge.

Williams, P. L. (2002) *Al Qaeda: Brotherhood of Terror*, Indianapolis, IN: Alpha Books.

—— (2004) *Osama's Revenge*, Amherst: Prometheus Books.

Wintrobe, R. (2002) *Can Suicide Bombers be Rational?*, Presented at the annual meeting of the McArthur Preferences Network, Philadelphia.

9

MAGHREB IMMIGRANTS BECOMING SUICIDE TERRORISTS

A case study on religious radicalization processes in Spain

Rogelio Alonso and Fernando Reinares

Introduction

On April 3, 2004 seven people committed suicide in Leganés only weeks after terrorists killed in Madrid 191 men and women, injuring hundreds. The suicide terrorists killed themselves when their flat was surrounded by police forces who were investigating the March 11 massacre in the Spanish capital. It is believed that the seven suicide terrorists were themselves involved in perpetrating and preparing the March 11 attack. This chapter will analyze how and why the seven immigrants from the Maghreb became the first suicide bombers in Western Europe related with the current networks of international terrorism.[1] Relying on research based on interviews with significant informants, as well as open secondary sources and judicial reports, the authors will examine the process of radicalization of the seven men. Factors such as their socialization experiences, family, and friends networks as well as the influence of religious, cultural, and political variables will be looked at in order to shed light on their real motivations and the rationale behind this collective act of self immolation. The importance that a neosalafist ideology had on their actions and their process of mobilization as members of the global *jihad* will also be assessed in order to understand how individuals already predisposed to suicide terrorism precipitated such a course of action due to conjectural factors such as the police siege.

The run up to the collective suicide: March 11, 2004

On March 11, 2004 Spain suffered its worst terrorist attack ever. Ten bombs planted in four different trains full of thousands of commuters on their way to Madrid went off between 7:37 and 7:40 am, killing 191 people and injuring hundreds. Since the late sixties Spain had been targeted by various types of terrorism, violence from the ethno-nationalist Basque terrorist group ETA (Basque Fatherland and Freedom) being by far the most intense one. However, never before had a terrorist attack in the country been so indiscriminate and lethal. Both characteristics showed that the way in which the terrorist attack was perpetrated did not represent the traditional *modus operandi* of ETA, the most active terrorist group in the country so far. As it would soon emerge, the killings on March 11 were carried out by a group of Islamist terrorists, some of whom were closely linked to individuals who were also part of the Al Qaeda network.

Only hours after the attacks took place, a van used by the terrorists was found outside one of the stations where the trains stopped on their way to Madrid. It is believed that some of the terrorists got on the train at that particular station in the town of Alcalá de Henares. Inside the van, detonators identical to the ones used by the terrorists were found as well as a tape with religious verses from the Koran, among them the third *Shura* which talks about "punishing the infidels."[2] That particular chapter of the Koran included verses that are also used by suicide terrorist in Palestine or Iraq and which read: "Do not say that those who have fallen for Ala have died, but that they live and that they are sitting besides him." Fingerprints of some of the terrorists who committed suicide were discovered in the van which had been stolen some months previous to the attacks in the Tetuán quarter, an area were one of Madrid's mosques is located which was frequented by some of those involved in the massacre.

The terrorists claimed responsibility for the attacks through a video tape which was left in a bin placed at a motorway that surrounds Madrid, not far from where the main mosque of the city stands. The video showed a man dressed in a white gown with his face covered by a white sheet, wearing dark glasses and a hat with a banner behind his back in which some Arab words could be read: "There is no other God than Ala and Mahoma is his prophet." Armed with a Sterling 9 mm L2A3, the terrorist read a statement he claimed to be "a warning from Al Qaeda's spokesperson in Europe, Abud Dujan Al Afgani." The terrorist, who was later identified as one of the seven men who committed suicide on April 3, 2004, Rachid Oulad Akcha, but whose identity has not been confirmed yet with absolute certainty, said:

> This is a response to the crimes you have committed in the world and particularly in Iraq and Afghanistan and there will be more if God so desires. (. . .) You want life and we want death. (. . .) If you don't stop your injustices there will be more and more blood. This attacks are very little compared to what may happen.[3]

For Spanish intelligence services such an ominous threat posed in such a fashion meant that suicide attacks were likely to happen in the near future.

It should be emphasized that the attacks on March 11 could have had even more terrible consequences since 3 of the 13 bombs left in the trains did fail to explode. The bombs were detonated by cell phones and left in backpacks and bags filled with shrapnel with the objective of magnifying the damage caused and prepared so as to minimise any risk or danger for the perpetrators. One of the bombs was deliberately primed to go off as one of the trains entered Atocha station, the main station in the Spanish capital which is a major focal point of the commuter train line and the metro rail system. A slight delay in the arrival time of the train on that particular day meant that the bomb went off as the train was slowly approaching the station but shortly before arriving at the platform. Had the bomb went off as expected by the terrorists, when the train was right inside the platform, the dome that covers the best part of the modern station would have almost certainly fallen down causing more serious personal and structural damage. These details expose a carefully planned terrorist attack in which the cruelty and high lethality pursued by the perpetrators should be emphasized in order to properly understand their minds and motivations.

March 11 was also a date of some kind of symbolism for those who perpetrated the massacre in Madrid. There were exactly 911 days between September 11, 2001 and March 11, 2004. In other words, and as pointed out by the terrorist who claimed responsibility for the attack in a video recording, two and half years had elapsed between those two attacks. The fact that the suicide terrorists who crashed their planes in the United States also chose four targets constituted another coincidence with the attacks perpetrated in the four trains in Madrid. Furthermore, it is also important to mention that the terrorist attacks took place three days before a general elections in the country to be held on March 14. Much speculation has been placed on the likely intentions of the terrorists in relation to this issue. Contrary to extended opinion, there is no evidence to prove that those responsible for March 11 aimed at destabilizing the government or even influencing the nation's vote in order to damage the party in power at the time. In fact, the relationship between electoral processes and terrorism is not uncommon, previous experiences exposing that very often the outcome of the terrorists' attacks does not fulfill the expectations of those behind them since violence can be, and sometimes is, counterproductive to those who perpetrate it.[4] It is reasonable to argue that had the Spanish government at the time of March 11 responded in a different way, avoiding the mistakes made in the management of the crisis, the electoral results could have been different.[5] Therefore, two points can be made. First of all, it is not possible to assert that the terrorists main motivation was to punish the Spanish government for its involvement in the Iraq war. Second, even if that had been the terrorist's intention, the final outcome was not only determined by the attack itself, but also by the response to it. The fact that a different response could have strengthened the Spanish government at such a critical time, puts into question that the terrorist intention was to change the sign of the election.[6]

The Popular Party (Partido Popular), led by the conservative politician José María Aznar, had one year earlier lent its support to George Bush when the US president struggled to get the backing of the international community on his policy toward Iraq. The judiciary investigation on March 11 records some opinions that suggest that the terrorist attack was motivated by the intervention in Iraq, a claim also repeated by Osama Bin Laden in April 2004 when he interpreted the mass murder perpetrated in Madrid as a consequence of Spanish policy in "Iraq, Afghanistan, and Palestine."[7] According to the judicial inquiry, Jamal Ahmidan, alias *the Chinese*, one of the suicide terrorists who was actively involved in the preparation and perpetration of March 11, believed that "the Arabs are the most powerful army." The judicial report quotes the dialogue between Ahmidan and the wife of the person who supplied the terrorists with the explosives, both of them Spanish citizens involved in ordinary crime. When Ahmidan defended the Al Qaeda attacks on September 11, she criticized him, to which he replied that many innocents were also dying in Iraq as a result of the decision of the Spanish president to send troops to the country.[8] Moreover, Basel Ghalyoun, one of the terrorist suspects interrogated and held for his alleged involvement on March 11, told the attorney that Serhane Ben Abdelmajid Fakhet, alias, *the Tunisian*, one of the leaders of the cell responsible for the attack and one of the suicide terrorists, assured him that he was going to perpetrate a terrorist attack in Spain because this was a country that was "against Muslims and involved in the war in Iraq."[9]

These opinions should be analyzed bearing in mind some important facts. First of all, it is difficult to assess whether assertions like these ones are part of a process of an *ad hoc* rationalization which would cast in a different light such an atrocious terrorist attack. Second, it should be remembered that Islamist terrorist had targeted Europe long before the intervention in Iraq. Previous terrorist attacks had been foiled as a result of good intelligence and effective police work. Third, some of the men responsible for carrying out March 11 seemed to have been committed to the *jihad* even before the war in Iraq. A report elaborated in 2001 by the office of the attorney of the Italian city of Milan defined Spain as "the main base of Al Qaeda in Europe."[10] The *Situation and Trends Report* produced by Europol in 2003 warned of the risk faced by Spain in the following terms:

> Various terrorist groups comprising the so-called Islamic World Front, under the leadership of Al Qaeda, as well as the advocates of internationalization of Jihad on a global scale, continue to pose the greatest threat to our interests as well as to the interests of the other EU Member States. The Spanish Government's support of the military intervention in Iraq by the United States and its Allies constitutes without doubt a further risk factor for Spain, even though it might not be the most decisive or dangerous one.[11]

Given the background to the activities in which the Al Qaeda network in Spain had taken part, which went back to the mid and late nineties, a different proposition could be advanced as a possible explanation for the March 11 attacks. As opposed to Iraq, but not incompatible, another issue could have acted as a stronger motivational factor: the major setback suffered by the network of Islamist terrorists when at the end of 2001 key figures were arrested by Spanish police. Such a strike against the infrastructure of the network could have triggered a strong feeling of revenge which would have materialized in the terrorist campaign initiated in 2004.[12] It should be stressed that March 11 was not a one-off from the terrorist's point of view. The bombs on that day were the beginning of a campaign that was going to continue for weeks and which was cut short as a result of the security forces successes that led to the siege of some of the terrorists in the suburb of Leganés and their collective suicide. The fact that the socialist José Luis Rodríguez Zapatero, the Spanish new Prime Minister elected at the polls on March 14, had decided to pull out the troops from Iraq did not deter the terrorists from carrying more attacks after his election victory.

On April 2, 2004 an explosive device placed at the railway line in the province of Toledo, near Madrid, was found. As it would be later revealed, the fingerprints of Anwar Asrih Rifaat, one of the suicide terrorists, were found in the plastic bag that contained the explosives which seemed aimed at derailing one of the high speed trains that covers the itinerary Madrid-Seville. The finding confirmed that, as police feared, the cell responsible for March 11 had planned more attacks. In the meantime Spanish police had managed to locate some of the terrorist suspects. The bag that failed to explode on March 11 proved decisive in the police investigations leading to some arrests two days after the attacks. Jamal Zougan was the first person to be detained. A Moroccan born in Tanger in 1974, he had lived in Spain for twenty years, where he had caught the attention of Spanish police forces. His name appeared in the judicial report written by Judge Baltasar Garzón in 2002 after the arrest of Imad Eddin Barakat, alias *Abu Dahdah*, regarded as the leader of Al Qaeda in Spain.[13] As a result of the investigations carried at that time, Zougam's surveillance demonstrated that he had regularly offered assistance to individuals linked to Al Qaeda. His house search proved quite revealing of his ideology and allegiance. Among the findings were a video tape entitled *Islamic Jihad in Dagestan* dated August 16, 1999, and another video tape entitled *The Islamic Movement in the West* which contained an interview with Osama Bin Laden. A couple of books in Arab were also found. One of them elaborated on the alleged campaign by the United States to finish off Islam and another one carried the revealing title of *News in Support of the Chechen Muslims*.

The suicide in Leganés on April 3, 2004

Jamal Zougam was the person who bought the phone cards used in the terrorist attack on March 11 which would allow Spanish police to track down the rest of the members of the operational cell, most of whom were hidden in a flat located in Leganés, a working-class area located in the outskirts of Madrid. On Saturday April 3, 2004, one day after the explosive device had been found at the railway line, police cordoned the flat. One of the terrorists identified police officers outside the flat, alerted the rest of the group before managing to escape from the scene. The terrorists initiated a shoot out and the GEO (*Grupo Especial de Operaciones*), the special unit of the Spanish police specialized in siege situations, was deployed. Two hours later, and after carefully assessing the situation, some members of the unit entered the building taking positions right outside the flat. As a member of the police squad who led the operation explained later on, a small amount of explosive was placed outside the door of the flat by police officers. Once the door was blown off the police attempted to negotiate with the terrorists to no avail, since they continued shooting from the inside while challenging the police to come into the flat. While the police outside was already considering the use of tear gas, more screams in Arab were heard before a explosion took place inside. Only seconds before the explosion inside the flat occurred, one of the terrorists announced they were sending an emissary who the police now believes was carrying explosives that went off too.[14] As a result of both explosions seven terrorists died and also one of the members of the police squad, Francisco Javier Torronteras.

According to the attorney in charge of the case at the Spanish National Court, Olga Sánchez, the terrorists only decided to kill themselves after realizing they were besieged and with no prospect of escaping. As it was revealed by the search of the house in the aftermath of the explosion, the terrorists had detailed plans for future attacks which they were going to carry out from April 4, 2004. This was the deadline established in a statement written by one of the suicide terrorists, *the Tunisian*, that was sent to the Spanish daily *Abc*. The communiqué, signed by Abu Dujan Al Afgani in the name of "The Death Battalion," demanded the withdrawal of Spanish troops from Iraq and Afghanistan and threatened with more attacks. As it was found later on, the targets included, among others, two recreational centres frequented by Jewish families and a British school, all of them in the Madrid area. Once again they had opted for soft targets particularly vulnerable.

It is also believed that one of the terrorists did not want to join the rest of the group in their collective suicide, as the finding of a body under a bed suggests.[15] The fashion in which the terrorists had claimed responsibility for the attacks on March 11 led the police and intelligence services to believe that a suicide attack was definitely contemplated.[16] According to Jorge Dezcallar, former director of the Spanish Centre for National Intelligence (CNI, *Centro Nacional de Inteligencia*), the dressing of the terrorist who claimed responsibility for March 11 was quite revealing. In his testimony to the Commission of Inquiry on March 11, Dezcallar emphasized that the video showed how the terrorist thought of himself as already dead and, in his opinion, the same could be said of the rest of the group. "The problem is that if they haven't killed themselves yet, they are going to do it. They already regard themselves purified and on their way to paradise," Dezcallar added. Only days before the suicide, on March 27, the group had recorded another video full of threats which was found after the explosion in Leganés. The video footage showed three terrorists who some sources have identified as three of the suicide terrorists, Sarhane Ben Abdelmajid Fakhet, alias *the Tunisian*, Allekema Lamari, and Rachid Oulad, heavily armed, dressed in white gowns and with their faces covered by balaclavas. The three members of the self named "Company of Death" appeared holding detonators connected to explosive devices which were stripped around their bodies.

Nonetheless, the collective suicide was not an immediate objective of the group before they took their lives on April 3, this outcome being a rational decision reached in the context of the siege by the police. In fact such a reaction under those circumstances was not without precedent, as previous acts of suicide in other places of the world indicate. According to some of the police officers involved in the siege, the terrorists wanted to die while killing as many policemen or any other persons as possible.[17] This was the same intention confessed by another Islamist terrorist under surveillance in the United Kingdom should he find himself surrounded by police.[18] A similar rationale was behind the killing of a police officer who died in March 2004 in Tashkent, the capital of Uzbekistan, when he approached a terrorist suspect who killed herself with explosives in order to prevent her arrest. On the very same day and city another suicide terrorist killed three policemen and a child in similar circumstances.[19] Only a day after, several policemen died in another incident involving three suicide terrorists. Another suicide terrorist killed himself in the Uzbekistan capital when his house was surrounded by the police.[20] In February 2004 another terrorist killed himself in Afghanistan to avoid arrest.[21] These and other precedents help to explain the awareness by British police of the dangers involved in arresting potential suicide bombers in the aftermath of the terrorist attacks perpetrated in London on July 7, 2005.

The radical neosalafist religious ideology of the seven men who killed themselves in Madrid was most certainly of great relevance in their behavior. Nonetheless, it could be argued that the context in which they encountered themselves constituted a precipitant factor in their decision in a way that other motivations beyond the purely religious ones were equally important.[22] According to the judiciary investigation the terrorists intended to prevent the police from carrying future investigations that could derive from the arrests and interrogations that would follow, deciding at that point, and as a result of such a commitment to his cause, to end their lives while trying to kill as many policemen as possible. Police officers who were on the scene have confirmed that although the terrorists shouted and screamed profusely when they realized they were besieged, the situation became quieter and before the suicide actually took place prayers and songs were heard. This change of mood has led the police to believe that the intention of the suicide terrorists was definitely to kill themselves and that their death was no accident. Some sources argue that their intention to kill policemen or other individuals was motivated by the fact that Islam prohibits suicide and, therefore, their act would be seen in a different light if what they regarded as infidels also died in the course of their immolation.

The seven suicide terrorists

Seven were the men who killed themselves on that day in Leganés. These were Allekema Lamari, Sarhane Ben Abdelmajid Fakhet, alias *the Tunisian*, Jamal Ahmidan, alias *the Chinese*, Asrih Rifaat Anwar, Abdennabi Kounjaa, alias

Abdallah, Rachid Oulad Akcha, and Mohammed Oulad Akcha. Some of them had been known to the police before the suicide took place since Spanish security forces came across their names while investigating Islamist terrorist networks in the country. All of them came from the Maghreb, mainly from Morocco with the exception of Allekema Lamari, who was an Algerian, and Sarhane Ben Abelmajid, whose country of origin was Tunisia. We will now outline some biographical details of each of the suicide terrorists.

Allekema Lamari was born on July 10, 1965 in Alger, capital of Algeria. He studied technical architecture at University in his home country, working for five years for a security department of the Algerian government at the town of Hydra before coming to Spain in the early 1990s.[23] He did not have a legal permit to stay in the country and worked as an illegal worker in rural areas. He settled in the small town of Tudela, in the province of Navarre. In 1993 he joined an Islamic association where, according to some sources, he would initiate his process of radicalization. Nonetheless, other sources point out that Lamari had come to Spain with the deliberate intention of setting up a logistic base for the Algerian terrorist group GIA (*Groupe Islamique Armeé*).[24] In fact his brother was a GIA militant who died in his country. Therefore, it is difficult to establish the exact period in which his process of radicalization took place.

According to people who knew him around that time, Lamari used to pray five times a day, attending the mosque every Friday.[25] Safwan Sabagh, a Syrian who acquainted him, believed that Lamari had never had a girlfriend or lover. The Algerian kept himself away from drugs, sex, or alcohol, regarding them as common vices of westerners that a good Muslim should refuse. He socialized with radical Islamists based in Valencia, where he would travel frequently and where he attended the mosque of the Islamic Cultural Association Alfath, a center which at the time allowed fundamentalist speeches. In April 1997 Lamari was arrested in Valencia as part of a police operation against the logistic and infrastructure of the GIA. The police believed that Lamari and ten other men who were also arrested at the time constituted a very important link between terrorists in Algeria and France. GIA internal bulletins, automatic weapons, forged documents, and radical Islamic magazines as well as videos on *muyahadin* were found during the arrests. In June 2001 Lamari was sentenced to ten years in prison accused of membership of a terrorist organization. He also received a two-year sentence for illegal possession of weapons and two more years for possession of documents and goods destined to fraud.

His time in prison was, according to the Spanish intelligence service, a key period in which his radicalization deepened. According to one of his lawyers, Lamari argued that his life was under threat from other inmates, fears that led his solicitor to say that the Algerian suffered some kind of mental disorder.[26] He socialized with other Islamic prisoners who saw Lamari with respect and authority to the extent that he was protected by some of them. After his release he would regularly send money to other inmates. He was held in Teruel prison from December 1998 to April 1999 before moving to another jail in the town of

Cuenca. During that period he didn't socialize much with the rest of the prison population with the exception of two inmates. One of them, Ali Mimoudi, was born in Tetuan (Morocco) in 1958 and released in 2000. He was not known for his religious radicalism, contrary to Nasser Ahmed who was born in Jadida (Morocco), in 1977, and who used to socialize with Lamari during his imprisonment there. Ahmed, who is still in prison, has had several conflicts inside the jail. He is well known for his radical religious views and constant reading of the Koran. On several occasions he has covered the walls of his cell with shuras from Koran, at some point even boasting that as soon as he leaves prison he is going to become a martyr.

The Spanish intelligence service believes that Lamari was committed to take revenge for his imprisonment which came to an end in 2002. In June of that year the Algerian was set free as a result of a procedural mistake made by judges who while working out Lamari's remission incorrectly believed that the prisoner qualified for early release. When a year later the mistake was discovered and the Court requested Lamari's return to prison, the Algerian failed to turn up and a warrant was issued. Around that time, it is believed that Lamari was already in Madrid in touch with radicals such as Sarhane Ben Abdelmajid Fakhet, alias *the Tunisian*. Sarhane acted as a substitute for the main imam of one of Madrid's mosques situated in the quarter of Alonso Cano which was also attended by Lamari. Both men would become the leaders of the cell that perpetrated March 11. According to informers from the Spanish intelligence service, Lamari had boasted in the late months of 2003 that he was preparing a major attack.[27] His friend Safwan Sabagh has said that Lamari assured him that he would never be caught alive. When Lamari said goodbye to Sabagh on March 27, 2004, two weeks after the terrorist attacks in Madrid and only days before the collective suicide in Leganés, he told him: "We will meet up in heaven. Ask our brothers to pray for me."[28]

Sarhane Ben Abdelmajid Fakhet, alias *the Tunisian*, was born in Tunisia on July 10, 1968. He arrived in Spain in 1994 in order to pursue his PhD in Economics at one of Madrid's main universities, *Universidad Autónoma de Madrid*. An agency from the Spanish government awarded him a grant which covered his accommodation and expenses. However, he left University and started working for a states agency selling and renting properties. His salary was not too high: 600 Euros (775 US Dollars) per month plus ten percent commission. His bosses and work colleagues regarded *the Tunisian* as quite a successful estates agent. On a particular month he managed to earn 3,500 Euros (4,500 US Dollars). The estates agency, *ARCONSA Gestiones Inmobiliarias*, was placed in the west of Madrid, in the quarter of Tetuán, an area with a big affluence of immigrants. His workplace was very close from the Estrecho mosque, also called the Abu Baker mosque, which other members of the Al Qaeda Spanish cell used to attend. Nonetheless, *the Tunisian* was a regular at another mosque, the one that stands by the M 30 motorway which surrounds the capital. He occasionally worked in the restaurant of this mosque, where he also acted as translator. He lived within walking distance from the M 30 mosque.

He was married to a Moroccan woman who attended regularly the same mosque. She was only 16 years old when she married, and used to wear fully in black with her face covered, following a strict religious interpretation of Moroccan tradition. She is the sister of Mustapha Maymouni, regarded as the leader in Spain of the terrorist group Salafia Jihadia, and who is currently in jail in Morocco accused of involvement in the preparation of the Casablanca terrorist attacks in May 2003 which killed forty-six people. Maymouni was a very close associate of *Abu Dahdah*, the alleged leader of the first Al Qaeda cell in Spain, and, according to judge Baltasar Garzón, he was responsible for setting up in 2002 two cells which would become part of Al Qaeda. One of the cells was formed in Morocco and the other one in Spain, being integrated by *the Tunisian*, as well as by two of the people currently imprisoned for their alleged involvement in March 11: Jamal Zougam and Rabei Osman, alias *the Egyptian*.

According to the religious leader of the M 30 mosque, Moneir Ali, at the end of 2001 *the Tunisian* asked him why governments in Muslim countries were not good believers and whether it was possible to change them by force. The imam replied that Koran forbids all sort of violence.[29] Nonetheless he felt that *the Tunisian* was radicalizing himself. At the same time Sarhane stopped attending lessons in the mosque and although he still prayed there he would often do it in the early hours of the morning. Some of those who acquainted him say that Sarhane gradually increased his criticism of other Muslims who did not view religion in the same way as he did. The police search of his house uncovered lots of papers with notes written in Arab which had been unloaded from radical Islamist web sites. He had been seen handing in propaganda at the end of the prayers outside one of the mosques as part of his attempts to attract people to his cause. According to a police source who had *the Tunisian* under surveillance for some time, "he was not somebody who radicalised himself and became a terrorist. He was a terrorist who used as cover his normal appearance and his routine job."

It seems that his process of radicalization deepened with the arrest of *Abu Dahdah*, becoming, as a result of it, an important figure in the terrorist organization who would lead and mobilize around him a group of Islamist radicals. According to one of the suspects interrogated by judge Juan del Olmo after March 11, *the Tunisian* was not very religious when he first arrived in Spain, his process of radicalization being highly influenced by his friendship with Amer Azizi, a leading Al Qaeda member in Europe who manage to escape police arrest. At one stage members of the Muslim community in Spain contacted Sarhane's family in Tunisia warning them of his gradual radicalization. His family failed to bring him back home when Sarhane's mother travelled to Spain in an attempt to convince his son to return, hoping that this would have stopped his radicalization.

In 2002 *the Tunisian*'s name appeared in the diary of Ahmed Brahin, regarded as a key individual in Al Qaeda's financing system who was arrested in Barcelona that year. Brahin referred to *the Tunisian* as "Sarhane, Islamic friend."[30] As the judicial investigation points out, Sarhane's friendships led to the police surveillance of his flat since March 2003. Another of his acquaintances, Moutaz

Almallah Dabbas, a Syrian who was arrested for his alleged involvement in March 11, told Judge Juan del Olmo that *the Tunisian* had explained to him that he wanted to assault jewelleries, banks, and police stations as well as to raise money he would destine for the *jihad* in Iraq and Chechnya. Fouad el Morabit Amghar, another Moroccan also arrested as a suspect who would have taken part in the massacre, told the judge that *the Tunisian* had expressed in the summer of 2003 his determination "to do something big in Spain." He was a regular at the meetings that took place in several locations in Madrid where the members of the cell received indoctrination and extolled the *jihad* through videos and inflammatory speeches. Sarhane's house was also a regular meeting point were he would show videos of what he described as "the suffering of Muslims" also delivering original speeches of Osama Bin Laden. Some of these meetings took place at the back of a hairdresser's in the quarter of Lavapiés were the terrorists would also purify themselves with water brought from Mecca in preparation for acts that could be offensive to Islam.

Jamal Ahmidan, alias *the Chinese*, was born in Tetuan, Morocco, on October 28, 1970. He arrived illegally in Spain in 1990 and got involved in petty crime and drugs' smuggling. He was married to a Spanish woman and was the father of an 11-year-old boy. Police sources believe his marriage with a drug addict was primarily aimed at legalizing his situation in the country. He spent time in prison between 1992 and 1995, and after his release was detained at least nine times for forging documents and trafficking with drugs. In 1999, while he was held at a detention center in Madrid were illegal foreigners were kept before being sent back to their country, *the Chinese* started a fire aided by an Algerian internee in an attempt to break away. When he went back to Morocco in 2000 he was sent to prison for three years for drink driving and running over a man while driving under the influence. His time in prison is regarded as a key period in his life where he radicalized himself becoming a religious fanatic. His brother Mustafa says that Jamal gave up smoking, heroin, cocaine, and alcohol, although he did not change the way in which he had earned his life so far. Shortly after being released in 2003 he acquired the explosives used on March 11 exchanging them for drugs and a considerable amount of money. He also managed to acquire weapons and ammunition through his contacts in the Spanish criminal world. At the same time he became a regular at the mosque in the Villaverde quarter of Madrid, where he would listen to the preaching of a radical imam, Samir Ben Abdellah, who shared with Sarhane *the Tunisian* strict views about Islam.

Asrih Rifaat Anwar, who was born in December 16, 1980 in Tetuan, Morocco, was the youngest of the group and did not have a legal permit of residence in the country. He was single. Spanish police's first knowledge of Rifaat was around 2001. Nonetheless, after March 11 a friend of his who was interrogated as part of the investigation assured that Rifaat had been in Spain for the last 7 or 8 years. If this information is correct it would mean that Rifaat arrived in the country at a very young age. He was first arrested years before March 11 with a car full of hashish. His fingerprints were found in the plastic bag that contained the explosives placed at the railway line which failed to explode one day before the collective suicide. He was sheltered by Moutaz Almallah Dabbas at this home in street Virgen del Coro, in Madrid, a place where other members of the cell would regularly meet to extol the *jihad* and where indoctrination took place, as demonstrated by police surveillance of the house carried out since the beginning of 2003. Almallah Dabbas' brother, Mohannad, was also arrested in London accused of involvement in the cell responsible for March 11. It is believed the two brothers were in charge of facilitating the movements in Spain and abroad of youngsters involved in their cause. Almallah Dabbas was a close friend of Sarhane, *the Tunisian*. It is believed that Sarhane brought Rifaat Anwar, together with Abdennabi Kounjaa, alias *Abdallah*, into the group. Rifaat's involvement in petty crime and drugs had led him to get associated with Jamal Ahmidan.

Abdennabi Kounjaa, alias *Abdallah*, was born in the Moroccan city of Taourit in 1975. He had been arrested by Spanish police in 1999 when he attempted to smuggle into the north African country a car stolen in Italy. Although he was expelled from Spain after that incident, he managed to come back and settled in Navarre where he was employed as a temporary worker in the country. He had no qualifications and he managed to legalize his situation in Spain in 2002. At that time he also taught children in the local mosque using, according to other Muslims, quite a radical rhetoric. He left his wife and two daughters in Morocco. One of the daughters was named Jihad. Before he died he wrote a letter to them which has been described by Judge Juan del Olmo as similar to a "farewell letter or testament." Writing in Arab the deceased thanked God for guiding him through the path he followed and assured his family that he left them behind in Morocco because it was "a decision made by God almighty." The letter shows how he asks his daughters not to emigrate to "infidel" countries like Spain equating it to "hell." While addressing his daughters Kounjaa asks them to follow the "*muyahadin* brothers throughout the world." He emphasizes that that's the fate he expects from them since "terrene life should not worry them." He goes on to say: "I can't put up with this life living like a weak and humiliated person under the scrutiny of the infidels and tyrants." He also adds that "this life is the path towards death," thus preferring "death instead of life." The letter concludes: "I hope you follow the words and the deeds, the *jihad* in Islam, since it's a full religion. Make of westerners your enemies. May God punish the tyrants."

Rachid Oulad Akcha was born in Tetuan, Morocco, on January 27, 1971. His brother Mohammed Oulad Akcha was born in 1975. Shortly after March 11 their sister Naima was also arrested but later released. Between March 5 and March 6, 2004 Naima withdrew from her bank 13,500 Euros (17,430 US Dollars) that she gave to her brothers. Their brother Khalid is currently serving a prison sentence in the Spanish prison of Topas (Salamanca) because of his involvement in petty crime and drugs' trafficking. Another brother, Hassan, is also under arrest in London after trying to get in the country with forged documents.[31] Both brothers were single when they died after committing suicide in Leganés. Mohammed arrived illegally in Spain in 2001, although a year later he managed to legalized

190

his situation. He had no qualifications and worked in the country for a while also taking up other menial jobs. Rachid arrived in Spain in 1995 with a legal status since he came over as a student who intended to continue his degree. However, in 1998 Rachid was also sentenced to four years in prison after being found guilty of drugs' trafficking. According to prison officers who met Rachid during his imprisonment he was not religiously radicalized but rather a "normalised inmate with quite a low profile." Nonetheless, there was a three-months period in which he was in the same prison, Madrid III, as one of the key figures involved in March 11, with Allekema Lamari, who also committed suicide. Some sources argue that this period could have proved decisive in Rachid's process of radicalization. After being released he worked as a builder at different sites in Madrid managing once again to legalize his situation in the country.

Both Rachid and Mohammed attended the meetings in which the group extolled the *jihad* and watched videos such as the one that showed the pictures of the seven agents from the Spanish intelligence service who were killed in an ambush in Iraq on November 29, 2003. This was not an uncommon exercise of reaffirmation as evidenced by the hard disk of a computer found in the explosion site in Leganés which contained pictures of the killing of the Spanish intelligence officers and footage of religious leaders in Saudi Arabia calling on the *jihad* as well as terrorist attacks against American soldiers in Iraq.[32] Information on weaponry and instructions on the preparation of explosives, as well as a manual on conventional, guerrilla, and nuclear warfare was also found at the site. One of the suspects interrogated by judge Juan del Olmo argued that Sarhane, *the Tunisian*, was highly regarded by both brothers, who described him as "an angel," a comment inspired by his assessment of the Casablanca killings in 2003.

Profiles and social networks

The analysis of the seven suicide terrorists' life patterns that have so far emerged expose characteristics shared by members of other terrorist groups throughout the world. Common factors can be appreciated when comparing the influence and recruitment processes of religious and secular organizations,[33] variables which are also evident in the seven examples considered here and in other individuals who participated in March 11. Structural, motivational, and facilitational factors merged in their process of radicalization and recruitment. They were all part of a closed community of activists poorly integrated in Spanish society who were kept together by a radical ideology. The dynamics that influenced these terrorists approaching and joining the *jihadist* movement do not differ extensively from the experiences of other participants in the *jihad*.[34] As Snow and Zurcher observed long ago when analyzing recruitment into social movements, the network channel is the richest source of movement recruits,[35] constituting a key issue in the case under study in which a social and family set of connections facilitated such a process. The genealogy of Islamic terrorism in Spain is one of interpersonal links strengthened by kinship and friendship through which social and group cohesion has been fostered. One particular incident may help to illustrate this point.

Three years before the terrorist attacks in Madrid took place, some of the main Al Qaeda figures in the country attended a Muslim wedding between a Spanish woman and a Syrian held in the capital. Three of the leaders of the organization, including *Abu Dahdah*, shared a table with Sarhane Ben Abdelmajid Fakhet, alias *the Tunisian*, who acted as a translator during the wedding. As it has already been mentioned, Sarhane was married to the sister of Mustapha Maymouni, a close associate of *Abu Dahdah* and a very influential individual in the Al Qaeda network as head of the group Salafia Jihadia. It is around these authority figures that ideological and social bonds were knit. Different mosques in the city enabled contact between individuals but did not represent the main meeting points where they gathered and conspired, other places such as restaurants, hairdressers, and flats being preferred for those purposes. The quarter of Lavapiés, with a great affluence of immigrants, provided some of these meeting points. A restaurant called *Alhambra*, the public phone booth *Nuevo Siglo*—owned by Jamal Zougam—and *Abdou*'s hairdressers were all situated in the same street and only meters away from each other. It was at these places that members of the cell regularly met. The back of *Abdou*'s hairdressers was where the radicals purified themselves with water from Mecca and a place where they used to meet for prayers since they did not wish to attend the local mosque which was controlled by a Pakistani who upheld an interpretation of Islam they did not agree with.

In the privacy of these locations the exaltation of the *jihad* took place, collectively endorsing the activists their radical views of Islam with literature and video footage which portrayed a victimized Muslim community as well as the violent and bloody response to their grievances that *muyahadin* inflicted on their enemies. This ritual contributed to strengthening the "culture of death," also evident in other suicide terrorists, which makes martyrdom appear as the right thing to do.[36] It is revealing that a copy of one of those video tapes used as a means of indoctrination and of reassuring their beliefs was found in different locations when house searches of Al Qaeda suspects took place.[37] The tape, named *Islamic Jihad in Dagestan*, showed the brutality of *muyahadin* against Russians. The video featured prominently Abdelaziz Benyaich and his brother Salaheddin, alias *Abu Mughen*, both dressed in combat fatigues leading a group of *muyahadin*. The Benyaich brothers had befriended Jamal Zougam in Tanger where all of them came from. *Abu Mughen*, who lost an aye fighting in Bosnia, became an iconic and venerated figure for the members of the Spanish cell and was welcomed in their homes when he needed refuge, as he did when he was operated on his eye at a Madrid clinic in March 1999.

Both brothers were later arrested and sentenced for their participation in the attacks in Casablanca in 2003. Another Benyaich brother, Abdalla, was also involved in the *jihad* and died in Afghanistan while American troops chased Bin Laden. Mohamed Fizazi, a religious figure imprisoned after the Casablanca killings who is serving a thirty-year prison sentence for his alleged involvement in that terrorist attack, is regarded by police as somebody who greatly influenced youngsters like Zougam and the Benyaich brothers who shared the same background.[38] The relevance of kinship in the *jihadist* structure is highlighted by the involvement of several group of brothers such as Rachid and Mohammed Oulad, both killed in the collective suicide, Moutaz Almallah Dabbas and Mohannad Almallah Dabbas, as well as Abdelgani Chedadi and Said Chedadi, the later arrested before March 11 and the former in the aftermath of the terrorist attacks, both of whom ran a shop just a few meters away from some of the main regular meeting points such as *Restaurante Alhambra* and Zougam's public phone booth, both located in a popular neighborhood of Madrid. Abdelkhalak Chergi and his brother Abdelhak were also arrested and interrogated under the suspicion of also being involved in the preparation and financing of the terrorist attack.

A run-down house outside Madrid also offered a meeting point where they socialized and reinforced their ideological commitments through the hatred and dehumanization of westerners encouraged by the means already outlined. It was owned by Mohammed Needl, imprisoned in Spain while awaiting trial since 2001 for his alleged involvement with Al Qaeda's cell and his leader *Abu Dahdah*. The house had been rented by Mustapha Maymouni before he was sentenced for his involvement in the Casablanca attacks and later on by Jamal Ahmidan, *the Chinese*, through the intermediary Sarhane, *the Tunisian*. The secrecy of the shack outside Madrid was used to prepare the bombs. It was also the place were some kind of celebration took place on March 21 shortly after the terrorist attacks had shocked Spain. On that Sunday the members of the terrorist cell and their families gathered together for a barbeque. In fact it was quite common for the group to get together at a country location in the Madrid province where for the last couple of years some of those involved in the terrorist attacks perpetrated in Madrid and Casablanca used to play football, swim in the river, cook, and pray, as the judicial investigation revealed.[39]

Family bonds seem quite important as the final hours of the suicide terrorists suggest. All of them, with the exception of Lamari and Rifaat, did telephone their relatives while they were besieged by the police and before killing themselves. Farewells are not uncommon in other suicide terrorist experiences,[40] in this case taking the form of rushed and probably unexpected telephone calls during the last minutes of their lives. The first one to make such a significant call was Sarhane, *the Tunisian*. He called his mother at 19:15 pm. and told her he was besieged by police forces and before saying goodbye he added that he was going to kill himself as part of his *jihad* in the name of Allah. Mohammed and Rachid Oulad called their brother in the United Kingdom and explained their intentions. Kounjaa also called his brother and asked him to pay off his debts.

Jamal Ahmidan, *the Chinese*, phoned her mother Rhama in Morocco and explained to her: "This is my last day. At the end of the day, we all have to die." Jamal's mother asked him why was he going to do it and he replied: "I don't know, mother. It's God's will." He hung up and she phoned back immediately. Another

193

person picked up the phone and passed it to Jamal, who retorted: "It's enough, mother. Do not worry about me and give me your blessing. Do not phone me back." A similar pattern was also present in the case of Mohamed Afalah, another of the terrorists directly involved in the March 11 massacre who, according to sources from the investigation, killed himself in a terrorist suicide attack in Iraq. Phone tapings have led investigators to believe that Mohamed Belhadj, another suspect who managed to escape the police and who had rented the house in Leganés, also fled Spain to Iraq probably with the intention of perpetrating a terrorist suicide attack. The Spanish Ministry of Interior has informed that one year after the massacre in Madrid Afalah phoned his father asking for forgiveness letting him know his intention to take part in a suicide terrorist attack in May 2005.[41]

It is clear that terrorism in general, and suicide terrorism in particular, is a group phenomenon and that the immolation of the seven men in Leganés was highly influenced by group dynamics.[42] Of particular significance may be the fact that one of the men did not seem in favor of a decision supported by the majority of the group, as the finding of a body hidden under a bed in the bomb site suggests. Although his identity has not been determined yet, police sources believe that he was either Rifaat or Mohammed Oulad, in any case, one of the youngest members of the group.

The information collected so far on the seven men allows for some general conclusions in relation to their profile as determined by some useful variables such as sex, age, legal and marital status, professional qualifications, and country of origin. They were all male and part of the same generation, the majority of them being born in the first part of the seventies (Jamal Ahmidan in 1970, Rachid Oulad in 1971, Mohammed Oulad in 1975, and Abdennabi Kounjaa in 1975), two of them in the second half of the sixties (Sarhane Ben Abdelmajid Fakhet in 1968 and Allekema Lamari in 1965), and only one of them earlier than that (Asrih Rifaat in 1980). Four of them were single with the exception of Sarhane Ben Abdelmajid, Jamal Ahmidan, and Abdennabi Kounjaa. All of the suicide terrorists killed in Leganés did come from the Maghreb, five of them from Morocco (Rachid Oulad and his brother Mohammed Oulad, Jamal Ahmidan, Abdennabi Kounjaa, and Asrih Rifaat), one of them from Algeria (Allekema Lamari), and one of them from Tunisia (Sarhane Ben Abdelmajid Fakhet). Most of them could be described as under-achievers with few or no qualifications. Three of them had some qualifications and second-or third-level education experience: Sarhane Ben Abdelmajid Fakhet, Allekema Lamari, and Rachid Oulad. Their professional background and activities did not differ greatly, probably with the exception of Sarhane Ben Abdelmajid Fakhet, whose university degree allowed him for a slightly more qualified work experience. The involvement in drugs and petty crime was a common characteristic of most of the suicide terrorists with the exception of Allekema Lamari and Sarhane Ben Abdelmajid Fakhet. Their illegal activities did not prevent them from legalizing their situation in Spain with the exception of Lamari and Rifaat who did not hold the legal permits required to stay in the country.

As in the case of other terrorist expressions, those who are sympathetic to religious extremism and terrorism in the name of Islam represent a small but a significant minority disaffected with the country in which they live. The process of radicalization and recruitment apparently occurs under great influence from individual manipulation carried out by extremist Islamists who preach and advocate a neosalafist ideology. Spiritual leaders or other relevant figures exert decisive influence on individuals who at certain points decide to participate in extremist activities espousing a violent ideology. Those leaders usually identify places and clusters for the socialization of potential recruits which will enable the radical ideology and doctrine to spread. Some are targeted by extremists but others get recruited through personal contact, often by chance. As the example of the seven men who killed themselves in Leganés shows, the ideological indoctrination precedes active involvement in terrorist activities. The influence of peers was for them a very relevant factor in their process of radicalization as it seems to be in other cases too. As with those involved in March 11, very often potential recruits are exposed to videos, books, songs, speeches, and other sources available through internet that justify the use of violence and the *jihad*, places such as mosques, prisons, Islamic institutions as well as other social and sports meetings becoming propitious for these type of activities which provide an environment for some to gravitate to terrorism. It is through the engagement in this gradual and regular process that the commitment to the cause deepens also leading to involvement in training and fundraising, both inside and abroad, strengthening solidarity bonds among those being radicalized.

Notes

1 Suicide attacks had previously occurred since the mid to late nineties in Croatia as well as Turkey and Russia.
2 José Maria Irujo, *El agujero. España invadida por la yihad*, Madrid: Aguilar, 2005, pp. 341, 343.
3 Transcription of the video published in *El Mundo*, March 14, 2004. See also *El Mundo*, September 13, 2004.
4 David Rapoport and Leonard Weinberg, "Elections and Violence," *Terrorism and Political Violence*, 12, 2000, pp. 15–50.
5 Rogelio Alonso, "El nuevo terrorismo: factores de cambio y permanencia," Amalio blanco, Rafael del Águila and José Manuel Sabucedo (ed.), *Madrid 11-M. Un análisis del mal y sus consecuencias*, Madrid: Editorial Trotta, pp. 143–146.
6 In fact some authors argue that opinion polls held in advance of the terrorist attack already indicated that the difference between the party in power and the socialist party was narrowing to the extent that a victory for the latter did not look unlikely. See Julián Santamaría, "El azar y el contexto," *Claves de Razón Práctica*, 146, 2004, pp. 28–40, and Ignacio Lago Peñas y José Ramón Montero "Los mecanismos del cambio electoral. Del 11 M al 14 M," *Claves de Razón Práctica*, 149, 2005, pp. 36–45.
7 *El País*, April 16, 2004.
8 *El País*, January 20, 2005.

9 *El País*, January 20, 2005.
10 *El País*, March 3, 2002.
11 *Terrorist Activity in the European Union: Situation and Trends Report (TE-SAT) October 2002–15 October 2003*, Europol, 3 December, 2003, p. 37.
12 Fernando Reinares, "Al Qaeda, neosalafistas magrebíes y 11-M: sobre el nuevo terrorismo islamista en España," Fernando Reinares and Antonio Elorza (ed.), *El nuevo terrorismo islamista. Del 11-S al 11-M*, Madrid: Temas de Hoy, 2004, pp. 36–37.
13 Juzgado Central de Instrucción Nº 005, Madrid, Sumario (Proc. Ordinario) 0000035/2001 E, September 17, 2003.
14 *Abc*, March 6, 2005.
15 *El País*, March 10, 2005.
16 Cortes Generales, Diario de Sesiones del Congreso de los Diputados, Comisión de Investigación, Año 2004 VIII, Legislatura Núm. 7, Sesión núm. 13, July 19, 2004.
17 *El País*, April 3, 2005.
18 Contents of the recorded conversation contained in the documentary *Al Qaeda UK*, broadcast in *Dispatches*, Channel 4, 2003.
19 *El País*, March 30, 2004.
20 *El País*, March 31, 2004.
21 Recorded in the MIPT Terrorism Knowledge Base.
22 On the combination of religious fanaticism and rational choice than can be appreciated in suicide terrorists, see Fernando Reinares, *Terrorismo global*, Madrid: Taurus, 2003, pp. 101–116.
23 *El Mundo*, August 8, 2005.
24 *Abc*, July 17, 2004.
25 *El País*, February 28, 2005.
26 *El País*, February 28, 2005.
27 *Diario de Navarra*, October 16, 2004 and *El País*, September 19, 2004.
28 *El País*, January 20, 2005.
29 *El País*, April 14, 2004.
30 Irujo, p. 205.
31 *Abc*, March 24, 2005.
32 *El País*, December 4, 2004.
33 See for example two of the most protracted cases of ethno nationalist terrorism in Europe, Fernando Reinares, *Patriotas de la muerte. Quiénes han militado en ETA y por qué*. Madrid: Taurus, 2001 and Rogelio Alonso, *Matar por Irlanda. El IRA y la lucha armada*. Madrid: Alianza, 2003.
34 See Marc Sageman, *Understanding terror networks*. Philadelphia: University of Pennsylvania Press, 2004. The profiles of the four terrorists who died on the terrorist attacks perpetrated in London on July 7, 2005 do corroborate this point.
35 "Social networks and social movements: a microstructural approach to differential recruitment," David A. Snow and Louis A. Zurcher Jr., *American Sociological Review*, 45, 1980, pp. 787–801.
36 See for example Ami Pedhazur, "Toward an Analytical Model of Suicide Terrorism—A Comment," *Terrorism and Political Violence*, 16, 2004, pp. 841–844.
37 Juzgado Central de Instrucción Nº 005, Madrid, Sumario (Proc. Ordinario) 0000035/2001 E, September 17, 2003.
38 *El País*, May 15, 2005.
39 *El País*, August 3, 2005.
40 See for example Andrew Silke, "The Psychology of Suicidal Terrorism," Andrew Silke (ed.), *Terrorists, Victims and Societies: Psychological Perspectives on Terrorism and its Consequences*. Chichester: John Wiley & Sons, 2003.
41 *El Correo*, June 16, 2005.

42 J.M. Post, K.G. Ruby, and E.D. Shaw, 'The Radical Group in Context: 1. An Integrated Framework for the Analysis of Group Risk for Terrorism,' *Studies in Conflict & Terrorism*, 25, 2002, pp. 73–100.

Bibliography

Alonso, R., *Matar por Irlanda. El IRA y la lucha armada*, Madrid: Alianza, 2003.

——, "El nuevo terrorismo: factores de cambio y permanencia," in Amalio Blanco, Rafael del Águila and José Manuel Sabucedo (ed.), *Madrid 11-M. Un análisis del mal y sus consecuencias*, Madrid: Editorial Trotta, 2005, pp. 113–150.

Cortes Generales, "Diario de Sesiones del Congreso de los Diputados," *Comisión de Investigación*, Año 2004 VIII, Legislatura Núm. 7, Sesión núm. 13, July 19, 2004.

Europol, *Terrorist Activity in the European Union: Situation and Trends Report (TE-SAT) October 2002–15 October 2003*, December 3, 2003.

Juzgado Central de Instrucción N° 005, Madrid, Sumario (Proc. Ordinario) 0000035/2001 E, September 17, 2003.

Irujo, J. M., *El agujero España invadida por la yihad*, Madrid: Aguilar, 2005.

Lago, Ignacio and Montero, José Ramón, "Los mecanismos del cambio electoral. Del 11-M al 14-M," *Claves de Razón Práctica*, 149, 2005, pp. 36–45.

Pedhazur, A., "Toward an Analytical Model of Suicide Terrorism—A Comment," *Terrorism and Political Violence*, 16, 2004.

Post, J. M., Ruby, K. G., and Shaw, E. D., "The Radical Group in Context: 1. An Integrated Framework for the Analysis of Group Risk for Terrorism," *Studies in Conflict & Terrorism*, 25, 2002a.

——, "The Radical Group in Context: 2. Identification of Critical Elements in the Analysis of Risk for Terrorism by Radical Group Type," *Studies in Conflict & Terrorism*, 25, 2002b, pp. 101–126.

Rapoport, D. and Weinberg, L., "Elections and Violence," *Terrorism and Political Violence*, 12, 2000, pp. 15–50.

Reinares, F., *Patriotas de la muerte. Quiénes han militado en ETA y por qué*, Madrid: Taurus, 2001.

——, *Terrorismo Global*, Madrid: Taurus, 2003.

——, "Al Qaeda, neosalafistas magrebíes y 11-M: sobre el nuevo terrorismo islamista en España," in Reinares, F. and Elorza, A. (ed.), *El nuevo terrorismo islamista. Del 11-S al 11-M*, Madrid: Temas de Hoy, 2004, pp. 14–43.

Sageman, M., *Understanding Terror Networks*, Philadelphia: University of Pennsylvania Press, 2004.

Santamaría, J., "El azar y el contexto," *Claves de Razón Práctica*, 146, 2004, pp. 28–40.

Silke, A. (ed.), *Terrorists, Victims and Societies: Psychological Perspectives on Terrorism and its Consequences*, Chichester: John Wiley & Sons, 2003.

Snow, D. A. and Zurcher, L. A. Jr, "Social Networks and Social Movements: A Microstructural Approach to Differential Recruitment," *American Sociological Review*, 45, 1980.

INDEX